Praise for *The Unexp...*

'Truthful, modern and real'

Stylist

'The first half of the book describes in graphic detail Gray's misadventures as a borderline alcoholic...but the second half jauntily and convincingly argues that sobriety can be just as enjoyable as intoxication.'

Jake Kerridge, The Sunday Telegraph

'She wants us to us question our reliance on drink and the way society pushes it on us. Mainly, though, without being remotely preachy, she wants to convince anyone who'll listen that a booze-free life isn't just worth living, it's better.'

Hilary Rose, The Times

'The appealing pitch of Gray's book is that sober life is not just good for you, it's actually better fun, too. Sobriety has had a bad rap, being equated since time immemorial with seriousness and dull, muted colours. In fact, sober life offers you the whole rainbow...She writes about her addiction with admirable honesty, and in a tone that is light, bubbly and remarkably rarely annoying.'

Alice O'Keefe, The Guardian

'This book is great. A balanced, informative and entertaining mélange of memoir, sociology and psychology. I identified very strongly with huge sections of it.'

Jon Stewart, guitarist of Sleeper and Leaving AA, Staying Sober blogger

'Sober is too often equated with "sombre" in our culture. Gray's book turns that idea on its head. Her experience of sobriety is joyful and life-affirming. A must-read for anyone who has a nagging suspicion that alcohol may be taking away more than it's giving.'

Hilda Burke, psychotherapist and couples counsellor

'Catherine Gray really captures the FUN we can have in sobriety. This book challenges the status quo; sobriety sounds as liberating as taking a trip to the jungle. Fun and inspirational. What an important book for our time! A joy to read.'

Samantha Moyo, founder of Morning Gloryville

'This book is a gamechanger. Everyone deserves to have Catherine hold their hand as they navigate the new world of not drinking – whether exploring alcohol-free periods or going for full on sobriety – and this book enables just that. Wise, funny and so relatable, The Unexpected Joy of Being Sober adds colour to the "dull" presumption that often comes with not drinking. A book for the times as sobriety continues to be the "wellness trend to watch". Keep it in your bag as you navigate the world of not drinking, and let Catherine lead the way for you as she re-defines sobriety in the 21st century.'

Laurie, Girl & Tonic blogger

the
unexpected
joy   of
being
single

aster   catherine gray

To my single buddies. There is nothing wrong – and everything right – with you.

An Hachette UK Company

www.hachette.co.uk

First published in Great Britain in 2018 by Aster, a division of

Octopus Publishing Group Ltd
Carmelite House
50 Victoria Embankment
London EC4Y 0DZ

www.octopusbooks.co.uk

Text copyright © Catherine Gray 2018

Design and layout copyright
© Octopus Publishing Group 2018

Excerpt from *Oh, The Places You'll Go!* by Dr. Seuss, TM and copyright © by Dr. Seuss Enterprises L.P. 1990. Used by permission of Random House Children's Books, a division of Penguin Random House LLC. All rights reserved. Reprinted by permission of HarperCollins Publishers Ltd © 1990

Distributed in the US by
Hachette Book Group
1290 Avenue of the Americas
4th and 5th Floors
New York, NY 10104

Distributed in Canada by
Canadian Manda Group
664 Annette Street,
Toronto, Ontario, Canada M6S 2C8

ISBN 978-1-91202-381-3

A CIP catalogue record for this book is available from the British Library.

Printed and bound in the UK

10 9 8 7 6 5 4 3 2 1

Some names and identities have been changed to protect people's identity.

Publishing director Stephanie Jackson
Senior editor Pauline Bache
Copyeditor Caroline Blake
Art director Yasia Williams-Leedham
Designer Siaron Hughes
Production Controller Peter Hunt

CONTENTS

PREFACE

Society tends to view single people with a furrow of the brow, a pang of pity, and a 'There, there, you'll meet someone soon' *Pats hand*. Articles about singles are often illustrated with a disgruntled woman downing a martini, or a lone man in a glittery hat with a birthday cake. [Insert sound effect of a mournful party streamer]

We live in a culture that tends to celebrate and exalt couples, but pigeonholes singles as outliers, misfits, oddballs who can't find someone to love them. Poor singles.

Yet, if being single is so terrible, why are more than half of us choosing it over coupling? Simple. Because it's *not terrible*. Being single for an extended period – or for life – can be incredibly empowering, fun and emancipating. Being single is a heckofalot better than panic-settling, that's for sure.

I didn't know this in my twenties, that single is not a failure, that I wasn't 'broken' somehow if I didn't have a boyfriend. I bought into the idea of the 'other half' hook, line and heart-sinker, and felt horribly incomplete when I was solo. I roamed around desperately seeking my missing half, like a bisected panto pony.

As a result, I was a totally batshit-crazy love addict. (Still am, sometimes.) Rather than love blooming over me like wisteria, it had me in a poison-ivy-esque chokehold, threatening my very wellbeing. This manifested in lovely behaviour such as internet stalking, fantasizing about marrying people I barely knew, clinging, raging arguments, cheating and snooping.

Why am I telling you all of this? I've now learned that when you share the darkest parts of your life, and find that thousands of people say 'Me too', it transmutes those black memories into spun gold. Sharing is like alchemy.

This book is not an attempt to tear down happy couples (I love happy couples), nor is it saying that marriage is claptrap, or claiming that being single is 'better.' Single isn't *better*. But it's definitely not less than either. It's equally as nourishing and joyous an existence.

Most books with 'single' in the title pivot on 'How to cure your singleness by finding a partner'. This isn't one of them. This book is about how to own being single, locate single joy and detach yourself from societal pressure to couple.

Singles are often treated as Peter Pans, overgrown adolescents, grown-ups in training, but actually, they're the ones who should be given Advanced Adulting awards, since solo life is often no cakewalk.

Shooting for single/couple equality will benefit us all. The widespread resistance to being single, the sad-sack stigma attached to it, means that people settle for, and stay in, relationships they don't truly want. As the acclaimed philosopher Alain de Botton says, 'Only once singlehood has completely equal prestige with its alternative, can we be sure that people can be free in their choices'.

In other words, campaigning for single equality is as much for the coupled-up, as it is for the single. Given it means the coupled will then have a newfound freedom chute; the option to be single without sorrow.

Maybe this is you. Maybe you're seeking an escape hatch from your socially endorsed, coupled-up form, that has begun to feel more like a cage, which is why you've picked up this book? Maybe you're digging deep to see if you have the guts to go single.

Read on and you'll see, there's nothing to be scared of. We'll talk later about how 'They lived happily ever after' should read 'They lived happily for a bit', given that research shows that marrying only gives a brief bump in contentment. We'll talk about how being attached only actually makes you one per cent happier. Our perceptions are that relationships are euphoria-givers, but the hard evidence, the reality, doesn't bear up to that wildly romanticized expectation.

Singledom is a choice. People aren't single because nobody wants them. They're single because they happen not to want the people who want them. Or maybe they're not even looking.

The question 'Why are you single?' is nonsensical. Because we just are. Sometimes you're in a relationship, and sometimes you're not, and there's no reason for it. Single is a result of a tangle of happenstance, choices and chance. Sometimes a relationship ends in marriage, and sometimes it doesn't, and that doesn't mean the relationship was a bust.

Similarly, a divorce is not a 'failure' of any kind. It's actually warrior-level brave to walk away from a marriage that's no longer working, given the way marriage is thrown up onto a pedestal in our society. Divorcees are rebels *with* a cause.

Being single should be just as validated and respected by society as being in a couple. Now that we're the majority, rather than the minority, maybe the stereotypes of 'sad single' and 'smug married' can be jettisoned once and for all, and we can see that both lifestyle choices come with their pros and cons.

Singles are not half people, we are full people, and perfectly complete exactly the way we are.

DRUNK ON LOVE

FEBRUARY, 2002

I've been on three dates with a charismatic, smooth, handsome older man – Daniel. I've decided that Daniel is The Guy. Every day, at work, I keep half an eye on my Nokia just in case its screen illuminates green and that wondrous little envelope appears.

Every night, after I finish work, I go home and dial-up the internet. Bing, bong, jjjjhhhhh, bong, bing, screeleebop, repeat.

Several minutes later, I am online. Booyah! I sit in front of my cathmermaid@hotmail.com* homepage and click on my inbox. I am looking for a fix. My substance. Relief from this constant craving. I am seeking an email from Daniel, ideally arranging our next date. It's not there. Fucksticks.

I sit there, for the next two hours, constantly hitting 'refresh' on the computer. Refresh, refresh, refresh. I really do.

When I get bored of my clicking, I read articles on vacuous websites with titles such as 'How to get him hot for you', or '21 signs he's nuts about you' or 'Men on their 19 date-dealbreakers'.

It's imperative I learn this poppycock, in order to bag Daniel. It's like I'm revising for a test. OK, so I need to: play with my hair, not respond straight away, be busy for the first two dates he suggests, reveal legs or cleavage but never both. Check, check, check. Refresh, refresh, refresh.

I am totally oblivious to the fact that I'm obsessively clicking my inbox like a rat in a laboratory cage. A rat with a button that dispenses a drug. I think my behaviour is normal.

My behaviour was not normal. I was a raging love addict.

Have you seen *Inside Out*? It's one of the most mind-bendingly profound films of the past decade. (I know it's meant for kids. #sorrynotsorry)

---

* Millennials: this was back in the days when we all chose ludicrous email addresses. Think hotrod1979@hotmail.com, lusciouslipslucy@yahoo.co.uk, beerpongbarry@outlook.com. Without ever thinking that these would have to go on our CVs. We soon learned.

Anyhow, the film sets up a metaphor whereby all of us have islands in our brains, islands that make up our personality. The little girl in it, Riley, has Hockey Island, Goofball Island, Friendship Island, Family Island… you get the picture. The islands are the most important things in her life.

When Riley turns into a teen, Tragic Vampire Romance Island, Fashion Island and Boy Band Island emerge from the water.

As I was watching *Inside Out*, I experienced an epiphany. If you had mapped my personality islands in my twenties, there would have been Booze Island, a Mordor-style isle filled with lost handbags, nightclubs like *Be At One*, slavering demons and bottomless abysses. But the island that would have been just as big, and just as malevolent, would have been Man Island. It was constantly illuminated, shaking and beset with thunderstorms, like a possessed amusement park.

When I gave up drinking aged 33, I decided it was also about time that I tackled Man Island. I needed to shrink Man Island into more of a dinky Isle of Wight, rather than a sprawling Ireland-sized realm. I needed to make it less dramatic, less fearful and less all-important. More of an aside kinda island. A pleasant destination, rather than a whole country.

So that's what I set about doing. And when I did so, I discovered a new island, an alternative, that I unexpectedly fell in love with. Single Island.

INTRODUCTION

Monomania: Exaggerated or obsessive enthusiasm for or preoccupation with one thing. (Extracted from the *Oxford Dictionary*)
Oneomania: Exaggerated or obsessive enthusiasm with finding The One. (Extracted from my head)

I'm going to level with you. I am still a love addict. I can't claim to be fixed. Nope. Sorry. That would be a bare-faced lie.

Alas, I am still the woman who stares saucer-eyed at her text messages, watching her phone like a TV, breathlessly awaiting a reply when those tantalizing iPhone dots appear. I still have to gently slap myself around the face to stop the Yosemite Wedding fantasy (woodland-themed, if you must know, a little bit Narnian, with harpists and flutists, and I will wear...oh rats, there I go again *gentle slap*).

I still crush like a paper bag whenever a man I've only had two dates with, and barely know, who I've spent a grand total of (drum roll) seven hours with, ghosts me. I'm still that person. I'm not going to pretend otherwise.

However, I have managed to dial my oneomania down from urgent, hysterical, phone-stabbing, triple-messaging ('Are you OK? Have you had an accident?!'). It helped enormously that I took a whole year off dating, during which I didn't so much as hold a man's hand.

It helped that I read as much as I could about why love addiction happens, all of which I will impart to you. It helped that I stopped giving people the power to puff or deflate me. When I was chronically love-addicted, I was like an inflatable person; reliant on praise to pump me up and shrinking into a glum little heap when I felt rejected.

A SPINSTER AGED 33

My first love rock bottom came a couple of months before my final alcohol rock bottom. My dad, now sadly departed, started calling me a 'spinster' aged 33. And no, he wasn't yanking my chain. This was no 'just rattling your cage!' joke. He was being straight-down-the-line serious that I was a spinster, and what the devil was I gonna do about it.

This 'You're a spinster' conversation came about because of a visit we'd just had to my aunt and uncle. During which, the question 'So, any danger of you getting married, Catherine?' was asked. I explained that I'd just split up with a guy who hadn't been treating me well, who I'd lived with for a year, and that I felt good about the decision. My uncle frowned and said 'Well, you're not getting any younger,' which my dad guffawed at.

When we left, I turned to my dad, laughed nervously, and said 'They've started treating me like a spinster!' He said, matter-of-fact, unflinchingly, as was his way: 'Well, *you are a spinster*.' We then had a huge argument in the car, during which I cried, said I wasn't a spinster, and he shouted at me that I was a spinster. It was bizarre.

I was utterly distraught. Later that day, I went for a long run along the River Lagan, sat on a leafy riverbank and full-body-sobbed. Once I'd cried myself out, I tried to figure out why this had wounded me so much. I knew full well, rationally, that this was ridiculous fifties *Mad Men*-esque misogyny, and yet it had cut me deep. I explored my wound and found a thorn buried deep inside. A thorn of Failure. That was it. Huh. This was what had scored my side so brutally.

I felt like I'd failed as a woman, as a person, because I hadn't found my life partner yet. I felt unchosen, unwanted, left on the shelf. While also knowing, intellectually, that this was nonsense. I knew that I had just finished a toxic relationship and was, at the age of 33, a mere youngster in the grand scheme.

A friend once informed me that my photo albums resembled an ego-fluffing trophy room. The sort of room somebody despicable has hidden away, replete with stag antlers, rhino horns and stuffed leopards.

I recently looked back over said photo album, with a discerning eye. She was right. It was basically a Rolodex of my exes, with the odd mate thrown in. It was a display cabinet. Of men who had found me to be worthwhile. Now that I look at this album, it's highly creepy. My catalogue of kills. I really did define myself by the men I'd slept with.

But, d'you know what? I completely understand why I was the way I was. I don't judge my twentysomething self. I'd been taught that romantic relationships are *the most important thing*, over and over, through subliminal (or blatant) societal messaging. As have you.

SETTLE DOWN, QUICK!

Here's the thing. We've been brainwashed into thinking that a happy-ever-after always involves finding a partner. The person. Our lobster. Our other half. How is it that, in the 21st century, getting married is still seen as a woman's greatest accomplishment? Is it my imagination, or is that undercurrent really there? (I think it's really there.) And, it's not just women who feel this intense pressure. Men feel it too.

Yet, despite this proposal press-gang, millions of us are increasingly choosing to stay single. The single population is growing at ten times the rate of the population in general. A typical British millennial is expected to live alone, without a partner, for an average of 15 years.

The most recent data, collated by Mintel in their *Single Lifestyles* 2017 report, found that 51 per cent of Brits aged 25–44 are now single (including divorcees). Back in 2016, the Office for National Statistics reported that the single/divorced slice of the population was 35 per cent. Could that seriously be a jump of 16 per cent in one little year?

We're leaving marriage later and later. The Office for National Statistics released a report in 2018 that said, 'For marriages of opposite-sex couples, the average (mean) age for men marrying in 2015 was 37.5 years, while for women it was 35.1 years.'

In other words, the average bride was 35 years old, while the average groom was circa 38. This revelation triggered a slew of press headlines, such as 'Rise of the Older Bride: average age for women to walk down the aisle is now over 35.' Out of these 2015 marriages, 75 per cent of the men and 76 per cent of the women were marrying for the first time.[*] Six in ten brides were over 30.

In 1970, average marriage ages were 27 for men and 25 for women.[**] So, compared to 1970, men are getting married 11 years later, while women are getting married 10 years later. Astounding, huh?

What's more, 42 per cent of marriages end in divorce. Meaning that almost half of those who walk hopefully and beaming down the aisle, wind up suddenly single later in life.

---

[*] *I couldn't locate a reliable, nationwide source of data for the average ages of first marriage.*
[**] *The 1970 mean marriage-age figures have been rounded up/down.*

SINGLE IS NOW THE NORM

Before I dug up this data showing that singles have now tipped over into becoming the majority, I wrote reams of cool stuff about norm-subverting, which then had to hit the cutting room floor, once I found out that *we are now the norm*. I didn't know that. Did you?

However, even though it *is* that way, it doesn't *feel* that way. It still feels rebellious, like trend-bucking, to be single later in life. Why? Because we are still living in the shadow of the nuclear-shaped family and groaning under the weight of our parents' expectations.

We'll talk more about this later, but during the raising and adulting of the Baby Boomer* generation, there was an almighty marriage spike, which is likely why our parents are so perplexed that we're not married *like they were* by our age. (If you're aged 25–50, you're most likely the offspring of Baby Boomers.)

Our parents and the media have taught us to fear being single. I know this fear, intimately. It's why I was never single in my twenties, and instead swung from boyfriend to boyfriend. I thought *any* relationship, no matter how toxic, was better than none.

When I wasn't with someone I felt flat and dark, like a pitch-black room that waits for someone to come along, flick on the light, and animate it once more. And ironically, given the paramount importance I awarded the preservation of relationships, I was a human wrecking ball. I snooped, cheated, started arguments, all that fun stuff. I would break up with people to push a lever for more attention.

In recent years, I've managed to stop all of that. I don't stay in unhealthy relationships, I'm no longer frightened of being single, I can date without losing my marbles, and I've now learned to luxuriate in my singleness, rather than look longingly at couples thinking, 'I want that. Why don't I have that?'

As I say, I'm not *cured* of love addiction. It's still running around inside me, growling for sustenance. But I've learned how to live with it. How to tame it, leash it, re-train it, even stroke it. And I'm now genuinely happy as a single.

* Baby Boomers are those born roughly between 1946 and 1964, or those who are between 54 and 72 years old the year this book was published (2018).

Working on my love addiction has led to me now feeling free of the need to be coupled. In my twenties I was single for a grand total of six months (which were basically spent interviewing potential new boyfriends) and in the past five years I've been single for three-and-a-half *years*. That's a rise from 5 per cent singleness in my twenties, to 70 per cent in the past five years.

LET THE REVERSE BRAINWASH BEGIN

So, what are we going to do in this book? How do we proceed?

We're going to de-programme ourselves by talking to psychologists and neuroscientists about the love-hooked messages we get from society, and what goes on in our crazy-in-love brains.

We'll dig around in the messages we get from literature, films and TV, that condition us to be obsessed with romantic love (The *Bridget Jones* trilogy ended with, of course, a wedding). These messages get under our skin, they dig into our subconscious, they make us think that our happy-ever-after has to involve a couple silhouetted against a sunset. Y'know what? It doesn't.

If you do want to date, I'm going to tell you how I learned to do it *moderately*, without turning into a deranged Instagram stalker, and without thinking I was in love with some dude I'd known for two weeks.

Most importantly, we're going to locate and free a spring of single joy. And make sure it never goes away again.*

* Please note: wherever possible, I have been gender-neutral, while also remembering that around nine out of ten of my readers are female. Any heteronormative clangers are just that – accidental – and I apologize in advance for them. All of my ex-boyfriends names have been changed, to protect the innocent and let the guilty off the hook. Namaste *bows*.

I: THE MAKING OF A LOVE ADDICT

LOVE ADDICTION DEFINED

The Priory, one of the most highly regarded addiction-treatment centres in Britain, defines love addiction as 'characterized by feelings of strong obsessive behaviours of which the sufferer feels compelled to repeat regardless of the consequences'.

My interpretation is this: any addiction is the insanity of doing the same thing over and over, despite the fall-out, and expecting different results.

Dr Vik Watts and Mel Davis, from The Priory's addiction team, pull out the classic behaviours of love addiction as:

'1. Clinging to an idealized relationship, despite a different reality.

2. Returning time and time again to an abusive and damaging relationship.

3. Placing responsibility for emotional wellbeing on others.

4. Craving attention from many different relationships and seeking new sources of attention.'

I can absolutely say that I identify with every single one of those four. Yep, yup, tick, did all of that. BINGO. I win at love addiction!

Let's go through each and I'll tell you what my symptoms looked like:

1. CLINGING TO AN IDEALIZED RELATIONSHIP, DESPITE A DIFFERENT REALITY
I fantasized about movie-style relationships, tried to get my relationships to that level, and felt disappointed when I couldn't. I was simultaneously an idealist and a critic.

I would do anything to avoid being single, including putting up with substandard treatment and/or dating people I wasn't that into. I put being in a couple above my own happiness.

2. RETURNING TIME AND TIME AGAIN TO AN ABUSIVE AND DAMAGING RELATIONSHIP
As you'll read later on, some of the behaviour I put up with – and exhibited myself – was extraordinarily screwed-up, because I was in denial as to what the reality was.

If I sensed a relationship was beginning to falter, I reacted by snooping and creating dramas. Which, believe it or not, were attempts at survival strategies. 'If I find out what's wrong, maybe I can fix it.' And: 'If I threaten to leave, maybe he'll beg me to stay and realize he can't live without me!'

But these invasive/mercurial tactics actually just ransacked the relationship, rather than 'saving us'.

3. PLACING RESPONSIBILITY FOR EMOTIONAL WELLBEING ON OTHERS

I hadn't the foggiest that my happiness was my own responsibility. Say what? If I was blue, it was my boyfriend's fault. He needed to *make me* happy. He was failing at his job. Bad boyfriend.

4. CRAVING ATTENTION FROM MANY DIFFERENT RELATIONSHIPS AND SEEKING NEW SOURCES OF ATTENTION

When I wasn't in a relationship, I sought one with the same level of urgency as you seek a place to live. My mates called me a 'love monkey' for swinging from man to man, like a monkey swings from tree to tree. Even when I was coupled, I solicited attention from other men. I confused sex with intimacy. I had sex, when what I wanted was intimacy. And sex was more like a moving art installation, intended to elicit approval and applause, rather than a loving act.

I am happy to report that I've now managed to cease all such behaviour. PHEW. But I still remain vigilant to any of this creeping back in. Always vigilant.

If you think that you too might be a love addict, don't feel disheartened by that label. 'I don't love the term "love addict" since it seems to imply a lifelong problem,' Dr Jenny Taitz, a certified psychologist and author of How to be Single and Happy, tells me. 'At any moment, we can choose a new action, and create new patterns of behaviour that link to our hopes. Our past doesn't need to dictate our future.'

I agree. I think of addiction more as experiential than defining of me. If I was going to be really pedantic, I would say that 'I have experienced love addiction, and am still prone to exhibiting signs of it,' but that's a bloody mouthful, and I can't be arsed to type that repeatedly, so just take 'love addict' as shorthand for that. I'm going to wear that label, but you certainly don't have to.

And most of all, if you feel like you might be hooked on love too, there's hope. Change is entirely possible. People change all the blinking time.

WHEN I GROW UP, I WANT TO GET MARRIED

When I am four, I am able to climb the towering oak tree at the end of our road, right to the top. None of the boys can do it. I'm the only one. I'm the king of the castle, while they're the dirty rascals. But then I realize, aged five, that I am a girl and, ideally, girls don't climb trees. Girls are meant to be *queens*, not kings.

Instead, I start making 'perfume' out of smushed up rose petals and tiny drowning insects. I carefully place my creation, tongue out with the effort of not spilling, into the hot press to 'bake.' And then I slather myself – and my grimacing mum – with it. Already, I am very aware that a girl's purpose is to attract. That my ultimate destiny is marriage.

Aged seven, my friends and I sit on the kerb of our street in Carrickfergus, working out our percentage compatibility with the names of boys we like, who are currently playing footie and don't give a flying monkeys about us. I swing like a confused compass between what I really want to do (tear around doing wheelies on my brother's BMX) and what I'm told I should want to do (play with the doll I have that pees when I give it a drink. That's literally all it does *rolls eyes*).

If my purpose is to achieve male approval, then I am already failing at it. I feel rejected by both father figures in my life. As I grow into a gawky tween, my father appears to be consistently underwhelmed by me. My parents divorce and my mum remarries when I'm 10; I acquire a stepfather who openly loathes me.

My new stepfather makes my brother and I knock if we want to come into the living room (we are banned from it after 7pm), types us letters with bullet points of what we are doing wrong (too much butter on knives in the dishwasher!), nicknames us 'the lodgers' and makes it crystal clear that we are moving out on our 18th birthdays, come hell or high water.

If friends of mine spontaneously ring the doorbell, he sends them away with a roar and a slam of anger, for not having a prior appointment to visit. I don't know what he expects; a scroll sent via a messenger boy on a horse?

I escape my home life by reading. By 12, I have read a contraband copy of *Forever* by Judy Blume about seven times. I am drunk on the romance it describes. One day, I will love a man so much that I will let him put his 'Ralph' inside me.

My stepfather reads my diaries. My best friend, Sam, and I creep out of the house the next night and cry dramatically as we lower the rest of my diaries, the undiscovered ones, into a pond in Dudley's Priory Park, as if we're burying a beloved pet. We walk home whispering frantically about running away to live in Birmingham, where we will shop at the rag market, pierce several parts of our bodies, date guitarists and go to Snob's every Friday.

Deeply unhappy, I ask my dad if I can come and live with him, on Islandmagee, in Ireland. My happiest days are summers spent there, skimming stones in the horseshoe bay, crunching cinnamon lozenges, playing Swingball, repeatedly watching the 4 Non Blondes video on MTV, and playing with his three Jack Russells. He says no. I am devastated.

Throughout all of this turmoil, I am incredibly close to both my mother and my stepmother (my dad's partner, Ruth). It's either a coincidence or a fait accompli that later, as an adult, I find forging lifelong female friendships a doddle, while with men, I never manage to make anything stick, even a platonic friendship.

APPROVAL-HUNTING

At 14, I replace my devotion to horse riding, with nightclubbing. One of my closest friends at school drops me, writing me a letter saying that I have 'become obsessed with boys', whereas I used to be all about bands, good books and having a laugh. I am hurt, but I reason that she's got it all wrong, not me. I swivel and point myself towards my other friends instead.

One day in our French lesson, the teacher asks us to stand up whenever we hear a French adjective that fits us. The class goes up and down like yo-yos as he calls out 'long hair', 'blonde', 'tall' and then 'pretty', which only the popular, smug girls stand up for.

Then he calls out 'ugly.' Balls. I have to stand up, don't I? Everyone can see that I am. I stand up. Nobody else does. The teacher tells me to sit down, says it was just a joke, and clumsily starts to tell me that he thinks I'm actually...before realizing he can't, and trailing off.

Something magical happens. My dumpy teenage frame stretches as I grow tall, cheekbones emerge from my doughy face, straighteners land in Boots and that nice man John Frieda brings us hair serum so that I can tame my nuclear cloud of hair.

I go to see my dad, and a visiting friend of his circles me as if I'm a horse, looks me up and down, and declares me a 'Thoroughbred'. My dad turns to me, surprised, and something shifts behind his eyes. Later he says, 'It stirred something in me that I'd never felt before. And then I realized what it was. Pride.'

My mum finally kicks my stepdad out when I'm 15, the trigger being him chasing me around the house threatening to lamp me because I've eaten something I wasn't allowed. He writes me a letter saying that he hopes we can all work things out, starting the letter, inexplicably, by saying that I am becoming an 'attractive young woman'. It's the first nice thing he's ever said to me, and I cling to it.

Soon after, my mum meets my current stepfather, Stewart, who is a king among men. He builds an extra wall in his house with his bare hands, in order to create me a bedroom of my own. From the day I meet him onward, I never feel anything but accepted, cherished and loved.

Stewart never admires – or derides – my appearance, other than to say amusing things like, 'You look like a....physiotherapist' when I ask him if he likes my new top. Who I am as a person, that's what matters to him. He rewards honesty and kindness and humour, and doesn't give a stuff what I look like in my Jane Norman dress.

But by then, my blueprint of seeking male approval, my expectation of rejection, is bone-deep. And given that my newfound passable prettiness once wielded the power to *turn disgust to acceptance*, I award my looks supreme appearance in my adolescent brain.

I AM A DOLL'S HOUSE
And so henceforth, all of my self-esteem depends on how I look. I purchase/shoplift my self-worth from make-up counters. By 17, I spend an hour-and-a-half getting ready for sixth form. Leaving the house

without a full face of make-up is as unthinkable as leaving the house stark-vagina-naked.

If I'm having a bad hair day, I simply don't go to college. Appearance first, learning second. If somebody doesn't fancy me, I take that as the Most Mortal Wound. I need everyone to fancy me, because I think that if they fancy me, it means I'm worthwhile.

I hop aboard a Rolodex of constant boyfriends. It's very important to me that my boyfriend-of-the-time thinks I'm the most attractive girl. 'You're the most beautiful girl I've ever been out with,' my boyfriend Tony offers. 'But am I the most attractive girl you've ever seen? I mean, apart from on telly?' He tries to change the subject.

I am like a doll's house that is for display only. An intricately painted façade, but with a dull cardboard interior, where you can see the staples and the scruffy seams. Wanting my boyfriends to find me more appealing than anyone else is an utterly unattainable chimera. But without that assurance, without them being complicit in that illusion, I feel adrift, lost, unanchored.

I fail to realize that people don't choose to go out with people based on their exteriors; they choose them based on the entire package. I don't crave approval of my personality, because as far as I am concerned, my only worth is in my outer shell.

Given the founding year of my acceptance by men was the year I started styling my hair, wearing make-up and pouring myself into tight clothes, it's imperative that I keep these game-changers up.

In the first few months of a relationship, I get up half an hour before him to apply foundation and mascara, and iron my hair, because I truly believe that if he wakes up next to the Actual Me, he'll be appalled. I need him to believe in Maybelline Me. Because there's no way in hell I was born with it.

SKETCHING BOYFRIENDS

A night out is 'pointless' if I don't pull. And thankfully, Nineties Birmingham is awash with #everydaysexism to prop up my self-esteem. Lines like 'If I say you have a beautiful body will you hold it against me?' or 'Love that dress. It would look even better on my bedroom floor' or 'Nice legs, what time do they open?' are still acceptable. I can't go out into the world without men shouting at me about my bum.

Boyfriends are empty pages of my sketchbook. I draw in heroism and magnificence, when all I have is a rudimentary outline. But they don't fall for the real me either. They may as well fall for Jessica Rabbit, given I'm just a collage of 'What Men Find Sexy' articles.

I read *A Streetcar Named Desire* by Tennessee Williams at university and feel a rubber-band twang of recognition when I read about Blanche DuBois. I style myself as a poker-playing, wisecracking, boozy broad. I seek out men who are a challenge. I love meeting a man who is indifferent to me, beating him at pool, and sparking all around him until I light a flicker of warmth in the cold coal of his eyes. Until the fireball-bright look of 'yes' passes between us.

I am a sexual vigilante who brags about sleeping nude and derides my best friend's soft PJs and cuddly toys. Bed is a stage, not a *cocoon*, forgodsake. I am more pop-up performance art, than person. I badger my university friends to play strip poker after nights out, so that the tone can turn from wholesome to wanton.

I am like the pouty, nearly naked person who parades about on Instagram, except I don't have social media to strut around, so I use Birmingham's Broad Street instead. I stride around like an open-mouthed Pac-Man, feeding on the compliments I gather as I go. When I drink, I feel ten-feet tall; being sober shrinks me.

At first glance, you look at me and see supreme confidence, a sway of the hips, exaggerated laughter, a game face. But if you're observant you'll see a person at war with themselves. An irritated tug at rebellious hair, feet shoved into too-small shoes, fingertips bitten to blood and superglued to fake nails. Beneath the swagger of this showpony, there's civil unrest.

I read Erica Jong's *Fear of Flying*, which constructs an erotic wonderland and gives me the term 'zipless fuck': shorthand for sex without strings, commitment or ulterior motives. That's what I tell myself I'm doing, but the truth is, there's nothing zipless about my motives. I want intimacy, affection, validation and I'm looking for it in all the wrong places, by letting my clothes cascade onto floors.

I drink to feel close to people and wind up too close. I pour wine into myself to feel sexy, and end up being too sexy. I don't know how to halt the intimacy acceleration halfway.

I wake up the next morning and for a blissful second, I don't know where I am, or who I'm with. Then I feel shame cover me. I don't want to do this, so why do I keep doing it?

Because I am addicted to them wanting me – the conquer, the overthrow. That underbelly snap of mutual attraction. Which sends lust swimming from my navel to my hip bone, where it pauses to tumble-turn, and then surges down the inside of my thigh.

A night on the lash and the lust comes with consequences; both appear to hate me come the morning. Sunrise smashes the spell, like a collective morning comedown at a rave. Last night desire pulled me into its lap; at daybreak it boots a bewildered me back into reality.

As Carl Jung said, 'Shame is a soul-eating emotion,' and that's how it feels. Like tiny moths eating at my spirit, moths that are hidden in the sad eiderdown of those mornings. I try to sleep it away, drink it away and laugh it away by turning my trysts into anecdotes, but the shame moths have burrowed under my skin and are now chomping away at my soul.

LOVE-ADDICT LULLABIES

To get to sleep, to erase these episodes from my mind, I compose love-addict lullabies. Montages of things I'd seen in movies, like [insert man of the month] chasing a car to stop me leaving, or diving into foaming white-water rapids to save my favourite necklace. I lie there tingling with *vorfreude*, imagining my future wedding, just as an aspiring astronaut pictures being the first to set foot on Mars, or a showjumper envisages clearing a tricksy water obstacle.

I listen to The Corrs 'What Can I Do', Extreme's 'More than Words', Big Mountain's 'Baby I Love your Way' and Aqualung's 'Brighter than Sunshine', and fantasize about making men love me. And they do. I am a hit. But I can't handle true intimacy; as soon as they come too close, look too close, I pull away and pivot towards my next conquest.

My first bona fide person addiction is the Daniel we've already talked about, the one of the constant email refreshing. I date him when I'm 22 and write down every detail of our dozen or so dates.

I read the date logs over and over and record every compliment he ever gives me diligently, like an accountant tallying profits. But when he tells me that he loves me, during sex, perhaps accidentally, I stare at him, horrified. The truth is, I don't love him, I love the idea of him.

My dad tells me I'm 'getting bingo wings' when I turn 24, so I panic and join a gym. (I spend the next five years thinking I have fat arms, when I definitely don't.) If I have a spot, he will say, 'What is THAT?', angrily pointing at the offending item as if I've tattooed a spider on my face. He's just trying to help me, I think. I'm failing him, by becoming unattractive.

I believe that female beauty is like a flower that only blooms for a short while, then browns and droops, and slowly drains of colour. I am terrified of this wilt, even in my mid-twenties. If anyone criticizes my appearance, I take this as a terrifying sign that my wilt has begun. And now what will I become?

My alcohol dependence and my love addiction prop each other up, like smashed people trying to walk home from a party. My drinking enables me to secure boyfriends, and when it all falls apart, my drinking is there to console me, or to catapult me on to the next conquest.

When boyfriends break it off with me, I react by crying and drinking until catatonic, while listening to the Foo Fighters' 'Best of You' or Radiohead's 'Creep' on repeat. When I break it off with them, I bowl out, get blotto and find a new bloke.

THE GIRL WHO CRIED THE ONE

There are plenty of men to serve as an energy source for my self-worth. By now, I am working at *Cosmopolitan* magazine as a writer, and I go out-out four or five times a week, to drink my head off and flirt outrageously.

My job gifts me with assignments like 'Find 35 men and convince them to pose naked for charity'. Basically an excuse to chat up random men in the street, on work's time and dime. I secure all 35 within a week and my colleagues give me a thunderous round of applause. I go on dates with several of them after the photo shoot.

I bring boyfriend after boyfriend home, like a proud cat with a mouse, so much so that my family stops learning their names and settle on 'Whatshisface' or 'Yer man' or 'Cath's new boyfriend'. I laugh when people call me a 'Maneater' and shrug when they exclaim, 'Another one, already?!' They shake their heads in disbelief when I swear that this one is different. I have become the girl who cried The One.

Time after time, my friends comment on how my relationships get 'intense' really quickly. And they do. We plan kids' names after just a couple of months – weeks even. I think it's because we're in a romantic spin, but really, it's a 'just add people' mix, the Instant Whip of relationships.

Men are potential suitors first, people second. If they're married, I simply stop talking to them. 'Bah. Irrelevant.' Birthday parties are not chances to celebrate my friend, they are a chance to meet heaps of potential new suitors. I look at who's checking me out on the train, rather than at the golden fields streaming past.

I am a deft catastrophizer, so much so that one boyfriend starts calling it 'Cathastrophizing'. If my boyfriend isn't answering the phone one evening, he's definitely having a threesome. If he wants to 'talk', he's definitely going to split up with me. I have a talent for doomscaping ice palaces out of the teeniest, tiniest snowflakes.

I am convinced that every other woman in my boyfriend's life poses a threat. I quiz them about their exes, convinced that if I can gather enough data about what went right/wrong, I can win the game. On high alert for love rivals, I scan any new environment for more attractive women. Whenever I do catch a boyfriend sneaking a glance at another girl, I feel it like a hot rod of pain.

A WRECKING BALL

When I'm 27, I meet Seb and fall deeply in love and, happily, he does the same. Finally, I've found a relationship in which we're both equally keen.

The preservation of the relationship is my ultimate goal. Yet, I fly it into a wall like a kamikaze pilot. Just as a teenage boy smashes a model airplane because it's not 'perfect', I blow things up on a regular basis.

I burn our bond to the ground, rebuild it, demolish it, reconstruct carefully, hack it to smithereens, piece it back together, and then wonder why it's a lopsided, fragile-as-fuck eyesore.

I do things like dump him in a rage, and then, when he asks for a few days for him to process our break-up-then-make up, I refuse to allow it. He screens my calls during his 'headspace' time, so I go to the payphone at the end of the street and repeatedly call him from that instead, tricking him by using a different number. I cannot stand not having access to him *at all times*. Because he is my *everything*. And that's how it's supposed to be, right?

Our relationship buckles beneath my movie-standard expectations. I carefully orchestrate date-cute scenes, by organizing weekends looking for wild ponies in the New Forest, or cocktails overlooking Santorini's caldera, and then feel disappointed when they're not what I expected.

I terrorize him with my demands, tantrums and bad drunken behaviour, until, finally, all of my Cathastrophizing comes true, and he dumps me three years in, shortly after my 30th birthday. He's done.

My heart is not just cracked in two, it's decimated. But my immediate response is to swivel and find a new boyfriend, as if I have just lost a job and need to find a new source of income pronto.

I am online dating within a month. When I can't get a date, I sit and drink-dial my roster of men from home. I am the female equivalent of the man who texts after midnight saying, 'You still up? Wanna come over?'

I don't really care who comes over, as long as someone does. Anything, other than being alone. I am in the market for a man who will provide the boyfriend experience, at 1am, while the men I dial are usually in the market for something entirely different.

STORYBOOKS AND SCREENS SHAPE LOVE ADDICTS

Let's step out of my story for a moment, and into the cultural landscape as a whole. To take in an aerial sweep of the messages I was – and you were – receiving. Kids are like Play-Doh. They are easily shaped. Here is a nice chat I recently had with a five-year-old.

Five-year-old: 'Where's your house?'

Me: 'Well, I don't have one, I do something called "rent".'

Five-year-old: 'You don't have a house?! MUMMMM, she doesn't have a house!'

Five-year-old, a few seconds later, once she's digested this shock: 'Are you married?'

Me: 'Nope.'

Five-year-old, hands on hips: 'Why not?'

Me: 'Because I haven't met anyone I want to marry.'

Five-year-old: 'OK. Do you have children? *Looks pointedly at my belly*

Me: 'Ummm, anyway, shall we go upstairs and play?'

I find it fascinating that a five-year-old already knows that these three things – property, marriage and children – are markers of a 'successful' adult. How do they know that?! These messages get encoded young, no?

One of the ways we are conditioned very early on is through fairytales. Let's consider some of the messages a five-year-old could glean from the most popular ones.

Snow White's stepmother is so jealous of her superior beauty that she tries to kill her – three times. But hey, at least Snow White (along with her band of enchanted woodland friends) is an excellent cook and cleaner for seven men.

Cinderella's only hope of getting away from the Ugly Sisters (ugliness is generally shorthand for being a bell-end, in fairytales) is to fulfil her dreams of going to the ball and landing the prince.

Sleeping Beauty is in a cursed coma until a prince kisses her and animates her. Even Ariel, aka the little mermaid, who is indeed a ballsy, father-defying heroine and saves the prince's life, trades her beautiful voice for legs (that feel like walking on knives) in order to hang out with him. She then dances for him, despite excruciating pain.

Beauty is always, always what enchants the princes in these tales. Many of the princes propose before they've even *talked to* the girl for longer than a heartbeat. Modern-day fairytales such as *The Princess Bride* and *Stardust* also slot into the narrative mould of beautiful damsel in distress being rescued by a courageous man.

One of the reasons Whitney Wolfe started *Bumble* (a dating app where women have to message men first) was to subvert this man-approaches-woman dynamic. Wolfe encourages women to swerve mean, and seek nice.

'We're trained to be attracted to meanness,' she says, citing the Disney dynamic. 'The little boy is mean to the little girl because he has a crazy crush on her. But then he goes home and writes love letters at night.'

Right? It's why we were told that the boy who pulled our pigtails in the playground had a crush on us. 'We've all heard "Oh, he's too nice," as if it is a bad thing. Why is that part of our culture?' says Wolfe.

Moana is lauded as being the most progressive Disney heroine yet, in which a 16-year-old Pacific Islander goes on a daring ocean voyage to break an ancient curse on her people. 'She has no love interest!' the marketing around the film megaphoned. (Guys, she's 16. That's no big whoop.) *Brave*'s Merida also tried to break the princess-shaped mould. And all credit to Emma Watson, who insisted on a feminist upgrade for *Beauty and the Beast*; the tweak being that Beauty is the genius inventor, not her father. But we still have a very long way to go.

For every sea-voyaging Moana or galloping-off-on-an-adventure Merida, we still have a thousand pink-hued 'Find a gown, land the prince' tropes being fed to our little girls. They hammer home the notion that Finding a Man is their ultimate goal. *Frozen*'s Elsa was upheld as a feminist icon given her lack of love interest and her 'You can't marry a man you just met' counsel to Anna (about time, Disney!). But as somebody clever pointed out to me, she's still rocking a dress with a thigh-high split, as well as a waist that would have no room for internal organs.

Of course, fairytales are emotionally unhealthy bedtime stories for little boys too. He's taught that he needs to lock down his emotions (emoting = bad), to be flawlessly brave (no room for fear here), an athletic action man (not a stay-at-home geek), he needs to rescue her (rather than have her rescue him) and most of all, he needs to secure an objet d'art, a beauty to denote his prowess (above finding somebody simply kind and nice).

A few years back, I was reading to my three year-old niece from her *Princess Annual*, and realized that it was already giving her 'Finding a Man is imperative' messages. So I started adding lines. 'But she also wanted to get a degree, as well as a dress.' Or 'But women can be just as happy single, as they are married.'

Penelope Cruz does this too. 'Fairytales matter so much because these are the first stories that you hear from the mouths of your parents,' she once said. 'So, when I read fairytales to my kids at night, I'm always changing the endings – always, always, always, always. Fucking Cinderella and Sleeping Beauty and all of this – there's a lot of machismo in those stories. That can have an effect on the way that kids see the world. If you're not careful, they start thinking: "Oh, so the men get to decide everything"'. Cruz takes it to the extreme and completely edits the ending. 'In my version of Cinderella when the prince says, "Do you wanna marry?" she says, "No, thanks, 'cos I don't want to be a princess. I want to be an astronaut, or a chef".'

But I have been complicit, in the love-centric shaping of a child. For my niece's christening, I bought and wrapped four of my favourite books, and marked them with the ages at which she should open them. These were *The Very Hungry Caterpillar* (I stand by that one, voracious eating is good), *Thumbelina* (which in retrospect is merely: 'tiny girl seeks husband'), *Rebecca* ('young wife lives in shadow of husband's dead wife') and *How I Live Now* (beautifully written, but ostensibly a 'boy meets girl' love story, albeit where the girl gets the chance to be a spitfire).

All of the latter three spin on the axis of a love story. Whoops. I've since attempted to undo my status as an accidental trope-feeding accomplice, by gifting her with *Good Night Stories for Rebel Girls*.

Stylist, one of my favourite magazines, subverted the fairytale in

December 2016 by featuring a sleeping beauty, with the coverline '...and then she woke up and went to host her TED talk'. Inside, we saw a slipperless Cinderella with the strapline 'And then she put on her shoe, went back up the stairs and collected her MBE'. It summed up so neatly how we need to be giving little girls different stories. As Lizzie Pook pithily said in the piece, our focus should be reaching the glass ceiling, rather than the glass slipper.

SCREEN-SHAPED DREAMS

I think most women, including me, spend their lives fighting a wave of disappointment that nobody has ever:

1. Fought over us in an Italian restaurant, à la Hugh Grant and Colin Firth in *Bridget Jones*.

2. Stood under our window with a boombox, like John Cusack in *Say Anything*.

3. Gone to our father, cap in hand, like Patrick Swayze in *Dirty Dancing*, to try and convince him that they're good enough for his daughter.

4. Turned up outside our door with a bunch of giant flash-cards, telling us that 'To me, you are perfect'. (*Love Actually*.)

5. Built us a house with a wraparound porch and a room for us to paint in, as per Ryan Gosling in *The Notebook*.

6. Changed their look from Greaser to Preppy, despite mass ridicule from mates, in an attempt to 'match us' better, like in *Grease*.

7. Stood outside our door for hours until we finish work, hiding behind a Xmas tree. (*How to Be Single*.)

8. Transformed, nay, *transfigured* from lady-hopping barman into ready-for-commitment guy having met us. (*He's Just Not That Into You*.)

THESE THINGS NEVER HAPPEN. They just don't. They've never happened to me, or anyone I know, or anyone they know. The reality of a fledgling courtship is much more like Jordan Catalano in *My So-Called Life*. We have no idea if they like us; sometimes they appear to, sometimes they don't. Mystifying at best. (And we never fancy Brian Krakow, even though he's totally emotionally available and into us.)

Even two of my favourite chick flicks, which were acclaimed for upholding female friendship above romantic love, contain love-addict conditioning. *Bridesmaids* for instance (the 'Help me, I'm poor' plane scene makes me cry with laughter). Why did Annie (Kristen Wiig) *have* to end up with a guy? Why?

Meanwhile, *How to Be Single* has so many spot-on moments such as Meg (Leslie Mann) giving little sister Alice (Dakota Johnson) a ticking-off for watching *Bridget Jones* when she's heartbroken. 'It feels good in the moment,' Alice wails. But the wrap-up (spoiler* alert ahead, people) drops a total clanger, by lingering on fortysomething Leslie Mann and saying 'Isn't there a danger that you'll get so good at being single, so set in your ways, that you'll miss out on the chance to be with somebody great.' Aargh. They nearly got it *so right*.

I was all like 'Men don't have to deal with this crap!'. Until I started thinking about the ultimate blokey films too. *The Hangover* ends with them all dancing with suitors. *Top Gun* pivots on a love story. *Die Hard*, the same. I could go on and on. The *Mission Impossible* films, the *Bond* franchise, the *Bourne* trilogy. The relationship is not the main focus, granted, and the love story is more of a 'foxy chick skydives through roof wearing leather catsuit' kinda vibe, but it's still THERE. Always there.

There is, of course, the odd film that bucks the 'and then they got together' ending trend. There's *Home Again*, *La-La Land*, *The Way We Were* and *Eternal Sunshine of the Spotless Mind*. But they're the extreme exception, not the rule.

THE BECHDEL TEST

Thankfully, we now have the Bechdel Test, in order to forage for films that are more groundbreaking.

The Bechdel Test originated in a cartoon published in 1985 by Alison Bechdel, called 'The Rule'. In the cartoon, one woman tells another that she only sees movies that meet three requirements. Firstly, there must be more than two women. Secondly, they need to talk to one another. Thirdly, they need to talk about something other than a man. 'Last movie I was able to see was *Alien*,' cracked the cartoon character.

When you hear about the 'rules' of the Bechdel Test it's tempting to

* While we're on the subject of spoilers, my favourite film spoiler story ever is this: in China, they renamed The Sixth Sense 'He is a Ghost'. They actually did.

think that most films must satisfy those three requirements, surely. But a user-edited database of 7,721 films (bechdeltest.com) found that only 58 per cent of them passed all three 'rules'.

Another study, by the Annenberg Public Policy Center at the University of Pennsylvania, showed that the ratio of male to female characters in movies has remained at about two to one for at least six decades. That study, which examined 855 top box-office films from 1950 to 2006, showed female characters were twice as likely to be seen in explicit sexual scenes as males, while male characters were more likely to be depicted as violent.

Now, ever-forward-thinking Sweden has incorporated the Bechdel Test into some of its film ratings. Things are moving in the right direction.

SINGLE SITCOMS

On the smaller screen, we grew up watching sitcoms with mostly single characters, such as *Ally McBeal* and *Friends*, but the storylines did obsess on them hunting their 'lobsters'. Whereas *How I Met your Mother* did away with all the pretence, and literally said it in the title.

Single women everywhere eagerly awaited the finale of *Sex and the City*, willing the creators not to cop out. 'It's not going to end with a four-wedding ceremony in Central Park,' promised the show's producer, Michael Patrick King. 'I would shoot myself. And single women everywhere would find us and kill us.' But still, three of the four protagonists were married by the close of the story. And five of the six *Friends* were either married by the finale, or on their way to the altar.

In today's world, we're now glued to *Love Island*, which is basically a load of fake-tanned love addicts sent to an island to bonk, like zoo pandas locked in a room until they finally *do it*. Meanwhile *The Bachelor* and *The Bachelorette* treat landing a partner like a gladiatorial sport, only with stilettos and aftershave instead of shields and swords.

Depictions of single freak-outs tend to feature people that are, age-wise, way below the freak-out stage many of us experience in Actual Real Life, which just makes us feel *even more* depressed. The character of Bridget Jones was just 32 in the first film. A mere whippersnapper.

'In 2011 I wrote a cover story for *The Atlantic* called "All the Single

Ladies", which went astonishingly viral,' says journalist Kate Bolick. 'The article and my resulting book, *Spinster*, both got optioned for TV by production companies. In both cases, they wanted to make the "me" character 30 years old, even though I was 39 when I wrote *The Atlantic* piece. It was maddening.' Seems they'd missed the point entirely.

Thankfully, things are improving. 'There's a comedy called *Spinster* (unrelated to my book) currently in production, and they've cast Chelsea Peretti as the lead character. Chelsea is 40 in real life, and the character she will play is 39, about to turn 40.' A few years back, that 'freaking out about being unmarried' character would have been in her early thirties, for sure. So, maybe the screen will start to reflect our realities back at us, at long last.

Nonetheless, in the grand scheme of Hollywood, happy endings are still couple-shaped, 99.9 per cent of the time. So is it any wonder we award such towering importance to our love lives? If anything, it's a wonder that we're not *more* obsessed.

'Oh, the dream. The goddammed man + baby dream. Written by the High Commission on Heterosexual Love and Sexual Reproduction and practised by couples across the land, the dream's a bitch if you're a maternally inclined straight female and not living it by the age of thirty-seven.'

— CHERYL STRAYED, TINY BEAUTIFUL THINGS

OUR BODIES AND BRAINS
TELL US TO COUPLE UP

Finding a mate and having a good hard shag is hardwired into us, just as finding water when we're thirsty, or food when we're hungry. It's a biological instinct, to make mini-mes, to be the little spoon or the big spoon. It's an urge that we can't turn off.

'Evolution-wise, it's written into our DNA that being in a couple is preferable to being single,' says psychotherapist Hilda Burke. 'We wouldn't have fared very well as solitary women or men in caves with wolves stalking around. If you were hungry, you would have needed to hunt the animal, skin it, get the fire going, *and* cook it. That's a lot for one person. Procreating was important, because when you got old, your kids went out and hunted for you.'

She says that it's coded into our instincts to live in a community, be in a couple unit and procreate. 'Industrialization and urban living has only unfolded in the past 200 years or so,' she points out, which is a mere blink in the eye of evolution. 'Modern fallbacks like convenience food and care homes didn't exist before that. Now, we don't need to be in a couple to survive or thrive, but that's going against thousands upon thousands of years of deeply-etched DNA that leans towards marriage as a preference.'

So, obviously, our body desires to couple up and make babies. But what you may not know is that the brain colludes with the body. And it's very cunning in the ways it gets you to chase a partner.

LOVE IS THE DRUG
The early stages of romantic love are very similar to a drug high. A paper entitled *Reward, Motivation, and Emotion Systems Associated With Early-Stage Intense Romantic Love* listed symptoms such as 'Euphoria, intense focused attention on a preferred individual, obsessive thinking about him or her, emotional dependency on and craving for emotional union with this beloved, and increased energy'.

'Infatuation is certainly like an addiction,' says Dr Alex Korb, a neuroscientist who has studied the brain for fifteen years. 'During the early stages of a relationship, your brain releases large amounts of dopamine, which drives you to keep pursuing them, often at the expense of other objectives in life. Your attentions and actions are guided by getting your next dopamine fix via this romantic interest, and if you don't get it, you then feel a withdrawal, a discomfort, a dysphoria, which is very similar to the withdrawal from a drug.'

So, Roxy Music's 'Love is the Drug' was spot on. Indeed, experts at Rutgers University said that a break-up causes an incredibly similar reaction to drug withdrawal. Brain-imaging scans showed similarities between romantic rejection and cocaine craving, which then leads to 'obsessive behaviours', the paper said. 'It shows that intense romantic love seems to function much like an addiction,' says Dr Aron.

Another paper, called *Intense, Passionate, Romantic Love: A Natural Addiction? How the Fields That Investigate Romance and Substance Abuse Can Inform Each Other* (snappy title, guys), said that, 'We have proposed that romantic love is a natural (and often positive) addiction that evolved from mammalian antecedents four million years ago as a survival mechanism to encourage hominin pair-bonding and reproduction, seen cross-culturally today in homo sapiens.' In layperson words, it's an addiction that has evolved to ensure people shag, make babies and hopefully raise said babies together. But it can morph into something negative.

WANTING VS LIKING

As with any addiction, wanting is different from liking. You can want something, even when you no longer like it. 'As in substance addiction, 'wanting' the romantic partner is different from 'liking' a pretty face and finding pleasure in a beautiful sight,' says the latter paper.

When liking someone/something tips over into an addiction, whether it's a person or a drug, Dr Korb says there's an interesting change in the brain's activity, in particular in the striatum.

'We know from MRI brain-imaging scans that whenever you show occasional, social drinkers pictures of alcohol, the nucleus accumbens activates, or the pleasure region,' says Dr Korb, who is the author of *The Upward Spiral: Using Neuroscience to Reserve the Course of Depression, One Small Change at a Time*. 'Whereas when you show a picture of alcohol to a dependent, heavy drinker, it's not the pleasure centre that lights up; it's the habit centre, or the upper part of the striatum. This is how we know that an addiction switches from something that is pleasurable, to something that people feel compelled to do, whether they are enjoying it or not. It gave them pleasure originally, but now that pleasure has gone.'

It's similar with a relationship that becomes an addiction, he says. 'It can stop being a pleasurable choice, and become an addictive urge. This tends to happen when a person feels an emotional lack, say if they're lonely, or they have a fear of abandonment. This means they're more prone to hook on a person like a drug, as a replacement for that empty feeling.'

HEARTBREAK PHYSICALLY HURTS

Heartbreak literally hurts, just as a smashed shoulderblade hurts, say neuroscientists. The reason? Our brains have evolved an 'attachment system', which becomes distressed whenever we're separated from the object of our affection.

Way back during the dawn of us, we developed a biological mechanism in the brain which neuroscientists now call 'the attachment system'. We have evolved to keep our 'attachment figures' (parents, partners and children primarily) as close as possible. Even though we live in a modern society, we still have many of these Stone Age sentiments governing our brains.

'The emotional circuits that make up our attachment system evolved to discourage us from being alone,' reveals Amir Levine, the neuroscientist who co-authored *Attached*. 'One way to nudge us back to the safety of our lover's arms is to create the sensation of unmistakeable pain when we find ourselves alone. Studies have found that the same areas in the brain that light up in imaging scans when we break a leg, are activated when we split up with our mate.'

In prehistoric times, having a partner and keeping them close was literally a life-or-death kinda thing. They were more on a par with a New York cop's 'partner', in that you relied on your partner to save your skin if shit went down. They would cover your back, clock that Komodo dragon over the head (yes, humans were once hunted by dragons: the Smithsonian says so), stop the fire from going out so you wouldn't freeze to death, or keep your kids alive (so's they could kill wolves for you to eat when you were too old to run around the woods with spears). Crucial stuff.

Because of this inherited attachment system, our brains still freak out whenever we can't get hold of our partner, or our kid has swan-dived into a ginormous ballpool and we can no longer see them. This results in 'protest behaviour'. Cue crying, panicking, repetitive calling, diving into ballpools ourselves despite advanced age. It's built into our brains to maintain contact at whatever cost.

Whenever we act completely loco in a romantic setting, it's because our attachment system has been 'activated', which causes great distress, or 'protest behaviour'. Our brains are wired to ensure psychological and physical closeness with whoever we have attached to.

And here's the kicker: our brains do this even if the person we've 'attached' to no longer wants to go out with us.

IQ-LOWERING
The thought of 'I'm going to be alone forever' can even impair your cognitive prowess and lower your IQ.

Three separate studies into the 'anticipation of loneliness' found something remarkable. They took a bunch of people and gave them a baseline IQ test. Then, they told the same people they would 'end up alone' – and promptly performed more cognitive tests.

The study observed 'significant and large decrements in intelligent thought' after they delivered the doomful 'alone' prophecy to the participants. So, the moral of this story is: never attempt to solve a mathematical equation while you're in an 'alone forever' cognitive cave.

THE DANCE OF VEILS WITHIN OUR BRAIN
There's a key difference between men and women during orgasm, and it's why women get more emotionally attached than men after sex.

Women release more of a hormone that bonds them to their sexual mate during orgasm: oxytocin, which means that we can perceive the person we've just had sex with as more trustworthy, more desirable, more ideal than they actually are. The oxytocin does a chiffon-veiled bellydance of seduction within our brain during the post-coital afterglow, which leaves us heart-eyed and seeking more, even if the person we've just had sex with is a total dipstick.

'This is true, and it can be unfortunate for women,' says Dr Korb. 'Their greater release of – and sensitivity to – oxytocin after sex, means they can feel emotionally closer than the man does. So, once a relationship gets physical, there's often an asymmetry, whereby the women bonds faster than the man. This isn't *always* true, but that's the tendency.'

TRAINING YOUR BRAIN

We tend to think of the brain as, well, brainy. We tend to trust what it tells us to do. Because it's our brain, right? The supercomputer in our heads. However, even though it's an ultra-sophisticated piece of kit, it needs steering, just like a NASA rocket requires human intervention to reach Mars. It needs your help, if it's going to come out of auto-pilot and do something different, something that's a break from pre-set programming.

'I would say that your brain does know best,' says Dr Korb. 'But, there are different parts of the brain, and it depends on which part you're listening to. The striatum is like the "dog" section of the brain, given it's pleasure-oriented and habitual, doing what it's been trained to do. The limbic system is like a toddler or a teenager, and can get really upset when it doesn't get its own way. While the pre-frontal cortex (PFC) is the adult in the room. Sometimes it's great to let the toddler/teen call the shots, you need to do that occasionally, for a balanced, happy life. But in general, it's wise to learn to listen to the adult, the PFC, which will pipe up and say "Er, maybe that's not the right decision" whenever you're wanting to have a drink, isolate yourself, or break up with someone on a whim.' The more we do something, the more it becomes encoded in the habit centre of the brain, he adds. Thus, the easier it becomes.

'When you do something new, it's scary and uncomfortable for the brain and creates more emotion,' says Dr Korb. Whether that something is *not* contacting your ex, counting your single blessings, or not chasing emotionally unavailable partners. 'But you *can* use your PFC to train your striatum to make better choices.'

However, your brain will try to snap back to the old way of doing things. Ingrained neural pathways are the route of least resistance. It's why we can tend to make the same mistakes over and over, on our voyage of self-improvement (we'll revisit this later, when I repeatedly make mistakes, oof).

Training your brain into new, healthier habits is exactly like a person training a dog. It's tiresome and takes endless repetition. You might have to say 'ball' or 'toilet' three thousand times before it sticks. You may even be tempted to wee in the garden to demonstrate what the command 'toilet' means and where 'toilet' should happen (Guilty. I came *so close*.)

But one day, the dog/your brain, will finally get with the program. I promise. Hopefully before you resort to having a wee in the garden.

WHY WE FANCY INDIFFERENT PEOPLE MORE

Are you like me? Do you fancy indifferent people more? Great, isn't it. Not.*

This is because of an *awful* psychological phenomenon called Reward Uncertainty. Droves of studies have demonstrated that when animals know they're going to get rewarded with food every time they push a lever, they will eventually slow down. Whereas, when the animal cannot predict the certainty of a reward, they become way more interested in getting it.

It's why unobtainable, unreliable people draw us in like moths to a flame. 'So pretty, ouch...so pretty, ouch...'. Repeat for ever.

It's Reward Uncertainty being a motherf*cker. We want them more, because we're not sure if we're going to get them. The moment we become sure we'll be rewarded, by a text message for instance, is the moment we start lying on the floor of the cage with our hands folded behind our head, like a lackadaisical rat wearing sunglasses, half-heartedly pushing the lever with our little rat feet.

There's more. In a terrifying social study, psychologists found that women are most attracted to men who are 'uncertain' about them, preferring them to men who definitely dig them, and men who classed them as 'average.'

'We know that an uncertain future and lack of control increases the limbic system's activity,' says Dr Korb. 'If someone is playing hard to get, that whole "Are they going to text me back?" uncertainty means you actually release more dopamine when they do. More than when someone is reliable.'

Basically, our brain's reward system lights up like a Christmas tree when somebody unreliable contacts us. And is slightly bored whenever somebody stable and reliable contacts us.

Brain?! Stop that mischief! You're making us fancy the *wrong people*.

* I'm trying to get Eighties term 'not' back in fashion. Let's do it, people! Don't frown at me.

II: THE UNDOING OF A LOVE ADDICT

THE TERRIBLE TWINS

Enough of all that. Let's talk about me some more. I'm now taking you back to the year 2010. Hop in.

I've just turned 30, and my alcohol dependence and love addiction are like terrible twins that intensify in tandem. As one starts to misbehave outrageously, the other follows suit, each daring the other to up the ante.

While drinking, I treat my body like they treat that ball that they throw onto the roulette wheel in casinos. I lob myself onto the wheel of Soho's nightland, sacrificing myself to its furious spinning, and see where I end up. I charge into the city, where the skyscrapers glint like jaws, and cast myself upon its mercy.

I grow gradually more disgruntled that my happy ending hasn't shown up yet, and more demanding as a result. The sane men detach themselves swiftly, sending me break-up texts such as, 'You're undeniably lovely, but crazy. Goodbye. P.S. Please stop calling me.' (This is a real text.)

When I do convince somebody to go out with me by acting sane for a spell, they soon learn that I am the High Priestess of Drama. I send so many, 'That's it! We're finished!' texts that boyfriends start acting like they haven't even happened, knowing that I'll have changed my mind in five minutes, or five hours at most. I dangle the threat of a break-up over their heads, like a guillotine, when actually, what I want is reassurance. And maybe a hug.

I cheat on almost everyone. Never in a premeditated way; usually when blackout drunk, and always followed by violent guilt, which claws at my mind for weeks, months, years afterward. But when I am out-out and drinking, the love addict rears up from within me, roars for attention and rip its shirt off. If my boyfriend isn't around, I seek it in the immediate vicinity, by falling on – or on to – the nearest attractive man.

Then, since cheaters always make the most suspicious partners, I become convinced that my boyfriend is cheating on me too. And I justify snooping on his messages, invading his privacy, in order to ensure that is not the case. My hypocrisy is unbelievable.

I live tyrannized by the fear that my boyfriend will find out about my blackout infidelities. The daily dread sits there, like a goblin on my shoulder, no matter how much I drink, or how sweet I am to my boyfriend in secret recompense, or how much I obscure my tracks with lies, or how often I tell myself, 'Everyone cheats, they just don't talk about it'.

Meanwhile, my jealousy drives a regime of digital self-harm. I scan Facebook photos of my boyfriend to look for evidence of *new women*. Is that comment from this Penny chick about 'last night' being 'fun' about them shagging? Must be. What else could it mean. I can't believe he shagged Penny!

I click on any suspicious new women he befriends, to check the threat status, on a thermometer scale of green to red. I sit there, inflicting cyber Chinese water torture upon myself. Drip, drip. Click, click. The too-much-information nature of social media nearly drives me insane. Harikari by Wi-Fi.

I quiz my boyfriends as to whether they really love me, and why they love me, and are they sure they love me, and whether they love me more than their exes. I'm sure it's really relaxing for them.

Given my bonkers behaviour drives away well-adjusted men, I end up in toxic relationships with...*not* well-adjusted men. And then I stay in these relationships long after I should have left (a whole year, in one case) because booze has eroded my self-esteem like battery acid, and I don't think I deserve any better.

All the while, I use alcohol to erase my inhibitions and get closer to men; then alcohol to soothe me when it all goes belly up. Alcohol – men, alcohol – men. It's a cyclical kind of hell.

I REACH FOR A MAN AS A SELF-ESTEEM SOURCE
AUGUST 2011

I wake up with that familiar 'dead furry animal' feeling in my mouth. Fuckinhell, I've done it again. Started off with a romantic 'one glass of wine in the garden as the sun sets' and wound up drinking an entire bottle, and then some. The debris in the garden mocks me, sitting there smug as a crime scene which clinches my guilt.

I check my phone gingerly, as if it's an unexploded bomb. I'm examining it to see what inappropriate messages I sent last night. One to my ex, Daniel. 'I've never stopped thinking about you and wondering what might have been.' I groan at the phone, and chuck it across the room. Thankfully, it finds a soft landing.

I stand, defeated, in the shower for half an hour, hoping the pounding water will cure my pounding head. Why did I send that? I'm not even sure that's true. In vino veritas is bullshit. In vino dramitas would be more accurate. I barely think about him, other than when I drink.

I retrieve my phone. He's replied. 'Hey, great to hear from you, it would be lovely to meet up as friends, you were always important to me, but I just got engaged.'

Even though I don't actually want to get back with him, it feels like yet another suckerpunch. Where is my engagement ring? Why am I not engaged?! I deserve to be engaged!

I sulk on it for an hour, and then turn to the only solution I know. Another man. I text a guy I've been on two dates with, and was 'meh' about seeing again, who I know is keen.

We drink hard. I don't particularly like him as a person. He's talking long term; about me moving into his flat, teaching me to drive, getting me insured on his car. I am doubtful I even want to see him for a fourth date.

I sleep with him anyway, to distract myself from loneliness. It's an attempt to reboot my self-esteem. I don't particularly enjoy it. I just do it, robotically. Like an overeater who eats that fifth éclair mechanically, all joy forgotten.

Does it make me feel better? No. But it makes me feel Wanted. It feels like I'm constantly trying to reach Wanted status. Like the polar opposite to a scoundrel in a Western.

SURREY'S ANSWER TO SID AND NANCY
MARCH 2012

I am in a relationship that can best be described as Surrey's answer to Sid and Nancy. Amy and Blake. Bonnie and Clyde. We are partners in crime and bring out the absolute worst in each other.

Enter Ralph. I fancy the pants off him, think he's cool as fuck, and we *are obsessed with each other.*

The first few months are louche bliss. We enable each other's recklessness, staying up all night drinking, smoking and shagging, and then going to feed the ducks in the park while still off our tits, laughing manically as runners wide-circle us suspiciously.

We say things like, 'Where have you been all my life' and 'You're my soulmate' and 'I can't imagine ever being without you now.'

*We're so besotted that we move in together after six months.**

I SHARE A BED, YET AM THE LONELIEST I HAVE EVER BEEN
SEPTEMBER 2012

I don't know how we got from there to here. From constant snogging, to daily savaging.

I am sitting up in the tower room of the loft flat Ralph and I rent. The room placed in a little turret of the tumbledown, characterful house we rent a slice of. It's where we smoke out of the window.

I drag on my cigarette, and stare at the people outside, wondering why they're so normal, and I'm so not. I feel like I'm waiting to be rescued, but in the eyes of society, I already have been.

'What more do you want of me?' Ralph raged last night, arms aloft in exasperation. He has a point, to be fair. 'I've told you I'm in, I've told you that we can even get married if you want to, even though I don't care about getting married. And still, you want more.'

He's right. I do want more. I don't know what the more is, but all I know is that even after we moved in together, I wanted more, and even though I now have a promise of future commitment, I want more. I'm never satisfied. It's exactly the same as my drinking. Every time I drain the current bottle, I reach for the next.

I don't know yet, but that is the hallmark of addiction, that flashing neon sign in your brain that blinks and fizzes and demands MORE. That moves further away, every time you inch towards it. That you're

---

* Which is a super idea, because we barely know each other, and have spent a grand total of eight hours together sober.

always trying to reach, and never successfully get to. It's an ever-moving destination. The promised land of satisfaction, when we've finally had enough. Have enough.

I have bought into the idea that coupledom is the cure for loneliness, but I am lonelier than I have ever been. I have distanced myself from friends and family because I can't tell them the truth about what is going on with Ralph. When I make the mistake of doing so, they tell me I should finish it.

I once told a friend that Ralph's new slogan was 'Cath doesn't know anything'. He would roll it out at dinner parties with other couples, when I showed up the glaring gaps in my general knowledge.

'Oh sweetheart,' she said. 'You need to get as far away from him as possible.'

But I don't. Life without him is unthinkable.

GASLIGHTING MAKES MY ADDICTION GO KA-BOOM
OCTOBER 2012
It's my one-year anniversary with Ralph and I'm at his ex-girlfriend's 30th. The ex-girlfriend that I know he still holds a torch for, because he told me on our second date, way before we were ever anything.

Why am I here? He told me that if I didn't come, he'd go without me. So, it was either spend our first anniversary alone, or come to his ex's birthday party.

I've brought two friends for moral support, and both are horrified. 'Cath, this is seriously screwed up, we should just leave.' The other chips in, 'It's like watching him have a date with her!' And it is. He's openly flirting.

Eventually they do leave, aghast at Ralph's behaviour, and urging me to do the same. But I stay. To wait for Ralph to come back to me, so that we can go home.

'Gaslighting' is a term based on a 1930s play. It depicts a husband who dims the gas lights by hanging out in the attic. When his wife notices the lower lights, he insists it's her imagination. He 'gaslights' her by saying it's her being a basketcase, rather than him doing something secretive.

'Gaslighting' is psychological shorthand for those who cry, 'It's not me, it's you!' when it most definitely is them.

I protest that it's definitely amiss to spend our anniversary at his ex's birthday party, and Ralph tells me I'm being unreasonable. That it's civilized – normal! – to stay friends with your exes. That I'm a 'psycho' for not wanting to go, or not wanting him to go. That it's no wonder he still has a thing about her, given the way I am.

My friends and family loved Ralph at first, describing him as twinkly, clever, funny. All things that he still is, but he is also casually cruel and unbelievably selfish. My gentle stepfather, who never hates anyone, decided he couldn't stand Ralph just a few months in.

Why? Open scene: I'm in hospital awaiting surgery, and Ralph is there when they suddenly decide to wheel me down for the op. I'm scared and crying, since I'm about to have the second of two serious operations on my hand (long story), but Ralph won't wait for me. 'I'll only be an hour, max,' the doctor says, raising his eyebrows at Ralph. 'I have plans with my brother,' he says, and leaves.

He later apologizes, and I let it slide, but my stepfather never forgave him.

Meanwhile, his family are insufferable snobs who openly reject me. I laugh along when they call people who haven't been to private school 'muggles'. Funny! Until I realize that they actually mean it; they actually believe that private schoolers are superior to those who went through the free schooling system. My face doesn't fit, and they make sure I know it.

I am far from innocent in all of this, though. Going out with me is, no doubt, an absolute nightmare. I am desperately insecure, melodramatic and throw insults at Ralph like daggers when I'm drunk.

Ralph is the pilot light and our relationship is the gas that combine to set my alcohol addiction ablaze. I start drinking five nights, six nights a week. I stop even attempting to moderate my alcohol intake.

I get the shakes in the mornings, and drink to try and curb them. One night, Ralph finds me on our doorstep, slumped like a sack of potatoes, unconscious, because I've lost my keys.

I don't know it yet, but our shared flat is going to get even dimmer, over the next six months.

THE THREE EXES
FEBRUARY 2013

I am sitting alone in my flat, while my boyfriend and his family have a cosy dinner at a restaurant a few minutes away. With his ex girlfriend.

Not Ex One (the one whose birthday party we went to, who he now sees regularly). Ex Two. Otherwise known as the private-schooled (!) ex-girlfriend that his family desperately want him back with.

The ex that his family invites round for Sunday dinners, to their birthdays, as a sledgehammer-subtle hint that they want me gone – and her back in. At first, Ralph boycotted these family-meetings-with-his-ex, but now he just goes along too. He tells me I should not expect his family to like me straight away, and that I need to 'earn' their acceptance.

It's not just her on the scene either. He started meeting up with Ex Three again a few weeks back. He didn't even bother to ask me if I was OK with it, and I didn't have the fight to point out this oversight.

I've become obsessed with finding out as much as I can about these rivals, these three exes, as if I'm sizing up a boxing opponent by watching videos of their upper cuts and left hooks. I stalk them on social media, trying to find out how I can be better, how to keep him, how to save us, how to dodge the knock-out punch.

It feels like Ralph is on a High Fidelity style road-trip, checking out 'The ones that got away'. Except, unlike John Cusack in the film, Ralph is not single. And I'm sitting with him in the car, growing gradually more paranoid as we stop at each ex.

When he's asleep and the duvet growls with snores, I creep cat-soft alongside the bed to pinch his phone, so that I can read his messages.

I find out something I don't want to know, almost every night. On the nights when I find nothing to wound me, I almost feel disappointed. It's the emotional equivalent of taking a razor and making tiny slices in my thigh. Death by a thousand text messages.

I LEAVE THE DARK FLAT
MAY 2013

I start sobering up, putting together three, five, seven days sober, and finally see Ralph and our demented relationship clearly. I realize that I have to hightail it out of here as soon as possible, before the gaslighting intensifies, and the flat we share becomes pitch black.

The final snap is tiny; just two little words.

It happens the evening I clean the entire flat for our quarterly flat inspection, and since I am currently making dinner, I ask Ralph to empty the bin.

'Fuck off,' he replies, nonchalant.

'Pardon me?' I say.

'Fuck off, do it yourself. I've been at work all day.'

So have I, but that doesn't appear to matter.

Ironically, given sobriety has given me the gumption to end this, I drink to pluck up the courage to actually do it. That weekend, he's away on a minibreak, so I mainline wine and compose him a text message ending it. (Yes, a text message. That's how mature my behaviour is.)

I also text mutual friends about our split, and de-friend his family on Facebook, as a madly petty, but admittedly effective way of torching the return-bridge. I know now that I won't go back on my decision.

And I don't. I move out, and back in with my parents, to get sober for good; to figure out when and why I became the kind of person that puts up with this kind of gaslighting shite.

THE AFTERMATH OF THE SPLIT
AUGUST 2013

The most surprising part of this is that there is none. No aftermath. Zip. I thought I couldn't live without Ralph and, yet, once we go our separate ways, I don't miss him for even a second. I feel nothing but relief that my entanglement with him (and his family) is over.

A few months after the split, I have counselling for my alcohol addiction. The counsellor asks me a lot of questions about Ralph, which I think strange, but still, I have a lot of stories, so I tell them.

I tell him about the time Ralph left the flat and shouted, 'Hope you don't find the whiskey!' when he knew full well I was addicted to – and trying to quit – alcohol. I then spent two hours upturning the entire flat, even looking in wellington boots, for the mythical whiskey in our otherwise-dry flat. 'Where is it?' I texted him. 'Oh, I was only joking!' he replied. Hilarious.

Then there was the time when...and the time when...it all spills out of me. It actually feels good, given I've never told anyone the entire fucked-up saga before.

The counsellor's face grows more and more stern. At the end of the session, he says, 'OK, so I'm going to tick the box on this sheet that says 'Domestic violence'. He shows me the box, and him ticking it. I'm gobsmacked.

'But, he never hit me!'

He tells me that domestic violence is often purely psychological. And that I have definitely been subject to it. Huh. I had no idea.

I CHOOSE MYSELF ABOVE A RELATIONSHIP
APRIL 2014

Just a few months after my split with Ralph, I am already in another serious relationship, with Jacob. Why? Love addict.

It's a 'tinderbox' relationship, in that it's incredibly quick to ignite. Within a fortnight, I'm spending most of my nights with him, and within a month, I'm on holiday with his family. It's a mostly lovely relationship.

But we're now six months in, and over the past few weeks he's been acting strangely, disappearing for days on end, losing his temper, putting me down. I told him we should have a break of a fortnight, for him to sort his head out, and tonight we are talking on the phone after said break.

As I sit there, listening to him saying that he's not sure, and he doesn't know how he feels, and to come down this weekend and we'll see, something within me rises up. I'm not the kind of person who puts up with this caper any more.

'D'you know what, let's just leave it, I'm done,' I say.

And just like that, we're finished. I know it's the right thing to do, and for the first time in my life I have finally chosen myself above the preservation of a relationship. But I fall apart nonetheless.

My falling apart is not really because of Jacob, or missing him, it's because of me. Because I still think that being single means I'm broken, I'm worthless, I'm unwanted. I still feel that the ending of a relationship signifies a failure of me as a person, as a woman. I am not fulfilling my main purpose of securing a man.

I'm prickly and short-tempered with my family, over the next few days. Until my mum finally manages to get past my defensive spikes and gives me a long hug on the sofa. The hug undoes me. Shuddering with sobs, I say things like, 'There's something wrong with me', 'Nobody's ever going to love me' and 'I'm going to be alone forever'.

I am floored by what I can only describe as 'collective heartbreak'. My heart feels like a tree that has had so many initials carved into it, that its bark is flayed and sore. I feel like there's no more room, that I can't take any more initials.

That weekend, I cancel my birthday party, a gathering of eight of my best mates at a restaurant with ping-pong tables, because of the split. My mum and stepdad insist on taking me out for dinner and when the restaurant brings me a cupcake with a candle, I nearly burst into tears.

I know that this isn't right. That something needs to change. And I suspect that something is me. I cannot continue to throw my happiness into the air and hope that some man catches it. I cannot continue to allow a break-up to upturn my mental health. I cannot rely on men as a self-esteem source any more.

It feels like my internal universe is collapsing, like I've been tipped into a ravine of cosmic chaos. But actually, a star is being birthed within me. I'm being rearranged on an atomic level.

I decide to not just break up with Jacob; but to break up with all men. With all relationships. And to be single, indefinitely.

'If you are trapped in a nightmare, you will probably be more strongly motivated to awaken than someone who is just caught in the ups and downs of an ordinary dream.'

– *ECKHART TOLLE*, THE POWER OF NOW

III: LOCATING SINGLE SANITY

I TAKE A YEAR OFF DATING

What happened was this. When I stopped drinking, I transformed sexually, becoming a sixth-date-after-STD-tests kinda girl. I went from fast to slow, from man-chasing to chaste, without so much as an ounce of effort. It was also a doddle to stop all the snooping and cheating, given all my phone-reading and infidelity had been while wankered.

So, that was wonderful. Finding out I wasn't a doggone snoopin', cheatin' maneater. However, my actual love addiction, the root source, was still rampant. My habit of reaching for a man to feel complete was still there, long after I'd stopped reaching for a drink to feel better.

I begin to realize that pouring a glass of wine and clicking on a dating app are the exact same process. They're a restlessness, an emotional void, that we attempt to fill by grabbing a substance/person outside of ourselves.

What's more, I discover that this is incredibly common. It's why Holly and Laura of *HOME* podcast call recovering from love addiction the 'second sobriety'. It's why people often describe addiction-wrangling as a game of whack-a-mole, given you thwack one into submission, and another pops up to mock you. It's why people will frequently give up cocaine, and discover a sugar addiction beneath it, or ditch internet shopping, and find themselves losing hundreds on a gambling app.

I GATHER UP MY TOOLS

So, I am a love addict. Huh. That's fun. But in a way, this is good news. As it means I already have the tools in my arsenal to beat this sucker.

I already know how to sit through an urge to drink, so I know how to become inert when my fingers want to text a bad man from my past. I use the 'drop phone and roll away' strategy more than once. I already know that a thought doesn't have to lead to an action, so I know that a 'I want to stalk my ex on the interweb' thought doesn't have to lead to me actually doing it.

I am aware that feelings are not facts, so I can let the 'broken', 'failure' and 'unwanted' feelings I have around my singleness, pass through me without believing them. I know now how to dismantle the stories I tell myself ('I need to drink to have fun!' or 'Nobody wants to marry me'), by asking 'Is this really true?' and then constructing a story that more closely resembles the reality. *I can do this.*

THE ESSAY THAT INSPIRES THE YEAR OFF

I tell my friend Kate about my resolve to undergo a man-ban, and she sends me an essay by Elizabeth Gilbert called 'Learn to be Lonely.' In it, a hairdresser is telling Elizabeth about how she has just kicked a no-good jerk to the kerb, and how she's going to go straight back out there and 'get myself something BETTER'. Elizabeth takes her hand and makes her swear to take six months off, before she so much as kisses another guy.

'Friends,' Elizabeth writes, 'at some point, we all have to learn how to walk into a party or a restaurant alone. Otherwise, we will be willing to walk in with ANYBODY (or worse, walk out with anybody). We have to learn how to endure our own company and hold our heads high. And sometimes, after enough time alone, we might even learn to enjoy ourselves.'

I feel ridiculously inspired. So inspired that a plan starts to hatch in my head. Goshdarnit. I should take a year off dating! A whole year, where I don't so much as hold a man's hand.

I tell my mum about it. 'But why would you do that? Why would someone do that?!' she says, visibly distressed. She bats every answer I give away like a wasp, and returns to 'But why?!' She's not on board.

In fact, I realize that my mum is a love addict too. She's never been single, for more than a year in total, over my entire 38 years of life. It explains why I once had to ban her from asking 'Has so-and-so been in touch?' because she was doing it daily, without fail. I once dated someone with 'Right' in his surname and she started calling him 'Rightman' despite my protests.

It explains why we once had this conversation about a different boyfriend:

Mum: 'You'll be able to work harder now, because you're happier now you've met Joel.'

Me: 'What does Joel have to do with my ability to do my work?'

Mum: 'Well, happier people are more motivated.'

Me: 'I'm not happier since meeting Joel, I was just this happy before meeting him.'

Mum: 'You are *happier!* You are. I'm your mother, listen to me. You're bouncier.'

I give up.

My brother and I used to joke about finding the most stereotypically unsuitable man we could, maybe a Satanist who wears little more than a leather thong, and bringing him home to introduce him to Mum as my boyfriend, so that she could find ways to justify liking him. 'He's just so...alternative! Gutsy in his style choices.' She would have found a way to approve.

But as Amy Schumer writes, in *The Girl with the Lower Back Tattoo*, 'Mothers are people – not angels from heaven or Ex Machina error-free service bots.' Christ knows I am responsible for my own reverse brainwashing.

However, all of my friends are totally into my year off. Not one thinks it's a bad idea. Many actually throw their hands up in the air and say things like, 'About time you were bloomin' single for once!'

And so I embark upon my year's dating sabbatical. And I do so with an urge to devour everything I can about love addiction, why we go loco in relationships, why we digitally self-harm and how to start to love being single.

Here's what I know. If you struggle with anything, be it singledom, disordered eating, spending beyond your means, drinking until you're smashed or depression, *learn everything you can about it*. Knowledge is power.

I read myself sober, and I read myself happily single. When you learn about something, and learn new ways of thinking about it, you are literally changing your brain and laying down new neural pathways, just as you do when you learn a new language.

In the next few chapters, I'm going to share everything useful I learned in my year's sabbatical.

THE SINGLE MOVEMENT IS A GLOBAL EVENT

The single revolution is not just on British soil. Globally, there are more single people than ever before. Across our beautiful planet, the amount of people living alone has rocketed by 80 per cent since the 1990s.

In America, 45 per cent of all American adults are now single. US jewellery companies are marketing right-hand diamond rings for single women who like their independence and want to put a ring on it. And talking of putting a ring on it, I discover that single female voters were so instrumental in putting Obama in the White House that they were nicknamed 'Beyoncé voters' (by who else but – Fox News). A slam dunk on behalf of single voters, I think you'll agree.

In Manhattan, nearly half of all households are now single, but this shift is also observed in less expected cities such as Cleveland, Seattle and Denver. 'This is a big change,' observes sociologist, Eric Klinenberg, author of *Going Solo*, in his TED talk *Living Single*. And it's more pronounced in wealthy societies. 'Why do the most privileged people on Earth use their resources to separate from one another and get places of their own?' He goes on to say, 'It is virtually impossible to go solo if you live in a poor nation, or a poor neighbourhood.'

A US grass-roots movement has taken seed, of single people dubbing themselves 'quirkyalones' as shorthand for 'a person who prefers to be single, rather than settle'. The founder, Sasha Cagen, writes on quirkyalone.net, 'When you're quirkyalone like me, you know that being single is not a disease. Being single doesn't mean you are broken.'

But the fact still remains that in America, couples have the edge. A former professor of psychology, Bella DePaulo, regularly points out the 'special status of married people' in the US and talks about how there are more than a thousand laws that only benefit and protect people who are legally married. Back in 2006, she dubbed this prejudice 'singlism'.

Over in Sweden, Stockholm's households are 60 per cent single. In one town, there's a commune where dozens of forties-and-up singles live in a honeycomb of single apartments, clustered around 400-square-metres of shared space, where they have communal meals and hang out on the roof terrace. Sounds dreamy.

I learn that marriage rates are declining at such a rate in China (in 2016 they were down by nearly 7 per cent) that the government is hosting matchmaking events and is offering to subsidize wedding costs, fearing a drastic drop in population. (Births dropped by 630,000 last year.)

This has given rise to the 'Shanghai Marriage Market', a weekly aberration where parents tout the vital stats of their adult children (height, income, Chinese zodiac sign), trying to flog them to other parents. Often without the knowledge (or permission) of their offspring. Google Image it if you dare.

Then there's Chinese Singles' Day, which is on the eleventh day of the eleventh month because the number one signifies a person standing on their own. Singles go shopping and spend literally billions on presents – for themselves. Yee-ha! On this auspicious day in 2015, Topshop recorded a 900 per cent year-on-year rise in profits.

However, on the flipside, in China unmarried women beyond their late twenties get called 'Sheng nu' or 'leftover women.' In the interests of fairness, single men do sometimes get called 'Shengnan' or 'leftover men', but more commonly, they're referred to as 'Guang gun' or 'bare branches'* signifying their lack of additions to the family tree.

(Do we have a 'Singles' Day' in the UK? Apparently so. On 11th March. But NOTHING happens on it. Like, diddly squat. It seems that there was (is?) also a National Singles Week in August, which appears to have slipped out of the door without saying goodbye, like an unwelcome person at a party. In Britain, we are failing miserably at celebrating being single.)

Being called 'leftover' or a 'bare branch' is nothing compared to what happens in Germany. Single 25-year-old women get called 'old boxes' and their mates blockade their door with a bunch of empty boxes, just for jokes. Custom dictates that if a man reaches 30 without getting wed, he has to sweep the steps of his town hall. Generally having been forced to wear a frilly dress, and at the stroke of midnight, while being

---

I'd probably go on a shopping stampede too, if I was described as 'leftover' or a 'bare branch'.

laughed at by onlookers. Meanwhile, the women get made to clean the doorknobs of the town hall with rags.

In Denmark, 25 year-old singles get tied to things and covered in cinnamon; on their 30th, this becomes upgraded to pepper. Single-shaming at its most bizarre.

Japan has a similarly single state of affairs, meaning that Japan's birthrate fell to under one million in 2016; the lowest rate since the 19th century. And that's despite the Japanese prime minster chucking £20 million at the problem in 2014, by funding matchmaking services to get people into the sack. Despite his best efforts, six in ten twentysomething and thirtysomething Japanese men identify as 'herbivores', a term for those who have zero interest in sex or relationships.

In South Korea, a similar 'crisis' is afoot. The crude marriage rate there (the number of marriages per 1,000 people) has dropped from just over 295 in 1970, to 5.5 in 2016. Young people who reject dating have been called the 'Sampo Generation'. 'Sampo' is a Korean portmanteau that means to 'give up three things'; that is courtship, marriage and childbirth, which are seen as the trio of a successful transition into adulthood. South Korean universities are now running 'Marriage and Family' courses in which it's mandatory for students to date three classmates, for a whole month, each. (It's unclear whether they get to choose who they date for four weeks.)

But why is this being presented as such a global 'crisis'? As far as I understand it, there are too many people in the world already, right? So surely it's a good thing if fewer babies are born? It might actually mean that properties drop in price too, so that buying a house is less like buying a bungalow made of *actual gold*.

YOUR 'OTHER HALF'

I learn that the idea of your 'other half' dates back to Greek mythology. 'Each of us is always seeking the half that matches him,' said Plato. According to Plato, way back when, there were not only men and women, but also spherical double-beings, with two faces and sets of legs like the spokes of a wheel.

They wielded terrible power, strength and ambition, so much so that they made an attempt on the Gods. Zeus spliced them, in revenge, to strip them of their sway. And so, the 'halves' spend the rest of their earthly time seeking each other out.

'And so, when a person meets the half that is his very own...' said Plato, 'then something wonderful happens: the two are struck from their senses by love, by a sense of belonging to one another, and by desire, and they don't want to be separated from one another, not even for a moment.'

So, there you have it. But, it has to be said, I'm not sure I believe that these terrible sphere beings ever really existed, just as I'm not quite sure that centaurs, harpies or cyclops were ever *real*. I'm also pretty sure that animals weren't shaped out of clay, Pandora didn't own a jar filled with all the evils of mankind, and Athenians didn't sacrifice 14 youths a year to a minotaur that lived in a labyrinth.

I think we can just chalk the 'other halves' thing down to a vivid imagination and possibly Plato getting off his face on some ancient psychedelic drugs.

WHY ARE SO MANY OF US SINGLE?

I happen upon some fascinating theories as to why so many of us are now single, thanks to *Modern Romance*, by Aziz Ansari with Eric Klinenberg, a brilliant investigation into the modern dating landscape.

Firstly, we want 'soulmate marriages', whereas our predecessors were willing to settle for 'you'll do marriages'. Way back in the 1960s, 76 per cent of American women (and 35 per cent of men) were willing to marry *someone they did not love*. Mind-blowing, right? But by the 1980s, only nine per cent of American women and 14 per cent of American men were up for marrying someone they didn't love. An incredible shift.

However, this ultimately makes it harder to find a person we want to marry. In a 2013 TED talk called *The secret to desire in a long-term relationship*, the psychotherapist Esther Perel analyzed how our expectations have risen to unprecedented levels.

Not only do we want a partner for life to give us children, social status and companionship, 'But in addition I want you to be my best friend and my trusted confidant and my passionate lover to boot, and we live twice as long,' said Perel. 'So we come to one person, and we basically are asking them to give us what once an entire village used to provide...Give me comfort, give me edge. Give me novelty, give me familiarity. Give me predictability, give me surprise.'

Whew, that's a tall order, no? And yet we want it. And can it please roll into our lives at exactly the right age, not too young, and not too old? Thanks, genie.

TOO-MUCH-CHOICE PARALYSIS

I also discover that, paradoxically, when we're given too much choice, we become paralyzed, dissatisfied, and less likely to choose at all.

It's the reason supermarkets make sure not to give us too many options on-shelf. It's been shown to bewilder and befuddle us out of making a purchase. We're more likely to skedaddle out of the shop empty-handed.

A wealth of studies back this up, but *Modern Romance* cites one that is perhaps the most compelling. A study offered shoppers either six different types of jam, or 24. When they were offered 24 jams, shoppers were more likely to stop and taste, but ten times less likely to buy. The six-types-of-jam stall sold ten times more than the 24-types stall. It really did.

So, apply that to today's dating world. In London, or any major city, I believe it's actually impossible to scroll to the end of Tinder. It's like being in some kind of Tim Burton-esque festive grotto, and having to choose just one present out of three million presents.

It seems like a dream, but it's actually a dystopian hell. We end up wandering around and shaking all of the presents, analyzing their shapes, weights, potential value – and never choosing an actual present.

SINGLE IS A SUPREMELY MODERN PRIVILEGE

But, more importantly than all of that, we're single because *we can be*. That pathway of choice has only recently been blasted wide open, particularly for women.

A hundred years ago, single women stared down the barrel of persecution, unflattering slurs, a sexless existence, and the fact they could very possibly die of starvation. Whereas men were always able to make money, buy houses or travel, regardless of their marital status. While many men undoubtedly felt pressurized into marriage by their peers, or whispered about as 'strange' if they never married, they still had the *choice*. This was not the case for women.

Only rich women had the luxury of marriage being optional. Women were treated like baby-making machines and expected to have as many as eight children. If you reached the age of 23 and weren't married, you were dubbed a 'spinster'.

Meanwhile, over the Atlantic Ocean in the US, if you, gasp-shock-horror, reached the grand age of 26 without betrothal, you were called a 'thornback' (a spiky type of stingray; not a compliment). Most of the women persecuted during the Salem witch trials were either single or widows. In the 1960s, during graduation parties, married women were given corsages, while single women were given – lemons.

Back in the 1800s, it was even worse. In 1817, Jane Austen wrote a letter to a friend about the fact that marriage was merely a survival strategy for many women. 'Single women have a dreadful propensity for being poor...which is one very strong argument in favour of matrimony.'

Many have speculated that Jane Austen's means of making money, and resulting great personal fortune (she never sold the rights of her books to publishers, and always self-published), was why she never married. She had the choice, y'see, just as we do today. And she chose not to. Other prominent never-married figureheads of Austen's time included Emily Dickinson, Florence Nightingale and Emily Brontë.

Going back even further, I find out that 'spinster' used to be a totally neutral descriptor, says the *Oxford Living Dictionary*. It originated as a literal term (a 'woman who spins' yarn for a living). Then, given it was often single women who became 'spinsters', it became a synonym for single. In the 17th century, I would have described myself on an official document as 'Catherine Gray of London, Spinster'. It was much later that it became a slur.

But 'spinster' wasn't the only term used to subjugate single women. Two million women were dubbed 'surplus women' after WWII killed so many of our men. And spare a thought for the 'Catherinettes', a French term for women of 25+ who were not married by the Saint Catherine feast on the year of their 25th birthday. A ceremony was held for the 'Catherinettes', whereby everyone wished them a speedy end to their spinsterhood. Can you imagine anything worse?! (The 'Catherinettes' ritual still exists, but it now appears to merely consist of single Frenchwomen making each other hilarious hats.)

THE SINGLE REVOLUTION IS A SIGN OF PROGRESS

The reality was, before the 1950s, if you didn't want to be penniless, you found yourself a husband quick-smart. Jobs for women were few and poorly paid. Some single-women reforms were scarily late.

For instance, Irish women couldn't buy a house outright, without a male co-signee, until 1976. Women couldn't open a bank account in their own name until 1975 in the UK. Single women couldn't apply for a loan or a credit card without their father's signature and permission (even if they earned more than their father!), until the mid-seventies.

The explosion of single people (particularly women) is not a crisis, it's feminism (otherwise known as equality) working its magic. The single revolution is a cheery, gigantic throng, visible from outer space, spelling out PROGRESS.

And yet, as a 27 year-old ~~singleton~~ simpleton, I once dramatically sighed and said this to a friend: 'I wish we could go back to the '50s, when all men wanted to get married in their twenties, and *everyone* got married. We'd be knocked up – or mothers – by now. Things were so much simpler back then.'

I want to go back and shake some sense into myself. Bemoaning the fact that we no longer *have* to get married in our twenties is equivalent to cursing the fact women can now vote. It would be like holding up our ballot form and saying 'Oh, this is so tiresome, how very *boring*.' *A thousand suffragettes turn in their graves*

Do we really want to go backwards? To dive into marriage when we're little more than children ourselves (the decision-making parts of our brain do not fully develop until age 25 – fact). Do we really want to marry someone our parents choose for us?

Women can now have sex outside of marriage without community banishment; we can have socially accepted children without a husband; we can ensure a roof over our heads without the signature of a man; we can have stellar careers and earn *almost* as much as equivalent men (don't get me started), and we can now choose not to marry without becoming an outcast.

Overall, single is a supremely modern privilege women can now enjoy without being driven to join a nunnery, so not wanting it is a bit like not wanting contraception. We pushed this boulder uphill, so let's sit and at least admire it. We can now be single without being too poor to buy food, or being landlocked, or being dunked in the river to see if we drown.

Standards often weren't an option for our ancestors; but they are for us. Waiting wasn't allowed back then; it is now. Opting out altogether was seen as insanity; now we can say 'actually...no ta'. And for that, we should be mightily grateful.

WHY OUR PARENTS HATE
US BEING SINGLE

The way the press presents the decline in marriage is as a sharp, continual downward line. But the reality is more of an up-then-down rollercoaster trajectory. It's true that marriage rates are *now* at an all-time-low, but it's more true to say that we've dipped back to the rates before the church-rush of the 1960s – and then deep-dived some more.

It's an urban myth that *everyone* got married in the 1950s. In fact, marriage rates were pretty low in the UK then; they spiked during the 1960s, when many of our parents were coming of age, or getting married themselves. (This is important; we'll come back to it.)

There was a sizeable spike either side of WWII, as couples married before soldiers were dispatched, or the moment they came home. Then in 1959, marriage rates had fallen really low, to a rate of 340,000. Rates then steadily climbed throughout the 1960s, reaching a high of 426,000 marriages in 1972.

'The figures are similar in the US,' says journalist Kate Bolick, author of *Spinster: Making a Life of One's Own*. 'In 1890 only 54 per cent of people got married, but in the 1960s it surged to 80 per cent, so yes, it's best described as a surge and then a decline. The notion of the nuclear family has been compounded as the norm within our generation, because of the peak marriage rate of the Baby Boomers, and the depiction of nuclear families in TV shows we watched as kids.'

In 2015 – the most recent figures available – the Office for National Statistics recorded only 239,020 weddings, a drop of 8,300 from the year before. This means that 22 men out of 1,000 got married, and 20 women out of 1,000. This is indeed the lowest figure on record at the Office for National Statistics (which started collecting data in 1862).

Basically, there was an altar-sprint, an aisle-stampede in the 1960s. So, it's fair to assume that, given our parents grew up in a mass 'let's get married!' race, they now have an ingrained notion that marriage is really, really important.

Perhaps that's why they're now so puzzled that we, their children, are not following suit. We live in an age when marriage is increasingly less popular, and less expected, yet we are being raised by those who grew up in the betrothal-boom. We're living both in the shadow of Baby Boomer expectations, and free from the pressures they experienced.

THE PSYCHOLOGY BEHIND THE CHURCH-RUSH

Half of my friends are still single, but the other half were part of a 33-ish helter-skelter church-rush. Many wanted to have kids, and had the age of 35 ringed in their heads with a black marker of doom as their fertility deadline ('fucccck!'). So that explains some of the rush, but there's also a psychological phenomenon known as 'herding'.

'Herding' is what it sounds like; following a crowd. We know from hundreds of psychological studies that people do things like stay in rooms filling with smoke, if others (paid actors) do the same, or cross the road (again, paid actors) when it's not safe, if others do so.

We're sheep, psychologically. It's an almost irresistible, invisible undertow. It's distressing not to be able to be part of the throng. But when you do drift off from that herd, by not marrying, I wonder if it becomes easier not to rejoin it?

And then, you begin to observe the reality of child-rearing, the seven-year cracks, the infidelities, the agony of divorce, and wonder if you want to even go there at all. Which feels a little like...freedom. Peeling off from the pack is unsettling, but also emancipating.

THE WEST'S 'YOU COMPLETE ME' CAPITALISM

The Western capitalist belief system says that if we try harder, work more, buy that app, wear that perfume, purchase that brand of clothing, then we will get what we want. 'The One' is dangled in front of us like a necklace we can buy.

We see it all the time, with the beatific model wife in the passenger seat of the sports car, or the dating-app advertisement with the 'inseparable' couple superglued together. Whereas Eastern philosophies see that our relationship status is much more of a roll of the dice of chance, a turn of the wheel of circumstance.

I read around Buddhist approaches to relationships during my year off, which helps me enormously. I learn that we become our thoughts, which is why it's so important to believe in a friendly, rather than a hostile universe. I learn that it's about the journey rather than the destination; that nobody is more deserving of your affection than yourself; that peace comes from within rather than from an app. That kinda life-changing thing.

Capitalism sells the idea that we can dodge sorrow and strife in life, that a scent or a sweater can 'cure' your singleness. The fear of being single, and the desire to couple, is a powerful advertising tool.

But the question of who you will love, or when, is one of the great mysteries of the universe. An unsolvable riddle. A cosmic conundrum. Which is certainly not on sale at the App Store, or in a department store. You can't order the perfect person to be delivered from Amazon, bang on the societally approved age.

'YOU HAD ME AT HELLO' IDEALISM

Coming back to our 'soulmate marriage' expectations, other cultures are much more roomy-minded and magnanimous when it comes to choosing who to marry. There's a scene in Elizabeth Gilbert's *Committed: A Love Story* that sums it up beautifully. She's talking to a roomful of married women from a Hmong village in Vietnam.

She starts asking them questions such as 'Did you know that he was special right away?' and is met with bafflement and titters of amusement. She then asks, 'When did you fall in love with him?' and the women burst out laughing. Confused, Gilbert persists, despite their mirth. 'And what do you believe is the secret to a happy marriage?' she asks. In response, the women practically pee themselves. 'Now they all really did lose it,' writes Elizabeth. 'Even the grandmother was openly howling with laughter.'

The joke was this. We are peculiar, in our Western quest for 'you complete me' perfection. In most other cultures, it's more 'they'll do' rather than 'they're The One'.

Personally, I'd rather live in our culture of 'soulmate marriage' loftiness, and potentially wind up not marrying at all, rather than be shipped off to someone I kinda like who lives down the road, but it's food for thought, no?

THE SCREENPLAY VERSIONS OF US

In the West, we weave and plait and dye our how-we-met relationship stories into gorgeous tapestries. We create tales that would make great screenplays; involving fateful meetings, drama, suspense, and either salvation or a takeaway lesson. 'Over the years, her narrative will have been either hammered into a golden epic myth or embalmed into a bitter cautionary tale,' writes Gilbert.

Right?! I've done that. Haven't you? Taken an awkward first date and crafted it into a meet-cute. Taken a chance encounter, melted it down, and remoulded it into a pretty intersection of serendipitous significance.

One of my happily married friends (who shall remain unnamed) read these two paragraphs and told me, 'I think we use those stories to validate the choices we've made, when it's too late to change our circumstances. We create our own fairytales because at least 50 per cent of marriage is donkey work and non-magical logistics, 30 per cent is rubbing along side-by-side, and ten per cent is wondering "What if?"... so the remaining ten per cent of "fairytale" is so necessary.'

So, we shape storylines. I'm not even sure I was fully aware that *I was doing this*, until right now. It's just what we do, for dinner-party plaudits. We don't hear the real stories; they get buried. But then they often tumble out, on the wine waterslide, normally circa 2am: 'I wanted my ex back, but he didn't want me, so I married X'. Or 'I wanted a baby and Y was the best thing about'. Some do genuinely get super lucky, and some settle, and often you truly can't tell which is which.

REPURPOSING BITTERSWEET BREAK-UPS

I learn about the Old Flame Fair, a monthly market in Hanoi. The recently split drop off mementos from their ex-lovers that they can no longer live with, such as perfume, books, clothes, and even framed photographs and love letters. The guy who set it up, Dinh Thang, did so to be environmentally minded (waste not, want not), and to help smash the taboo of break-ups in Vietnam, where they're still frowned upon.

There are also Museums of Broken Relationships, in Croatia and LA, permanent showcases of love tokens, which see footfall of around 1,000 visitors a week. The curators of the Croatia branch say that Britain is the nation that donates the most to its coffers. Exhibits include 'a drawing of us by a stranger on a train', 'a packet of gastritis tablets', a 'stupid frisbee', a sailor's cap and shorn dreadlocks, all with fascinating stories from the givers.

The act of transforming something brittle into something beautiful really appeals to me. It honours our ended relationships rather than shoving them in a shoebox under a bed. It not only speaks to the power of letting go but also shows how we can turn what once would have been trashed into treasure.

There's a segment on their website for sharing break-up stories, which reminds us that even though a break-up can feel like *nobody has ever been through this*, literally everyone has, even those we regard as above heartbreak. 'Share a break-up story, lock it away if you need to take your time, or simply pin a break-up on the global map of broken hearts,' says the write-up. 'You are not alone.'

DEALING WITH FERTILITY FEARMONGERING

'The tyranny of time is a serious attack on freedom.'

– JEAN D'ORMESSON

Being a maternally minded single over the age of 30 is about as relaxing as being a bomb-defuser in *The Hurt Locker*. 'Tick tock, which wire do I cut, red or blue, REDORBLUE?!' It is indeed like feeling tyrannized by time. Chased by it.

And if you dare to forget the urgency of your predicament, don't worry, because countless of people will remind you that you 'Best get on with it' or 'What are you waiting for'.

Why do people do this? Well, it's their civic duty to remind you of your ageing womb, because otherwise you may become the woman in the Lichtenstein-style cartoon, who cries, 'Oh my God! I forgot to have a baby!' They need to remind you that your sperm swimmers flag with age, otherwise you might accidentally end up without an heir to continue your legacy. You ought to be thankful to them.

Heavy sarcasm aside, I realize during my sabbatical that this fertility fearmongering is definitely something driving my single panic, even though I am not sure *whether I even want kids*. When I turned 33, my dad told me that he was redirecting money previously allocated to my 'wedding fund' into an 'egg-freezing fund'. Yep. Seriously.

So, in order to soothe my fertility panic, I start digging around, and am very surprised by what I find.

Why do we think that our fertility takes a cliff-dive after 35? The chilling and oft-cited statistic is that one in three women aged 35–39 will not get pregnant even after a year of trying.

However, the source of this data? French births between 1670 to 1830. When antibiotics, electricity and fertility treatment were yet to be invented. So, these figures should have been shelved under 'antiquated and not relevant to modern science' around 150 years ago, rather than still being wheeled out now.

'Why would they exaggerate', I hear you cry? Well, fearmongering headlines sell papers. And fertility treatment is a massive money-making machine. Many, many companies profit from 'baby panic'. The truth is, there is no real rhyme or reason to fertility. A woman in her forties might get pregnant within a couple of months of trying, whereas a woman in her twenties might face several years of negative pregnancy tests. You just don't know, until you try.

A Boston University study followed 2,820 women and found that 78 per cent of 35–40-year-olds got pregnant within a year, compared with 84 per cent of 20–34-year-olds. Only a 6 per cent drop. Not quite the plummet we've been led to believe, hey. (Later, we'll talk about another study that showed *only* a four per cent drop.)

And while it's undeniable that fertility is indeed a window that eventually closes, we now live in a Britain where more than 2,000 babies a year are born to mothers aged over 45.

I know many people who are frightened of regretting not having children. Personally, I am frightened of regretting having them. I'm not sure my personality is compatible with kids, I'm not sure I would be a good parent, and by all accounts, my five big loves (sleeping, exercising, travelling, reading and alone time) will be torpedoed by kids with all of the tenderness of a nuclear missile.

From whence has this fear of regretting *having them* sprung? I suspect, this. Both of my parents independently told me that had they their time again, they're not sure they would have had kids. 'But back then, it was *expected*' they both said, separately, as if from a script.

Maybe I'll capitulate if I ever meet someone I want to make a baby with, but for now, all I know is that I'm not like a friend of mine who has spent thousands of pounds on freezing her eggs, to try to future-proof her fertility.

I recently said to her, 'If I had £4,000 to spare, I wouldn't spend it on egg-freezing, I'd spend it on...ooh, going to see the Northern Lights... maybe a Lapland safari with huskies and reindeer....and probably diving with Beluga whales! So, does that mean I'm not bothered enough?' Possibly. (Man, I really want to go on *that holiday*.)

As a kid, I mostly ignored dolls and played with animal toys: My Little

Pony, Sylvanian Families, Keypers (which for the record, definitely do not keep secrets safe from your big brother – false advertising). Plus, I like that you can leave animals alone for a few hours without being prosecuted by the authorities.

'If I had kids, my kids would hate me,' Oprah Winfrey once said. 'They would have ended up on the equivalent of the *Oprah* show talking about me.' And she's clearly a very maternal person; she's practically the mother of America. Which just goes to show that a maternal streak can co-exist with the knowledge that biological children are not for you.

Thankfully, we live in a society now where it's not *as* expected. A society where I feel that I do have a choice. And it looks like I'll have plenty of childfree company, if I do opt out. I discover that one in five people are still childfree by 45, these days, a figure that is only mushrooming.

WHAT MY YEAR OFF FELT LIKE

In two words? Bloody relaxing.

One of the most enjoyable things is how innocuous my phone becomes. When I am in the early stages of dating someone, my phone is like Frodo's ring. It is a thing of devastating power. It has the might to make my mood soar, or to smite me down with a single chirrup.

I have been known to 'go to the loo' while at dinner, just so's I can check my phone, if I'm in the early throes with someone. (I wouldn't read my texts at the table, I wasn't raised by wolves.)

Affirming treasures and terrible fates no longer reside in my phone, so it no longer holds that sway over me. It is like a dethroned king, an ex-boss, a wand-less wizard, an overthrown empress, an impeached president. I no longer watch it like a TV.

I stumble across a quote from writer Mark Simpson, who calls singles who spend hours a day trawling dating apps, 'the unpaid secretaries of desire'. I feel a buzz of recognition. This sabbatical feels a lot like being retired from the dull-ass admin of secretary-ing desire.

LEARNING WHO I AM

Without a plus one, I start to learn what I really like doing, and who I really am.

Coupled-up me was like a Picasso face: a composite of various boyfriends. Or, to use a less elegant simile, I was like Mrs Potato Head (Miss Potato Head doesn't exist, sadly), with interchangeable features. I start to realize that I was never single long enough to figure out *who I was* and *what I wanted* without someone else in the frame.

I develop a newfound love for failing at handstands in yoga; for spending hours roaming art galleries; for taking photos; watching TV absolutely intended for American teens (*How to Get Away with Murder*, *Riverdale*); spending days sunbathing and reading. I have acres of time and I can do whatever the Dickens I like with it. It's liberating.

Denied of a boyfriend to withdraw compliments from like an ATM, I learn to tap up my own reserves of approval, like learning the art of tapping a tree. I read Eckhart Tolle, who says, 'Stop looking outside for scraps of pleasure for fulfilment, for validation, security or love. You have a treasure within that is infinitely greater than anything the world can offer.' It's empowering.

I RE-WROTE THE STORIES I TELL MYSELF

Once I get some distance from my love life, I start to see it clearly, I start to see that the victim-esque stories I've been telling myself, like 'Nobody ever wants to marry me', are quite simply not true.

Eckhart Tolle theorizes that we're held up by the scaffolding of the stories we tell ourselves. Without that scaffolding, we feel insecure, wobbly, like we're a building that's about to rumble to the ground. Here's the peculiar part. The scaffolding can be negative, like 'I'm unlucky in love' or 'The opposite sex never fancies me'. We even hang on to *negative* scaffolding, for dear life.

Basically, the stories we tell ourselves are narratives that shape our existence. Like pouring jelly into moulds, or using a cookie cutter to make a blob of dough into stars. It makes our life neat. And often we hang on to stories, predefined narratives, that no longer apply.

We force our lives into shapes that they don't actually fit into. Because it's unsettling for our lives to be a wibbly mass of jelly or a random clump of dough. Without the shapes, potential existential angst awaits. 'Why am I here? What am I doing? What is the meaning of all this?!' That kinda fun.

The times when we're rejected, when we're hurt, when we're cheated on tend to stick in our minds, whereas the times when the opposite happened slide away into the forgotten files. As a psychologist, Dr Rick Hanson, famously said, 'The brain is like Velcro for negative experiences, but Teflon for positive ones.'

The story I've been telling myself is not the truth of why I'm single. I'm single because of a breakdance of chance, a hopscotch of choices. There have been a number of men I've dated who talked about marriage, and had I stayed, would have produced a ring. But I didn't. I could have gotten married aged 20, 26, 30 and 36, given there were men offering a potential lifelong pledge to me at all of those ages. Who would have committed, had I wanted to. But – I didn't.

I chose to bounce instead, because there were bigger yeses burning inside of me, those of book-writing, travelling and freedom. And do I regret it? Not for a hot second.

If you've been telling yourself 'Nobody wants me' try delving deep to find out if that is really true. You're trying to tell me that you have never finished with anyone? That there isn't anyone out there who would hop on the 'To Marriage' path with you tomorrow, if you picked up the phone and called them and said 'I've made a terrible mistake...' Hmmm. I don't believe you.

If you've been telling yourself that your singleness has been thrust upon you, start to question that story. Dare to take away the scaffolding. The reality is, sure you might have been dumped, as have I, many times, but I bet you've also walked away from things that weren't quite right. Or maybe 'Time is running out' or 'I'm happier in a relationship' are your stories. Dismantle them. Take a long hard look.

I used to tell myself that each break-up made me weaker. Whereas now, I know that my many romantic run-ins have given me grit and pluck. The knocks have strengthened me just as micro-tears gird a muscle. And I'm willing to bet my bottom dollar that they've strengthened you, too.

AN ODE TO MY SOULMATES

Amy Poehler on meeting Tina Fey –

'I finally found the woman I want to marry.'

My year off was also interesting, in that I didn't feel any less loved, or cherished, or wanted. Why? Because my life is already rich with soulmates, and I got the chance to behold that. You don't have to shag someone for them to be a soulmate.

We don't just need one person, says psychologist Jennifer L Taitz, author of *How to be Single and Happy*. 'Actually, we need a core group, not a single person. Robin Dunbar, a University of Oxford anthropologist, famously said that in order to be happy, people need to deeply bond with roughly five people. Not just one.'

Five people. And I bet you have them already, right?

During my sabbatical, I don't orbit whoever-I'm-seeing like the Earth slavishly circles the Sun, so I start circling the soulmates *I already have*. Who have been in my life a hell-of-a-lot longer than all of my exes put together. Allow me to introduce them.

My first love was undoubtedly the wickedly funny and endlessly loyal Sam, whom I met at secondary school aged 11. Our bond was instant and intense. Given we were either thick as thieves, or having scorching rows, our classmates nicknamed us 'The married couple'. 'They're at it again,' they'd say, rolling their eyes, if we were deep in an arms-folded silent treatment, or passing notes to each other and doubling over with hilarity.

It was a romantic relationship in many ways. We would share beds and trace letters on the others back, guessing what it was. We'd use our lunch money to buy an entire frozen Sara Lee gateau and then lie around eating it (still frozen) like a couple of budget Marie Antoinettes. Sam pushed me out of my introvert comfort zone, daring me to do things like stand up on a packed bus and sing 'Eternal Flame' by The Bangles. I did it, too.

It's still our song. We recently walked down La Rambla in Barcelona, singing it hand-in-hand. We endlessly tease Sam's husband that we're going to elope. We call each other ridiculous things like 'sugar tits', 'wonderbum' and 'bintface.'

I fell in love with my other best friend, Alice, when we met at university. We hated each other on sight, being polar opposites of ironed-jeans-and-glossy-highlights (Alice) vs band-T-shirt-and-hangover (me), but then we were slung together on a degree project, and forced to talk to one another.

I've lived with Alice for longer than any boyfriend (three years in total). We call each other 'wifey' and other friends 'mistresses.' Alice pretends to be a princess, but is a roll-your-sleeves-up trooper. She's so utterly quotable that I made a quotes book for her birthday recently, stuffed with gems such as 'You two will get on. She's into dogs and vampires and fantasy and all that nonsense too', 'I didn't think *Noah* the film would be ALL about Noah', or 'I just had a slightly traumatic wait for a bus'.

There's Wonder-Woman-esque Kate 1, who is my style twin, writing soundboard, 'accountability coach' whenever I want to get shit done, and my favourite person to do yoga and walks with. There's the adorable Kate 2, who is literally like Phoebe from *Friends* given her infectious, childlike wonder and enthusiasm. There's my 'Kick-ass Angel' Helen, a smart cookie so christened because of the Ash song and her black belt in tae kwon do, who I've loved since I was 11, and can phone at 2am if I have a crisis.

There's snacks-obsessed raconteur Laura, who I lived with for two years and love like a sister. And Gemma, whose wry wit and generosity of spirit never fail to astound me; I recently ran out of peppermint tea and she turned up on my doorstep with two boxes of the stuff, as if it were nothing, no big deal at all. Lovely Laurie, who knows more about the day-to-day machinations of my mind than anyone else. Legendary Jen, who will often drop me a text like, 'Just a quick one to say: You are magic. You are fucking glorious. You are so, so loved. Whatever you're doing today – SMASH IT. OK? OK. As you were.' Jen is officially the most romantic friend I have.

I'm a lucky badger, friend-wise. I have romance in my life every day without fail. Just not from people who I have sex with. And that's OK. Why does sex have to occur, for soulmates to be forged? I don't buy it.

These are the people that I will be cackling with in my eighties, should we all live that long. There's zero chance of me dying alone. I'll die with a throng of friends around my bedside, preferably having performed some glamorous stunt that saved the world.

FAMILY SOULMATES

And what about family? My warm, clever, funny mum, who's just been on the phone telling me that she's convinced the big ginger cat (who keeps trying to live with us) has figured out how to post itself through our letterbox, since it keeps showing up in the hall: 'Cheeky article. Anita said it's the smuggest cat she's ever seen.' Not to mention my wonderful aunts and uncles, my sister-in-law, my niece and nephew, my stepfamily, my close-as-sisters cousins, and my second cousins; I really won the jackpot when it comes to family.

I used to automatically sling my boyfriend to the top of my 'male loves totem pole'. But now, the three men at the crest of my male totem pole are my stepdad, brother and granda (Irish for 'grandad'). And it's going to take someone pretty spectacular to dislodge them.

My stepdad was the first father figure who was unreservedly *there*, who made me feel cushioned and held. He leaves peanut M and Ms beside my bed, gleaming like magic beans, because he knows I love them. We compete to think of the most ridiculous name for the remote control (the 'thingamybob', the 'whatchamacallit', the 'scoodmalaflip', the 'skidamadoo' and the 'bobbydazzler').

Since we're both tuneless, we have an imaginary band called the ToneDeafs. We do silly little dances and sing ear-bleeding harmonies in the kitchen, and schedule imaginary jam sessions, and pretend we are locked in a bitter rivalry as to who should be lead singer.

Then there's my brother: the person who supported me the most when Dad died; he was my safety net throughout, despite battling his own grief. He is the best father you've ever seen, we regress to childlike competitiveness when playing *Monopoly*, and our relationship has evolved from hair-pulling to gentle and respectful.

Third on my male totem pole, is my 92-year-old granda, who now sometimes forgets our names ('My memory's not as good as it once was, Anne...It is Anne, isn't it?'), but still manages to outwit us with his wry observations. 'What's this film about, Granda?' I recently asked him. 'Well, there's this fella here with long hair. No doubt he'll meet a woman and be away to bed with her.' A few seconds later he exclaimed, 'Jeepers creepers, they're already at it!'

If the measure of a soulmate is a) feeling totally accepted by someone, b) knowing they will always be there, and c) the happiness far outweighing the angst, then these soulmates beat any boyfriend I've have ever had. Hands-down. They have a royal flush to his pair of jacks.

I'm far from lonely, and I'm willing to wager you're not either, if you take the time to count your soulmates. Take a look. They're all around you.

IV: GROWING
SINGLE JOY

26 WAYS TO SOURCE SINGLE JOY

'Il vaut mieux être seule que mal accompagné'

– FRENCH PEOPLE

The French make everything sound better, non? Sexy feckers. This, roughly translated, means 'It is better to be alone than poorly accompanied'. RIGHT?! *Mais oui! Certainement.* Somebody put that on a fridge magnet, pronto.

I've discovered that single joy is like a garden. It's something that I need to plant, cultivate, water, feed and make sure it gets enough sun. I need to weed out the single sorrow and discontent regularly, hacking away at any growing grumbles as I would take down thistles threatening to choke foxgloves.* I need to talk to, tend to and coax the joy up out of the ground, toward the sun.

Societal messages tend to be like acid rain for single joy. People's opinions tend to beat down on it like a merciless sun, parching it. It's up to you to keep your garden lush.

Here are the gardening tools I reach for, when my fledgling single joy garden starts looking a little forlorn.

1. I REMEMBER THAT ROMANTIC LOVE IS NOT THE ONLY TYPE
Love songs. I used to feel a blank space next to me whenever I heard them as a single, or they would unlock a room of pain and longing in my head whenever I was getting over someone. I now take what are meant to be romantic love songs and apply them to the many types of love I have.

When I hear Aerosmith's 'I Don't Want to Miss a Thing', I think of my niece and nephew. My mum is my 'Wonderwall'. Bloc Party's 'I Still Remember' reminds me of when my tremendous mate Kate and I pogo-ed around to it at a gig in Brixton. 'Island in the Sun' by Weezer makes me think of 'running away together' with my mate Sam on holiday.

Try it. (If you suspect I point-blank ignore most contemporary music, you suspect right.)

* I say all of this as if I'm green-fingered. I would be more aptly described as 'death-fingered'.

2. I BAN ROMCOM-WATCHING WHEN I'M SAD

It's our go-to when we want reassurance that there's a Happy Ending out there for us, isn't it? I can't tell you how many times I've sat snivelling through *The Notebook* or *Pretty Woman*, or *Dirty Dancing*, or *10 Things I Hate About You* thinking, 'If only I met a guy like Noah, Edward, Johnny or Patrick'.

This just medicates my single sadness with the thing that caused it in the first place: an overemphasis on romantic relationships to make me happy. It makes no sense. It would be like treating a frostbitten finger with a bagful of ice.

I now switch these for anti-romcoms, with unexpected, empowering endings, like the series *Big Little Lies* or films *Begin Again*, *Like Father* and *The Break-up*.

3. I REMIND MYSELF THAT I HAVE AEONS OF TIME

I used to think of my life as something that would become static come 40. I used to think that I needed to achieve the golden triad of societal expectations (Spouse! House! Babies!) before that age, otherwise I may as well just crawl under a rock and die.

Now, I remember that given female life expectancy is 83 for women and 79 for men, even if it takes until age 50 to meet him (or her, if I switch sides, never say never), I will still have 29 l-o-n-g years with that guy (if we are the same age and he dies right on schedule).

29 years! I mean. The longest relationship I've ever managed thus far was three years, and it was hard to even keep that alit, so that 29-year hypothetical relationship is going to be a humdinger of a challenge. I can wait. Is fine.

4. I PLAN DOGS, RATHER THAN BABIES

On that note, for the childfree (not child*less*) among us: unless you want to go down the artificial insemination/surrogate route (and if you do, I tip my hat to you and your child-bearing wherewithal, you total badass) then we have no control over when we meet the person, or whether we meet them, and if we'll be able to procreate. NONE. Zero control.

Now, my motto is 'I'd rather have dogs/cats with the right person aged 55, than kids with the wrong person now'. Seriously. Having kids with a dud dad/mum is such a bad idea. Caitlin Moran put it pithily when she said, 'If you have children, you can only have as much career and happiness as your partner will help make for you.'

You are handcuffing yourself to someone for life, emotionally, financially and timetable-managing-wise, when you make babies with them. You will live with them, sleep next to them, make house with them. Assuming they stick around to see out the child-raising. It's the one partnership you really, really want to get right. Make your choice a good one.

But, I can plan to have dogs. So I choose the breeds and the names, rather than imagining any future kids that might not happen. The dogs can definitely happen, because they're not dependent on the puckish universe, plus the intricacies of my/his body.

5. I LET GO OF COMPLIMENTS

Did a builder tell you you're a stone-cold fox today? Did a woman on the bus stare at your arms? Great. But – let it go. I literally used to think that the solution to my limp self-esteem was to write down all the compliments people gave me. So I did that, in my teenage diary. I felt like it helped, but it was a bit like watching the romcoms. It made me more dependent on the compliments.

When you're too dependent on compliments, any kind of criticism can swipe your legs from underneath you. I used to be able to remember, with vivid clarity, any time *anybody* criticized my appearance. I would re-play these in my head, as if listening to a song over and over. Then I realized: the only weight I need to lose is the weight of other's opinions.

I no longer believe the hype, whether it's that I was the 'best sex they'd ever had' (bet they've said that before, and will say it again, to someone else) or 'too high maintenance' (for having basic standards).

I love what the artist Georgia O'Keeffe says: 'I have already settled it for myself so flattery and criticism go down the same drain and I'm quite free'. Let it wash over you like a bracing shower and then spiral down the drain, rather than sit in it for an hour like a bath.

6. I STOP LOOKING AT MEN TO GAUGE THEIR REACTION

I was (all too) recently bouncing down Putney riverfront on a run, when I caught myself doing something that was very 2008. Scanning the faces of men I passed, to see if they were checking me out. Looking for that attraction flicker.

Fittingly, I was listening to 'I Want You to Want Me' by Cheap Trick. Which was pretty much the dating anthem of my twenties.

Now that I'm in my late thirties, men have mostly stopped looking at me wolfishly, hungrily, almost angrily, and have started looking at me more gently. If at all. But then again, I did run around Shoreditch in little more than a bra and pants in my twenties.

I actually like the shift, it feels more respectful. But the ideal would be that I don't notice at all. Back in the early 1900s, a sociologist named Charles Horton Cooley coined the groundbreaking term 'looking-glass self' to capture this feeling of the gaze of others upon us. When we have a 'looking-glass self', our self-image is based on what others think of us, or what we imagine they think of us. Rather than who we actually are, or what we think of ourselves. But this is an extremely fragile place to live. When my self-esteem is based on the reaction of others, it's like having confidence made of ghostly gossamer. So easily ripped asunder by a negative comment, or a bad skin day.

I now seek to make my self-esteem like a rope, composed of thousands of fibres, which I have wound, bound and plaited myself. Something that's tough, difficult to snag and impossible to snap, even if ten men were to pull on it.

I sometimes imagine myself in an invisibility cloak, in order to encourage my outward-facing gaze. To stop myself from basing my self-worth on what I see reflected in mirror-ball pupils.

7. RECLAIMING THE MUSIC THAT HURTS

I used to hear songs that reminded me viscerally of an ex and feel a twist of pain inside. Seb and I once danced along a street to Madcon's 'Beggin'' after a night out, and as a result that song pierced me in the heart every time I heard it.

When I split with Tom, the two songs that caused that twist were 'Melody Calling' by The Vaccines (because we jumped around at their gig to it) and 'Under the Pressure' by The War on Drugs. I used to flip past these songs in my Spotify, or switch the radio station, to avoid the twist.

It took a while, but now I've reclaimed these songs and can sit and have a half-smile as I remember the good times. With exposure therapy, I've turned them from sour into sweet.

8. REMEMBER – IT'S A CHOICE

It's rough when you feel like single has been thrust upon you without your say-so, by an infidelity, or cooled ardour, or somesuch shock. I know; it's happened to me several times. However, choosing to remain single is generally your choice.

I bet you have somebody you could go out with right now, but you just don't want to. You could hop online and stack up a queue of dates, but you just don't want to. You could get back with that ex, but *you just don't want to.*

The thing stopping you? Keeping you single? Standards. Free will. It's really important to remember that single is a choice; you're not a put-upon victim who can't get a date.

9. SELF-DISCOVERY IMMINENT

Look up 'chameleon changing colour with sunglasses' on YouTube for a treat. You'll see chameleons becoming turquoise, pink or black depending on what shade of sunglasses they sit on. Maybe that was you, depending on who you were with. Now you can become whatever damn-well colour you like.

Our viewing habits, living situation, meals and sporting activities tend to mesh with whoever we're going out with. I think you only truly discover who you actually are and what you actually like, once you're alone.

Being single allows you to develop into a full picture, like a blank photo that is swirled around in developing fluid in a darkroom. The longer you're single, the more detailed that picture becomes.

10. HEALING, RATHER THAN HURTING, YOUR SINGLE SORE SPOTS

Remember my chat with a five-year-old (see page 30)? A few years previous, that chat would have triggered an existential crisis in me. I've realized that when someone prods a spot like this, the only time they can hurt me is when I've been poking said spot myself.

If I've been consciously soothing and healing these delicate areas, they don't hurt, but if I've been re-bruising them myself, all it takes is a guileless, round-eyed question from a child – 'Why aren't you mawwied, Auntie Caffwin?' – to make me wince.

11. FEEDING YOUR 'SKIN HUNGER'

We need physical touch, so much so that psychologists call the lack of it 'skin hunger.' It's why the recent trend for 'cuddle parties' or a 'cuddle buddy' is not as crackers as it sounds.

One study found that 'skin hunger' results in higher levels of anxiety and depression.

When I'm single, I get about 90 per cent less skin-on-skin contact. I hug friends, but only for a heartbeat. So, it's up to me to make sure my 'skin hunger' gets sated somehow. I have certain friends who I can walk along a road with holding hands (Hi Helen) or curl up with on a sofa. I can give my granda a little shoulder rub while he says 'lovely...lovely'. I can go for a facial and bliss out while someone basically strokes my face for a half hour. I can have my niece brush my hair. I can lift a dog and make it hug me.

If you're able to have casual sex without growing feelings (I'm incapable), and while staying safe (both emotionally and physically), then you might find that a shag buddy is your personal solution to 'skin hunger'. Whatever works. You do you. Or should I say – you do them.

12. SHUT DOWN THE ENVY STAB

If you are riven through with envy when you receive a notification that a school friend has gotten engaged, there's a solution. You can teach yourself to be happy for other people.

There's an ancient Buddhist technique called 'Sympathetic Joy', which was talked about in a book called *Lost Connections* by Johann Hari.

The meditation goes like this. You start off by imagining something terrific happening to yourself, and feeling the ensuing joy buzz. Easy peasy. Second up, you envisage someone you barely know, but see regularly, having some life win. Maybe a random colleague getting a promotion. And summon the joy buzz for them. Thirdly, this is the tricky part, you picture somebody you don't like experiencing a personal triumph, say falling pregnant after years of trying, while trying to conjure the same trill of pleasure.

You do this three-stage process every day, for 15 minutes, until it starts to stick and becomes second nature.

'Sympathetic Joy' is a muscle that you can strengthen, and by doing so, there's a win-win. You get a free bliss rush, even though all you've done is see a total stranger on the steps of a church. As Johann writes in *Lost*

Connections, 'Part of the point of sympathetic joy meditation is that you feel less envy, but an even more important part is that you start to see the happiness of others not as a rebuke, but as a source of joy for yourself, too.'

13. I CHECK MY SLEEP / FOOD LEVELS

My brain is most likely to chant 'DOOM, DOOM, DOOM' at me like a wild-eyed medieval peasant clanging a bell, when I need a nap or a snack. I was recently walking up Montjuïc in Barcelona silently crying behind my sunglasses because *I'm not married*. Then I sat down to eat a couple of cookies and an apple, and whoosh!, just like that, my unmarried angst disappeared.

Hunger triggers a stress response in us that feels a lot like sky-caving-in doom. 'Humans are built like all the other animals – and animals get very unhappy when blood sugar is low,' says naturopathic expert Dr Peter Bongiorno. 'It is an evolutionary mechanism that is designed to make finding food a priority.'

A few days later, I had a meltdown over the cyclingworldproblem of having to fix my bike chain, because *other women have boyfriends to do this*, and then I remembered that I was knackered. (There's a man on my street who likes to do bird calls between 2am and 4am, and reader, I suspect it's not because he's a bird enthusiast. I think he might be a *whisper it* drug dealer.) I scrubbed the oil from my hand, had a nap and felt grand. I mean, of course I can fix a chuffing bike chain.

Realizing that an emotional Greek Tragedy often has a forehead-slappingly simple solution pierces its power.

14. ALLOWING SINGLE SORROW IN

It may have been a case of misdiagnosis, but I still did the right thing by allowing myself to weep when I felt the single sorrow arise. It's futile trying to sidestep a negative emotion as you would swerve a ball in dodge ball. That ball is coming to get you, no matter what.

A study by the University of New South Wales told some participants to suppress an unwanted thought before sleep, while a control group could think about whatever they liked. They found that the suppressors dreamt more about the shoved-away thought than those who didn't dodge it. They call this 'Dream Rebound'. Essentially, even if you pluck a thought/emotion from your conscious thought patterns, it will still take root in your subconscious.

Another study entitled 'The Social Costs of Emotional Suppression' found that inhibiting emotional expression leads to less closeness to others, and lower social satisfaction. In a nutshell, if a friend asks you how you're doing, be honest.

Negative emotions simply grow, if they're stoppered. I think of my sadness as being like a reservoir behind a dam. If I hold it there, it amasses, and starts to spiral and froth, shapeshifting from an innocent pool into a lethal body of water.

Emotions are an inescapable part of the human experience. If you're sensitive, like me, it likely means you feel the swoop of sorrow more acutely. But, you probably also feel the soar of euphoria more keenly too.

I love what Matt Haig wrote in *Reasons to Stay Alive* about his thin skin. 'But would I go along to a magical mind spa and ask for a skin-thickening treatment? Probably not.' Thick skin is over-rated.

15. TIMED SELF-PITY BATHS
There's a difference between allowing an emotion to move through you, and getting stuck in day-long negative ruminations. There are times when it's simply not practical to feel all your feels. I mean, your colleagues are going to be somewhat alarmed if you burst into tears in a meeting and tell them you're 'terrified of winding up alone'. You'll end up in HR with a kindly woman called Margaret.

If the sorrow is all-consuming, try scheduling a time to let it roam. A Paralympian once told me that it's a common athlete trick to 'schedule worry time' at the advice of their sports psychologists. 'I'm not thinking about this now, I'll think about it at 5pm.' They set aside a specific time to set those worries loose, to give them licence to sprint around their brains.

I found this idea so intriguing that I started having 'self-pity baths'. Back when I was devastated by my split with Tom, I needed someplace to put that sorrow; I couldn't let it fold over me all day long.

So, I would wait until I was in the bath, and then let it roll. I would play tear-valve-trigger songs, such as 'While My Guitar Gently Weeps' by The Beatles, 'I Found You' by Alabama Shakes, and 'Use Somebody' by Kings of Leon, and really let the single sorrow cascade out of me for a half hour. It was like super-efficient emoting. Like the HIIT version of crying.

I then got out of the bath, dried myself off and put on my PMA (positive mental attitude) once more. It worked like a charm.

16. I WRITE A 'FUCK YOU' LETTER
Let's face it, one of the blockades to single joy is often residual anger towards an ex. Somebody very dear to me gave me a stellar piece of advice, on how to deal with repetitive 'I can't believe he/she' loops.

She told me to write a 'Fuck You' letter, whereby I freed every single resentment that I kept replaying in my brain. Of course, I would never send it, but that wasn't the point. It wasn't for them, it was for me.

Repetitive thought patterns can feel like a ball darting around a pinball machine, whirring, dinging and pinging. Writing it all down is the equivalent of letting the levers flop, so that the ball can fall and finally rest. Game over.

Incidentally, there's a brilliant function on the free *Happy Not Perfect* app called 'Letting Go', whereby you can write a 'Fuck You' letter, and then use your finger to raze it with fire. So satisfying.

17. I WRITE A 'THANK YOU' LETTER
Famed yogi Seane Corn says, 'We can't skip past the "fuck you" to get to the "I forgive you". Seriously, you can't. Stillness only comes after you allow your inferno of rage to burn out.'

I found that once I was halfway into my 'Fuck You' letter, I would start springing to the ex's defence. My fiery steam would falter, like a slowing train, and I would chug to a shuddery halt. I'd arrived at forgiveness, by hammering through the town of 'Fuck You'.

There's something about seeing all the animosity in black and white on paper, or on a screen, that helps you get from 'Fuck You!' to 'But hold up, that's not totally true'. You start to realize that they're a nice person as well as a cheating butthead.

So after having a pop at whichever-ex, I would then write them a 'Thank You' letter. I've found that turning my ex into a Lucifer figure is not the answer to moving past them.

18. SHRINKING THE TAMAGOTCHIS
Speaking of which, fixations on exes are just like Tamagotchis. Those titchy digital pets on key chains, where we hatched the egg and called

it something ridiculous like Eggward or Lovechi. Then it was up to us to feed, water and stroke our pixelated pet, otherwise it would die.

If we don't feed or water a fixation, it will eventually die. Really, it will. This is why I now delete exes from all of my social media, no matter how friendly our split. I block them on Instagram, so that I can't see their stuff. I also export our text chats to documents (WhatsApp has an 'export chat' function), which I email to myself. I'm not comfortable with deleting the chat chains forever, but I can export them without freaking out.

Funny thing. When the message chain is there, alive and kicking in my phone, I do tend to dip back into it. Archiving it doesn't work. Whereas, when I have it on a random document on my computer, I never look. 'Out of sight' on social media/on my phone, really does lead to expedited 'Out of mind'.

19. LETTING NATURE RECLAIM YOUR BODY
Male readers, excuse us for just a tick.

Women: I don't know about you, but my sleepover-date prep is about as time-consuming as that scene in *Game of Thrones* where Daenerys Targaryen preps herself to meet her future Dothraki husband. It takes half a dang day.

Except my ceremony features less braiding by half-naked maidens, less wistful bathing in marble pools, and more scorching of permitted hair and deforestation of non-permitted hair (insert gif of a bloke with a growling chainsaw).

Defuzzing half of our bodies takes an epic amount of time. It's so tiresome. 'Hair? Oh no, we don't have any hair, only on our heads, where it is full and lush, but everywhere else? NO HAIR. We mysteriously have the ability to only grow hair where you think we should have hair.' *Beams*

When you're single, you don't have to do any of that shite. You can let your body be reclaimed by nature, like a mossy, ferny glade. You can kick back in the bath and eat a Flake and listen to a TED talk, while it becomes all furry and warm. You can put aside that excruciating epilator, and relegate that hot wax, and only shave the bits you'll show in a dress. Hell yes.

I read a piece in a magazine recently, in which a female writer claimed

she goes for fortnightly bikini waxes even when she's single. What?!
I practically chucked the magazine out of the window in disgust.
Sacrilege! And also *coughs* bullshit.

Men, you obviously have your own hair-removal woes, which you can
now happily let go of. Back-waxing, chest-shaving, so on. And while
we're here, I need to tell you that women really don't care (unless
they're on *Love Island*) if you have a few patches of fuzz between your
navel and your neck.

20. INSTALLING AN OPINION FILTER

Opinions on our singledom. Like exit tunnels in their bottoms,
everyone has one. Sigh.

I love how author Brené Brown literally carries around a list of people
whose opinions matter to her. She calls them her 'Move the body'
mates. The ones who would help you get away with murder. I've now
done that too, by mentally drawing up a list of around ten people
whose opinion I will actually allow into my psyche. The rest? Nah.

Almost every time I tell someone I'm single, they express an opinion,
whether it's that I'm 'too picky' or 'all about your career' or that my
'success is intimidating to men'. My singleness seems to invite people
to opine all over it. But whatever. Once I home in on the people who
truly matter, and make the rest of the 'single blah' chatter into white
noise, I feel a lot more sane.

Take my hairdresser. Who looks slightly panicked when I say 'No' to
their gossipy 'So are you seeing anyone?' And then consoles me with
'Oh well, what a shame. But don't worry, he'll come along soon.'

I used to let this opinion deflate me a little. Oh well. My life is a shame.
But now, I have a brand spanking new opinion filter, buddy. So – ping!
That opinion shoots away as 'irrelevant.' I no longer need to suffer
through the slings and arrows of their unsolicited opinions.

21. TREATING MYSELF LIKE A TREASURED GUEST

Last night I ate my sushi dinner standing up in my kitchen while reading
and wearing a onesie. It's so easy to slide into constant takeaways, or
microwave meals, or cereal, crackers and cheese, when it's 'just me'.
Right?

In Rebecca Traister's *All The Single Ladies*, she reveals that Norah

Ephron once confided that during her single years, she would lay on the occasional elaborate solo banquet. Replete with courses, napkins and serving platters. As if she were having a VIP over for dinner. 'This was how she reminded herself that she could be alone but not have a diminished domestic experience,' writes Rebecca.

I dig it. Tonight I'm making myself a lasagne. It'll take me four days to eat it, but this lasagne makes me feel like Norah Ephron, so y'know, details.

22. TURNING MY BRAIN INTO A BOUNTY HUNTER

Gratitude has become a self-care cliché because it works. Reams have been written about how it does remarkable things like deepen your sleep, make your heart healthier, lower your cortisol (aka the stress hormone) by 23 per cent, and nix depression by 41 per cent. The research just keeps coming; it now resembles a mountain.

If you asked me what has been most transformative for my mental health, I would answer like a shot: exercise and gratitude. Even when I've had a beast of a day, I can always find at least fifteen things that were beautiful. When I first started writing gratitudes, I would struggle to find three. But, with repetition and practice, I have turned my brain from a worry-seeking instrument, into a bounty-hunting machine.

My mind wants to look for potential disaster, impending calamity, the prospect of being mugged, my dwindling bank balance. Now, I force my anxious little mind to alight on the good. Just as I scan my day to find pretty or cool things to pop onto Instagram, gratitude is the exact same treasure hunt.

A kind man who gave me 5p because I was short in the supermarket, a bulldog puppy bounding up to me, an undulating murmuration of starlings, or the dozens of other things that fall out of my brain when I'm not paying attention.

23. DIARIZING ENOUGH

Do you live alone like me? Now that I'm not in a house-share and I also work from home, I have to be careful. Even though I need alone time like I need oxygen, I also need people, so I schedule at least four social things a week, even though I don't always feel like doing so. Once I'm in them, I enjoy them, and it stops me talking to my 'pet fly'. (True story. I once spent four whole days alone, and started to have dialogue with a fly. I called him Desmond.)

24. DEEP DIVING INTO THE 'SHOULD HAVE'

It's so easy to be taunted by 'What ifs' and 'Should haves', of the ilk of 'What if I'd treated him better' or 'I should have stayed with her'. It's particularly mentally tormenting when you know that had you behaved differently (in my case, not been a drunken nightmare) or had you not split with them, you know it would have ended in a wedding.

Ain't no changing the past. That is GONE, my peach. Here's the thing. We made the best decision we could, with the information available to us at the time.

There's only been one guy I've ever come close to wanting to marry, and when we split he said 'I know we'll get married if we stay together, because I do love you, but I don't think we'll be happy.' And he was bang on the money.

That sentence nailed what our future would have looked like. If the person-he-was had married the person-I-was, we wouldn't have been happy. We needed to go our separate ways to find happiness.

So, when I really walk around in that 'What if' and deep-dive into the unfathomed depths of that 'Should have', I know that our split was the right decision. If we hadn't split, I would have been married by 31, mortgaged by 32, probably pregnant by 33, and everything would have been right on schedule, societal-expectation wise.

Ensconced in that partnership, protected from the consequences, I probably would have continued drinking well into my 40s. My addiction would have taken a lot longer to reach chronic levels, which basically would have meant a much slower, more painful unravel. We would have fought bitterly, I would have been a snippy parent, and we would have slid slowly towards divorce.

I also would have resented being caged, albeit in a beautiful golden gilt cage, so young, pouting like a child made to leave a party. 'Do not reach the era of child-rearing and real jobs with a guitar case full of crushing regret for all the things you wished you'd done in your youth,' says Cheryl Strayed.

The chapter close of that relationship was the start of a whole new book for me: sobriety, living in different countries, learning who I was, getting published. Without the bad, mad and sad times that spiralled off from that split, I wouldn't have been razed to the ground and rebuilt. I wouldn't have discovered my gumption, carved my current character, or drawn an intimate self-knowledge map.

When I give myself the *Sliding Doors* choice of going back and living that parallel life instead, I know I would choose *this life*, even though society looks slightly askance at it. Ask yourself, would you really go back and hop on that alternative train instead? And miss out on being on this train? Really explore that. The answer might surprise you.

25. SEEKING OUT SINGLE ROLE MODELS

I've noticed that when I'm, say, sat at an airport or on a beach, I will find the happy couples. Instead, I've started seeking out the singles, just as I hunt gratitudes.

It's meant I saw the city exec rollerblading in his suit and singing Guns N' Roses. It's meant I noticed the twentysomething having a chai latte and utterly absorbed in her book. The elderly man eating alone and smiling benevolently at someone on their 40th birthday wailing 'I'm so old!' and probably thinking 'Honey, you're a mere whippersnapper. The only people who get to call themselves *old* are 80+, like me'.

Of course, I have no real way of knowing if these people are actually single, other than a quick hand-scan, but seeking them – seeing them – helps me.

Also, it's made me think about how I assume people see me. I assume they look at me, clearly on my own flying to Barcelona, and think 'Oh, poor single loser'. Whereas, I stood behind an apparently-single thirtysomething lady while getting on a flight recently, and all I was thinking was, 'I really like her combo of crochet top, stone-wash denim cut-offs and gladiator sandals'. It didn't even occur to me to wonder why she's on her own. Or to pity her.

26. THE GALACTIC POSSIBILITIES OF THE UNWRITTEN

We've already covered how narrative arcs in TV, film and literature tend to end with wedding bells. 'That's a wrap folks.' Happy ever after, tick. However, before the ding-dong church finale, protagonists tend to remain single, or mostly single, until the last ten minutes, last season, or last chapter.

They might have an on-again, off-again love interest (Ross and Rachel

Friends, Carrie and Big SATC, Alicia and Peter The Good Wife, Barney and Robin How I Met your Mother, Emma and Dexter One Day) or an unrequited frisson with a co-worker (The Mentalist, Unforgettable, The Killing, Elementary, pretty much any detective drama in fact), but they spend the bulk of the storyline single.

Why? Because it gives the scriptwriters so much more scope. So much more wriggle room. Single characters are, bluntly put, so much more interesting, plot-wise. They can uproot and go anyplace; they can date the prime minister/a secret serial killer; they are more fun to puppeteer. Their endings are unwritten.

'I always hated it when my heroines got married,' writes Rebecca Traister in All the Single Ladies. Laura Little House, she points out, was always bowling down a hill, or chucking snowballs, or whooping while riding a horse. Until she got married, when she become 'stationary and solidly shod, beside her husband; the baby she held in her arms was the most lively figure in the scene. Laura's story was coming to a close. The tale that was worth telling about her was finished once she married.' Which adds a fresh, askance perspective to the 'they got married, the end' status quo, no?

Now, it's not that married couples have writing all over them, their endings are unwritten too, for real. But their story-spinning possibilities are more set, rooted and constricted than your renegade single, who could truly end up anywhere, with anyone, doing anything.

You can see the unwritten nature of your ending as a positive, rather than a negative. As a tantalizing choose-your-own-adventure tale, rather than a fear-filled empty page.

Don't play it safe, in your imaginings. Write a list of things you long for, that don't include any kind of romantic entanglement, and then go after them with all of the caution and trepidation of a comet.

'Tell me, what is it you plan to do with your one wild and precious life?'

– MARY OLIVER

SINGLE JOY INSPIRATION

PODCAST SERIES
A SINGLE THING, *ON ITUNES*
Hosted by Natalie Karneef, this drops truth bomb after truth bomb.
Natalie was in constant relationships from 20 to 39 and, in the wake
of the demise of her marriage, found that she had no idea how to be
single, let alone enjoy it. The motto is 'Let's be alone – together.'

TASTER: 'If being single was as revered and as aspired to in pop culture,
as much as love, couplehood and romance, would we stay in these
relationships, even though we know they're not right?'

TED TALK
ERIC KLINENBERG'S LIVING SINGLE
In this talk, the funny, warm and crazily insightful social scientist who
co-wrote *Modern Romance* reveals how he had to fight against his
publishers, who wanted him to call *Going Solo* the spectacularly
depressing *Alone in America*. Here, he excavates compelling (and
outrageous) research into perceptions of single people, plus delves
into the growth of the American single-by-choice demographic.

TASTERS: On Edward Hopper's *Nighthawks* painting, which he imagines
would have illustrated the jacket, had he relented on *Alone in America*
(the painting depicts a lone man with his back to us at a coffee bar,
sitting opposite a front-on couple). 'We look at the guy whose back is
to us and we project onto him this sense of loneliness...it's interesting
that we don't see his face, because in fact he could be smiling, having
the time of his life...I've always thought the couple in the back is who
really looks lonely and sad. It is not a love connection for these guys.'

KATE BOLICK'S TALKS
SEARCH FOR HER NAME IN PODCASTS/ON YOUTUBE
Featured on *Lit Up, Ideas at the House, It's a Long Story* among others.
She is a game-changer and often talks about the 'duelling desires for
intimacy and autonomy'.

TASTER: (from *Ideas at the House*): 'Today there are more single
women than ever before in history. In America, 53 per cent of women

are unmarried. It's an unprecedented demographic shift. As marriage historian Stephanie Coontz has put it, "Today we are experiencing a historical revolution every bit as wrenching, far-reaching and irreversible as the Industrial Revolution". And singledom is central to that story, but until very recently it's a story that was rarely told.'

YOUTUBE
REASONS TO REMAIN SINGLE *BY THE SCHOOL OF LIFE*
Philosopher Alain de Botton ponders society's pressure to couple up, and the encouragement of single fear. This short animated sketch delves into empowering and thought-provoking pro-single arguments.

TASTER: 'It's simply not thought possible to be at once alone and normal,' says Alain. 'But this sets us up for collective catastrophe, because it means that a huge number of people, who have no innate wish to live with anyone else and are at heart deeply ill-suited to do so, are every year press-ganged and shamed into conjugal life.'

BELLA DEPAULO'S TEDX TALK
WHAT NO ONE EVER TOLD YOU ABOUT PEOPLE WHO ARE SINGLE
I challenge you to watch this and not feel whole-body tingles of inspiration. Bella has been described by *The Atlantic* as 'America's foremost thinker and writer on the single experience'. She's the Harvard-educated psychologist behind books such as *Singled Out: How Singles Are Stereotyped, Stigmatized, and Ignored, and Still Live Happily Ever After.*

I love how she opens this lecture with 'I'm 63 and I have been single my whole life' and then takes a little bow. The perplexed audience pause, then get with the program and clap. This pregnant pause so neatly demonstrates how single is not routinely celebrated.

She then talks about how we get brainwashed into hunting 'The One' even if it's not what we want or need to be happy, and the lack of life-affirming stories about content single life. She upturns the myth that single people aren't happy, by calling on an arsenal of research that says different.

TASTER: 'In my twenties and thirties, I knew I was supposed to get married, and I knew I was supposed to want to be married. Even now, I keep on getting reminded...but living single was my happily ever after.'

SOLO BLISS* PLAYLIST

HOLD BACK YOUR LOVE *BY WHITE LIES*
'You know that I've had my doubts, wanna see what I'll feel without.'

GYPSY *BY FLEETWOOD MAC*
'Back to the gypsy that I was.'

TIMES LIKE THESE *BY THE FOO FIGHTERS*
'I'm a new day rising, I'm a brand new sky.'

EASY *BY THE COMMODORES*
'Why in the world would anyone put chains on me?'

THE COME ON *BY CRAZY P*
'I'm too long in the tooth, to be messed around.'

SHE *BY GREEN DAY*
'She's figured out all her doubts were someone else's point of view.'

I'M ALL RIGHT *BY MADELEINE PEYROUX*
Delves into walking away from an abusive relationship:
'It's fine, it's OK, it was wrong either way.'

I WILL SURVIVE *BY CAKE*
This droll indie cover of the Gloria Gaynor classic is spectacular.
I like their insertion of 'fucking' lock, rather than 'stupid'.

I'M COMING OUT *BY DIANA ROSS*
'The time has come for me to break out of the shell.'

* In retrospect, this title makes it sound a bit like a masturbation playlist, which was not my intention, but hey, you do whatever you like with it ;-)

SINGLE READING

The stand-out single books for me, in no particular order, are the following:

ALL THE SINGLE LADIES (more for women) by Rebecca Traister.
An impeccably researched, flawlessly written, tracing of single women through the ages. Guaranteed to make you feel like a single superhero.

MODERN ROMANCE: AN INVESTIGATION (all genders) by Aziz Ansari with Eric Klinenberg.
An international bestseller and deservedly so, since it's a witty and searingly insightful look at dating in the Noughties landscape.

HOW TO BE SINGLE AND HAPPY (all genders, but aimed at women) by Jennifer L Taitz.
Written by a psychologist who seriously knows her single stuff, fusing expert advice, hundreds of fascinating psychological and case studies of her clients. I finished this book feeling a resounding heart-glow about being single.

GOING SOLO: THE EXTRAORDINARY RISE AND SURPRISING APPEAL OF LIVING ALONE (all genders) by social scientist Eric Klinenberg.
This is a fascinating deep-dive into the rise of Americans choosing to stay single, with 300 case studies. When we can afford to live alone and remain single, we tend to, given the fact that it's the wealthiest societies that have the most singles.

SPINSTER: MAKING A LIFE OF ONE'S OWN (more for women) by Kate Bolick.
This is exquisitely written, by a renowned journalist and editor at *The Atlantic*. It's structured around her Awakeners, or historical figures who have shown her something she wouldn't have seen on her own. 'Whom to marry, and when it will happen – these two questions define every woman's existence' is the brilliant opening line.

V: DEMOLISHING SOCIALLY-CONSTRUCTED SINGLE FEAR

SINGLE SCARCITY

'People convince themselves that they have been robbed when they have not, in fact, been robbed. Such thinking comes from a wretched allegiance to the notion of scarcity – from the belief that the world is a place of dearth, and that there will never be enough of anything to go around. The motto of this mentality is: Somebody else got mine.'

– *Elizabeth Gilbert,* Big Magic

I was recently sent a round-robin joke, in which a woman is shopping in a 'Husband Department Store'. It has six floors, and she can only go up, not down. She can only visit each floor once. As she takes the escalator up through the floors and browses, the husbands get better and better.

The punchline? She heads on up to the sixth floor, intrigued as to *how good* the husbands up there will be, and is greeted with a sign saying 'There are no men on this floor. This floor exists solely as proof that women are impossible to please'.

Haha, right? Or maybe not haha. Because we've been told this our entire lives, that if we wait too long, are too choosy, don't snap one up on floor four, we'll get to a floor where there are no husbands/wives left.

This is utter bullshit.

WOODY AND TWINKIES

Have you ever seen *Zombieland*? If not, you need to see it, because it is a masterpiece of a zomcom that features Woody Harrelson, Bill Murray and Emma Stone, who are three of my favourite actors ever. Anyway, in *Zombieland*, Woody's character is on a feverish hunt for Twinkies.

Twinkies are like America's version of Hobnobs. They are everyday staples, humdrum treats, available everyplace. However, we are in the midst of the zombie apocalypse, yo! Which means that all the Twinkies are going off, and Woody's only hope of satisfying his fixation of chowing down on some fresh Twinkies is to find some encased in a refrigerated van. He becomes utterly obsessed with finding Twinkies.

When you're told that something is running out, it triggers a panic to bag one up right now. It's why people panic-buy when a cosmetics line is being discontinued, it's why consumers stampede over fallen shoppers on Black Friday to nab a half-price flat-screen; it's why the frequently wheeled-out line 'All the good ones are gone' strikes fear into the heart of single people.

But you're not Woody, and nor am I, and single suitors are not Twinkies. Dating is not a 'Get it before it's gone' sale. The single men/women are never going to run out. Promise.

Opposite are some actual numbers on single Britain. I do love a bit of factmongering to shoo away the bogeyman of fearmongering...

 **51%** OF BRITS AGED 25–44 ARE SINGLE.

98% ARE SINGLE IN THE 18–24 CAMP.

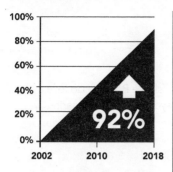

92%

100%		
80%		
60%		
40%		
20%		
0%		
2002	2010	2018

THE NUMBER OF OVER-55s WHO HAVE NEVER MARRIED AND DO NOT COHABIT, **HAS RISEN BY 92 PER CENT SINCE 2002.**

 TWO THIRDS OF WOMEN UNDER 30 ARE SINGLE.

 ONLY **ONE** IN TWO MILLENNIALS ARE EXPECTED TO MARRY IN FUTURE.*

 SINGLE HOUSEHOLDS IN BRITAIN HAVE MORE THAN **DOUBLED IN THE PAST 40 YEARS.**

7.7 MILLION

HOUSEHOLDS IN BRITAIN ARE ONE-PERSON. THAT'S 28 PER CENT (UP FROM 17 PER CENT IN 1971).

28%

So, you see, there is no scarcity. There's an abundance, in fact.

Says a think tank. Harry Benson, research director of Marriage Foundation said: 'On our own current estimates, 90% of 60-year-olds have married at some stage, whereas only 50% of today's young adults will do so'.

POOR JEN AND PLAYBOY LEO

'If a woman is not wed, it's not because she's made a set of active choices, but rather that she has not been selected – chosen, desired, valued enough.'

– REBECCA TRAISTER, ALL THE SINGLE LADIES

I was at a housewarming recently when it walloped me, square between the eyes. How differently single men and women are perceived.

We played a game whereby we had to guess who the celebrity was, based on quick-fire one liners. 'Unlucky in love actress,' my friend threw out. 'Jennifer Aniston,' yelled three of us triumphantly in unison, including me. Later in the game, Jennifer Aniston's ex Brad Pitt came up, when the clue '*Fight Club*!' was chucked into the ring.

Later, it struck me. Even though at the time Brad was also single and going through his second divorce, the clue for him would never be 'Unlucky in love actor'. Would it? Never ever. Isn't that odd?

It got me thinking about the different lexicons we use around single men and women, and the powerful effect that has. Single women are unlucky, to be pitied, they cut a lonely figure, and can't possibly have chosen their Godawful solo fate. People often say 'She can't hang on to a man' (heck, I've said it myself), but we'd never say 'He can't hang on to a woman.' Or at least, I never have.

'Desperate', 'needy' and 'broody' are words almost exclusively used to describe women in relationships. Men don't get called these things, or at least very rarely. Let's also lob 'high-maintenance' and 'demanding' into that mix.

WOMEN DEFINED BY MEN

Another thing about that party game. Jennifer Aniston was defined by her love life, whereas Brad was defined by his career. Even though 'Rachel *Friends*!' would have immediately worked as a clue, we auto-pilot to her love life first.

Women are defined by the men they're with, in a way that men just aren't. I once saw a scene in *Scandal* that summed it up. Now, I appreciate the scriptwriters of *Scandal* are not sociological experts, nor is *Scandal* real life (wish it was though, Olivia Pope for president over that buffoon!). But nevertheless, indulge me. Abby is talking to her boyfriend, Leo. They both have equally high-powered careers.

Abby: 'Every article that comes out about me has your name somewhere in it. Because apparently there's this rule. In order to mention my name they also have to report to the world that there's a man who wants me. My work, my accomplishments, my awards...I stand at the most powerful podium in the world, but a story about me ain't a story unless they can report on the fact that I am the girlfriend of DC fixer Leo Bergen. Like it validates me, it gives me an identity, a definition. They can't fathom the concept that my life doesn't revolve around you...property of Leo Bergen. Tell me, when they write articles about you, Leo, how often do they mention me?"

Right?! Damn straight! She nailed it.

POOR JEN

OK, so back to real people and real press. Jennifer Aniston and Leonardo DiCaprio, who are both single at the time of my writing, hugely successful and in their forties. Why am I plucking them out in particular? Because they are walking, talking personifications of how society perceives single men/women wildly differently.

Every time Jennifer splits with someone, she is portrayed as wretchedly sad, dragging a heavy heart and an urgently ticking timebomb of a biological clock. Meantime, Leo bounces out of a split unscathed, unready to settle, bellowing 'FREEDOMMMM' (*Braveheart* style) and bee-lining for the nearest lingerie-model convention.

'The Jennifer Aniston tabloid narrative – in which she is not a person but a character, a woman smiling and fit, and happy yet apparently deeply sad that she's unmarried and childless – is a haunting reminder,' writes Dodai Stewart on *Jezebel*. 'That if you're not doing what's expected of you – pairing up, mating, reproducing – you must be doing something wrong. Actually: *There must be something wrong with you.*'

The press's breathless womb-watch of Jennifer Aniston has affected single women everywhere. Why? Because there are messages buried there, invisible-ink beliefs that ever-so-sneakily fall into our brains. 'She must be unhappy' the invisible-ink message says. 'So therefore, *you* must be unhappy.'

Jennifer Aniston herself has gotten so fed up with the scrutiny, that she's issued a number of (very articulate) ripostes to the press. 'The sheer amount of resources being spent right now by press trying to simply uncover whether or not I am pregnant (for the bajillionth time... but who's counting)' writes Jen, 'points to the perpetuation of this notion that women are somehow incomplete, unsuccessful or unhappy if they're not married with children.'

PLAYBOY LEO

But, men get typecast too. And to ignore that would be like going on an equal-pay march and then rocking up to a dinner date and expecting the man to buy (equality means equal bills too, people!).

They're 'ladykillers', 'playboys', 'studs', 'commitment-phobes' and 'players'. They're predators that read *The Game* and lure unsuspecting quarry back to their bachelor pads where they supposedly seduce with Sade, revolving beds and satin boxer shorts. Ugh. They're 'ladies' men' whereas we simply don't have 'gentlemen's women'.

Let's look at the press circus around newly split Leo. It's laughable. 'Heartthrob' Leo is surrounded by 'a bevy of beauties', has women 'eating out of the palm of his hand' and 'laps up the single life' like some kind of big cat with a massive bowl of cream. He's even nicknamed the cringingly bad 'Leo-thario' by certain corners of the press.

GEORGE AND AMAL

Another neat comparison is how the press treats engagements. Let's look at how the media framed the engagement of Jennifer Aniston to (now ex) Justin Theroux. 'Aniston's announcement came with relief-oriented headlines like "FINALLY," and one cover declared she was "HAPPY AT LAST," as though everything before had been utter misery and despair,' writes Stewart, on *Jezebel*.

Meanwhile, George Clooney's engagement to Amal did not come with any FINALLY or HAPPY AT LAST headlines, at least not for him. The *Daily Mail* ran with a shot of Amal and 'Look that says "I've hooked the man who hates commitment": Glamorous British barrister is the woman to finally tame George Clooney.'

See the difference? The language and framing make it crystal clear that, in society's eyes, single men carry a higher value than single women. She is an acclaimed human rights lawyer, equal if not higher than him in the 'catch' category, and yet she has 'hooked', 'bagged', 'tamed' and 'landed' him, the press says.

Amal has since given a speech wittily saying how thankful she was that she met George, because 'I was 35 and starting to become quite resigned to the idea that I was going to be a spinster.'

On one hand, I love that she admitted her spinster fear (way to go Amal, nice vulnerability), but on the other hand, I was struck by the double standards. Can you imagine George giving a speech thanking her for coming along and saving him from bachelordom? Nah.

And while we're talking about age, the age gap between them is 17 years. I haven't seen one article that has thrown shade on him for this. But do you remember the hoo-hah the press made about Sam Taylor-Johnson marrying Aaron, 24 years her junior? Obviously, they called her a 'cradle-snatcher'. Or when Cheryl Cole got together with Liam Payne, who was 11 years younger? Cheryl was declared a 'cougar uncaged' when they eventually split. Apparently, the older man/younger woman dynamic is OK with the press, whereas when it switcheroos, the press flips the feck out.

Also, when a couple splits, it's often just presumed that the man did the splitting. It's why celebrity couples take pains to say that the decision was 'MUTUAL Y'ALL, YES REALLY' in their split press statement. Because of the propensity of the media, and society beyond, to pounce on the assumption that the man did the walking.

CARS AND HOUSES

All of this just compounds the absurd notion that women depreciate with age, while men appreciate. Women are cars, while men are houses. Older single men are portrayed as lesser-spotted snow leopards: elusive, high value and glamorous. While older single women are what, probably lone gazelles? Lost, vulnerable, confused. It's sexist, ageist, antiquated claptrap.

Imagine a world whereby *People* magazine runs a male line-up of celebs under the headline 'Are these men left on the shelf?' It would never happen, right? And yet, as recently as the 1980s, that magazine ran a line-up on the cover with 'Are these women old maids?' (Google Image it, if you're curious).

Imagine a world where a scrum of men at a wedding tussle over a thrown handkerchief that signifies who will get married next? (I always go to the loo during the excruciating bouquet-toss in any wedding.)

CAREER WOMEN

The 'single crisis' is laid squarely at the feet of single women. We are to blame. Just so you know. We're told that it's because we're 'career women'* who are 'putting babies on ice'. Usually illustrated by a woman with a briefcase (I've literally never seen a woman with a briefcase) and a baby in an ice cube (ditto, and if I did I would definitely call the police).

Never mind that men are also choosing to be single, men also have jobs, and men freeze their sperm. That's not important, mmmkay? Look at the women. The women who are selfishly choosing to be 'career women' in order to do things like buy food and put a roof over their heads.

I also recently saw the headline 'Britain is becoming a nation of Bridget Joneses!' Aaargh! RUN. I can just imagine them, attack of the 80 foot singles, selfishly stomping on the Tower of London with their stilettos, causing a tsunami down the Thames by waving their giant pay cheques around. Why is the headline not 'Britain is becoming a nation of Bridget Joneses *and* Daniel Cleavers'? The single men are conspicuous by their absence.

And then there was the headline 'Bridget Jones singletons threaten housing crisis'. We've caused the housing crisis now? Crikey! How did we manage that? When you read the article, this 'crisis' (which isn't a crisis) turns out to be caused by 'single households'. Ummm, aren't there men in around half of those single households? But, the men aren't the ones causing the housing crisis, it's the women, OK?

So, in summary, here's what's happening. Single women are so tired from lugging their briefcases around, and from trapping babies in giant ice cubes, that they are not getting married, and have caused a housing crisis. OK?

* *'Career men' is not a thing, just so you know. Men with jobs are just 'men'. Glad we got that straightened out.*

FORFUCK'SSAKE.

Excuse me, while I just go and meditate to calm down.

Brief intermission with panpipe music

THE MEDIA'S REACTION TO HAPPY SINGLENESS
I'm back. Thanks for waiting.

What's more, there's often a backlash when people come 'out' about being happily single in the press. In 2011, a then 39-year-old single journalist called Kate Bolick appeared on the front cover of American magazine, *The Atlantic*, with the coverline, 'What, me, marry?' Her brilliant accompanying article went viral. But Kate was deluged by negativity.

'The men were saying, "Who do you think you are, you uppity bitch, do you think you're too good to marry someone?"' says Kate. 'They got really defensive. But then I had dinner with a male friend-of-a-friend and he threw some light on why that could be. He said, "If women are no longer obsessed with getting married, then what does that mean for my identity? I was raised to be a provider and to look after a family." It made me think.'

Unexpectedly, Kate was also trolled by women. 'Many said the same thing as the men, "Do you think you're too good for marriage?" But with the addition of, "You'll regret it. It's easy for you to say that now, at 39, but when you're older you'll feel differently." And maybe I will,' reflects Kate.

And therein lies an important point, no? We have the right to change our minds as casually and unapologetically as a taxi flicks on/off its roof-top light. 'Because we're trained to think about our lives in the form of a "Forever marriage", there can be a tendency to think singledom is a "Forever choice" too,' Kate says. 'I got a lot of people saying, "So, you're going to be single for life, then?" I said, this isn't about marrying myself to the single state, this is about allowing myself to question these received assumptions. The reality is, there's very rarely any "forever" now, our generation is spending stretches of their lives single, and chunks in serial monogamy. The point is; both are to be celebrated. We shouldn't over-celebrate one, or the other.'

WE BECOME CLICHÉ-FULFILLING PROPHECIES

So, the press is responsible for many of the single man/woman stereotypes. I wonder how much this affects men, as well as women. We're always speculating as to what the 'Poor Jen' narrative does to women, but we never stop and think about what the 'Playboy Leo' stuff does to men.

Women. Suspend your disbelief for a minute and imagine being told, over and over and over, that you will feel 'trapped' if you get married, that your modus operandi is to chase male tail, that you won't be able to keep your vagina in your pants, that all men are trying to get you pregnant, and that commitment is anathema to you.

At what point do you stop trying to dress yourself, and start just putting on the cliché outfit being laid out for you every darn day? At what point do you forget who you are and what you want, and start just becoming what you're *told you are*?

I often wonder how many women think they want to get married and have kids, or feel sad when they're single, simply because we've been told repeatedly that *we want that* and *we are that*. On command, we all march towards the marriage goal, or cry into a tub of ice cream.

Equally, I wonder how many men think they're frightened of commitment, simply because they've been told over and over that they're going to hate it. It would be like presenting somebody with a slice of cake and saying 'Do you want some cake? You won't like it! This cake will make you feel trapped. What do you mean, you don't want the cake?'

I believe marriage-hungry women and marriage-swerving men are largely a social construct. Just as little girls are encouraged to play with toy kitchens and wear pink, while little boys are given tractors and blue, we are built from infancy by society. Constructed by either pink or blue blocks. And hence, we often become walking cliché-fulfilling prophecies.

We need to torpedo the 'poor Jen' narrative, for real, but we also need to jettison the 'Playboy Leo' narrative. Why can't we just be individuals, millions upon billions of us, who are vastly different within our gender? Rather than being called Bridget and squashed into bunny-girl outfits, or shoved into slick suits and told we're Daniel Cleaver.

THE REALITY OF SINGLE MEN

It's so mind-bogglingly reductive to tar all single men with the same 'player', 'Peter Pan', 'just after sex', 'commitment-dodging' brush. It drives me up the wall.

I've dated my fair share of knuckleheads, but I don't assume all men are knuckleheads. Any more than people should assume that all single 30+ women are gagging to get pregnant. We women know how annoying that is, so let's not homogenize half of the population, OK? It goes both ways. So on a quest to balance the books, I asked a couple of real single men to tell me about their experiences.

IAN SAYS: 'There *are* Tinder-terrorizing men leaving a trail of destruction and STIs in their wake, but that is far from the majority. Most single, 30+ men have just not found the right person, have been through a tough time, think a lone-ranger adventure is needed, or have realized you don't have to "hurry up and get married" any more.

'Hell YES I get asked "Why are you single?" I think it's a personal question that shouldn't be asked unless someone knows you well. Nevertheless, I reply honestly, that I'm doing my own thing, building an amazing life that I'll hopefully share one day, with the right person.

'I've seen that Mel Gibson movie about *What Women Want* and I'm guessing that's in no way factual, so I'm here to say: most single men simply want the same thing as most single women.'

ERNEST SAYS: 'I know just as many women who have casual hook-up partners as I do men. I feel pressured to couple up by my married friends all. the. time. As the only bachelor at a wedding recently, I was repeatedly told various incarnations of "Don't worry, you'll find the right one eventually". Being divorced tends to inoculate me from too much "Why are you single?" questioning, but when I am asked, I usually use humour to diffuse the situation ("I wouldn't want to put ANOTHER woman through that.") Or if I know them well, I just reaffirm that I'm happy, and enjoying concentrating on my career and children.

'The truth is, there are happy single men, lonely single men, happy married/partnered men, and lonely married/partnered men. I have been all four of those men, at some point. Ironically, I'm probably more ready for a serious relationship now than I've ever been, simply because I don't need one and am genuinely happy.'

'WHY ARE YOU SINGLE?'

This chapter isn't going to be mature, or zen, or magnanimous, but to those who think I should always be mature or zen, I magnanimously say, bore off ;-) We need to talk about this, because it's something that winds single people up *no end*.

When you tell people you're single, particularly married people, it's as if you've told them you have a mysterious ailment and they are a doctor who now urgently has to diagnose ('why?!') and cure your malady ('let's fix this!').

When people ask 'Why is a great girl/guy like you single?' the subtext appears to be 'So what's secretly wrong with you? What fault are you hiding behind that pretty dress/sharp suit? What's the deal, hmmm?' Bridget Jones summed it up when she deadpanned: 'It doesn't help that underneath our clothes our entire bodies are covered in scales'.

I get it, definitely, because I also did this 'Let's fix you' to single people when I was an unrepentant love addict during my twenties. I was horrified when people were single and sought to rescue them from their terrible plight. 'Here! Grab on to this piece of flotsam advice from me! It might save you! Or, maybe you would like to date this man on my Facebook that I would never dream of dating myself, whaddyathink?'

The feeling of failure over being single is created by a thousand paper cuts of the sympathetic 'Oh wells', or the 'You'll meet someone' reassurers, or the 'Have you tried?' fixers. People can't seem to let single people *just be*.

There's a peculiar social quirk to being single, much the same as when you don't drink. When you're single or alcohol-free, people feel like they deserve some sort of explanation. Single people are fair game for questioning, just as sober people are. It's odd.

It's not just singles though. Couples who have been together for yonks, but have chosen not to get married or have kids, are fair game too. As are those with one kid, weirdly. Couples with rings and double kids are allowed to cast aspersions on their life choices, and talk about them at length after they've left the dinner table.

There's also the unfathomably intrusive 'Why are you divorced?' A friend of mine says she gets the overwhelming urge to ask 'Why are you still married?' in response.

Basically, if you haven't chosen the traditional path of marriage plus two kids, you'll need to defend your choices to society, okay?

THE MOST COMMON THINGS PEOPLE SAY
They say: 'Why are you single?'

I want to say: 'Oh, I dunno. While we're asking probing, very personal questions within a few minutes of meeting, why did you get married? Were you guys ready? Do you think either of you will ever cheat? I hear you have separate bedrooms, why is that? Let's lay this all bare, shall we.'

Within the 'I can't believe you're single!' statement is an assumption, particularly if you're female, that you haven't been chosen. Which is why people are like – 'How can this be?!' – when you're super eligible. It's actually a compliment wrapped up in an archaic societal assumption.

I actually say: 'Oh, I have terrible taste in men. My loins find the most emotionally unavailable man in any room.'

(I find that when I take the blame square on the chin right from the get-go, they tend to laugh and then leave the subject alone, rather than try to 'diagnose' or 'fix' me.)

WHEN I'M DATING
They say: 'It'll happen when you're not looking for it.'

I want to say: 'You're so right! I shall stop meeting the gaze of any men and lock myself at home with some needlepoint.'

I actually say: 'So, I'm guessing you two didn't go on any dates?'

They say: 'Oh no, er, we did.'

I actually say: 'Then how does that work, exactly? You were dating too, just like I am?'

They say: 'Well, yes, I guess so.'

I actually say: 'Well then. I'll carry on, shall I?'

They nod. And nervously scout around for someone else to talk to

WHEN I'M NOT DATING

When I'm dating, I'm single because I'm dating. When I'm not dating, I'm single because I'm not dating. Either way, it's *something I am doing wrong*. Got that? Cool.

They say: 'Have you tried dating apps? What about that one, Bumble? My friend met someone on that and they've just got engaged!'

I want to say: 'Dating apps, you say? What is this modern sorcery? I have never heard of Fumble! Please, illuminate me with some more of your novel and groundbreaking ideas! I'm sure if I get this Fumble wonder I will end up just like your friend!'

I actually say: 'Yes, I've tried Bumble. Thank you! That's great about your mate.'

WHEN I'VE BEEN DUMPED

They say: 'Oh, you poor thing! Have you read *The Rules*? They changed my life. It's how I got him.' *Tips head at husband*

I want to say: 'The one looking down the waitress's top because he's ultimately turned on by what he can't have?'

I actually say: 'I have! I found them pretty antiquated and sexist, to be honest. Thanks though!'

WHEN I'VE DONE THE DUMPING

They say: 'Y'know, you're just too picky. You need to lower your standards.'

I want to say: 'Yes, you're absolutely right. The next time a Tom, Dick or Harry swivels to check out my ass in the supermarket I should totally just get with him, because he wants me, and despite my not wanting him, beggars can't be choosers.'

I actually say: 'I'd much rather be single than lower my standards, to be honest.'

I actually had this exact conversation yesterday, with the twist that after I said, 'Well, I'm not willing to compromise. I'd rather be single forever than shack up with someone less than extraordinary,' the married lady said, 'You sound just like my mate who's been single for ten years. Neither of you will ever marry anyone! Anyone!'

Said lady is actually a really lovely person, but I felt like she'd just pointed a wand and shot a curse at my head, dooming me to a lifetime of singledom because I dare to be choosy about who I share my bed and life with. It was *bizarre*, but sadly not unusual.

REMEMBER THEY'RE ON A 'NEED TO KNOW' BASIS

So, yes, I know how irritating it is when people feel that they're on a 'Right to know' rather than a 'Need to know' basis. But you don't have to play the 'Right to know' game. You don't have to give them a lengthy explanation, or excavate your love life thus far for them to squint at and appraise, or justify your decision to be single.

I still find myself 'explaining' my single status to people. I catch myself in the moment and ask, 'Why am I doing this?' Generally, it's because I'm overly concerned as to what this person thinks of me. So, I let go of that.

Nowadays, I tend to just say 'I'm single', with an unapologetic, sphinx-like expression, batting back their nosey questions, and remaining enigmatic. Am I asexual? A spy? They just don't know. Or am I single because I killed and ate my last boyfriend, thus should be called The Black Widow? I enjoy that air of mystery. I like how the eternally elusive Kate Moss's rule of thumb is 'Never complain, never explain'. That's my new motto.

I identify hard with Bryony Gordon's exasperation towards single-fixers in *The Wrong Knickers*. 'Oh fuck off. I mean *really*. Who do you think you are? Oprah freaking Winfrey? When you tell me I'll only find love when I'm happy in myself, I want to parrot it back at you in the tone of a five-year-old boy, while pulling a face.'

Instead of telling them to sling their hook, I pretend I'm a rock. I nicked this from my mate Holly, who once matter-of-factly said 'I practise defencelessness and pretend I'm a rock', which made me howl with laughter. I could just imagine her sitting there, a very pretty rock with eyes, using rock voodoo to make slings and arrows bend around her in a graceful arc.

And ultimately, once I/you reach a place where you're truly comfortable with your choice to be single, nothing anyone else can say will bother you. As Gandhi said, 'Nobody can hurt me without my permission.'

I repeat this to myself often, to help it fall into my sensitive, easily wounded skin. I find that I can't seem to help things hurting me in the first instance, but whether they continue to hurt me is indeed my choice.

So, why do they do it? Ask 'Why are you single?' I think simply because we like it when people make the same choices as us, and find it tricky to wrap our heads around those who *aren't* the same. Myself, I find it really hard to comprehend people who don't like to travel, or who don't like animals, and I try to talk them into travelling/liking animals, when actually, they're entitled to their own choices and opinions.

Psychologist Bella DePaulo sums it up nicely. 'People who like being single, who choose to be single, are threatening cherished world views about what people should want.'

The 'Why are you single?' lot don't do it out of malice, or even mean to patronize, they're just trying to get you onto the coupled-up bandwagon with them, because that validates their choices and is less confusing to them.

I'll leave you with this awesome piece of wisdom, which deserves to be on bumpers and coasters everywhere.

'People can't wind you up if you don't give them the key.'

– My Mum

VI: I FORGET AND RE-LEARN LESSONS

THE DORY OF PERSONAL DEVELOPMENT

Despite all of my epiphanies, all of my 'Aha' moments where the sun broke through the clouds and illuminated everything it touched, my re-entry into the dating atmosphere, after the serenity of my single year, was bumpy at best. [Insert emoji of monkey hiding its face.]

Why? Learning is not linear. It's best described as circular, even loopy. Here is a real aerial time-lapse of me learning stuff.

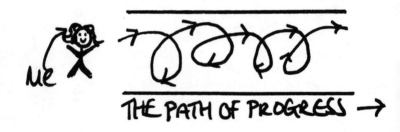

I have to re-learn lessons over and over and OVER again until they stick. I learn something, forget about it, learn it again, and realize 'Oh yeah, I learned that back in 2014!' I am the Dory of personal development. Seriously.

Turns out that dating sensibly, is a lot like trying to drink sensibly. It's easier to not date – or drink – at all. I found it harder to hang onto my single joy, once I hopped back on the extreme fairground ride that is dating.

I once had a chat over email with Eric Zimmer (the legendary host of podcast, *The One You Feed*) about this. I said, 'Turns out mental health is less of a linear narrative, and more of a confounding spiral!' Eric, as always, is the wisest in his reply: 'But hopefully an upward spiral. I seem to come back to the same challenges, but I'm at a slightly higher level each time.' YES. He's so right.

Why is learning loopy? It's just neuroscience. It's your brain trying to go down well-trodden pathways, the routes of least resistance. Remember, from page 41? It's why you have to go, 'Hold up brain, I don't date indifferent people any more, I like the keenos these days' and gently steer it in the right direction. Or, 'Hang on brain, we know that we're not incomplete single' when it tries to plunge into that habitual ravine.

And that's the point isn't it, to keep reaching, keep striving, even if you do find yourself on a downward trajectory all-of-a-sudden. You will have days where you are utterly consumed by single sorrow (I still do! For sure), and then days where you feel like the She-Ra/Spider-Man of single. That's OK. That's normal.

On the following pages, I present to you a bunch of diary entries, whereby I forget things I already know and re-learn them, in the years after I start dating again.

THE ONE WITH THE WAITING PLACE

I feel like I've spent most of my adult life waiting for somebody-I-fancy to text me back. Honestly, I do. I have half-lived days with half-an-eye on my phone. I have spent months refreshing emails, in the vain hope a missive will pop up from them. I have turned the notifications 'Off!' for a dating app, because I am much too busy and important to be bothered by this dating app...and then I've checked it ten times a day.

I've spent actual years in The Waiting Place. Feeling like my life is about to begin, if only he would message me back. Feeling like happiness is something that can be delivered in a WhatsApp message. Like life satisfaction arrives on the wings of a bluebird tweet.

It's not just me. I have a friend who has stayed in a job that bores her for more than a decade, rather than seek a more interesting role elsewhere, because of the 'excellent maternity leave'. The longer she stays, the better the maternity leave pay gets. Except, my mate is currently single and not remotely pregnant.

The Waiting Place is no place to live. It's a half-life.

– THE WAITING PLACE BY DR SEUSS

Waiting for a train to go or a bus to come,

or a plane to go or the mail to come,

or the rain to go or the phone to ring,

or the snow to snow or waiting around for a Yes or No

or waiting for their hair to grow.

Everyone is just waiting.

Waiting for the fish to bite

or waiting for wind to fly a kite

or waiting around for Friday night.

I DECIDE TO MOVE FROM THE WAITING PLACE TO BRUGES

APRIL 2015

*I've decided to come and live in Bruges for a while, despite the fact I've been spending time with someone I'm really into. I'm keen, but he's confounding. He disappears for days on end. *Camera pans to reveal nothing but tumbleweed and vast stretches of corn, accompanied by a soundtrack of crickets**

Then my phone trills into life and he leaps into the foreground of the shot, suddenly all up in my grill, jumping around saying how much he wants to see me and what am I doing tomorrow?!

He's making my head hurt. So, I've decided to take him out of the picture. To swivel my focus away from him altogether. For me, this is huge progress. Two years ago, I never would have done this. He doesn't sound happy when I tell him I'm going to Bruges. 'Oh. How long for?' But that's not my problem.

D'you remember when the press dubbed Kate Middleton 'Waity Katie?' Because apparently she was sitting there, looking pretty, anxiously twisting her ring finger, Googling frothy wedding dresses, eagerly awaiting Prince William's proposal? I mean, maybe she didn't give a toss, or maybe she was the one who wasn't ready for engagement; it's just another example of the press pushing a couple into a stereotypical box.

My point is this. I realized that I was really, really tired of being 'Waity Cath'. I realized that we only get this glorious life once and to spend it kicking about in the UK, when what I really wanted to do was go live in Bruges, just because a hot man may/may not want (delete as appropriate) to date me, was madness.

I felt like he was interviewing me for a girlfriend role, except the interview process was taking months, and I was no longer willing to stick around waiting for an answer. Sod that for a game of soldiers.

Before I go to Bruges, we're meant to go away for the weekend. He ghosts me, leaving my texts unopened. After I've actually moved to Bruges, he resurfaces, saying sorry. Six text messages, in total, with reasons and excuses. I tell him that I'm done. Onwards.

D'you know what, it feels deliciously good. Realizing that I don't have to wait around in the wings, seeing if he wants me to finally step onto the stage. Realizing that I can leave the theatre altogether.

I go for a bike ride along the canal and feel the freedom whip through my hair, not unlike Keira Knightley in Begin Again, *except I look nothing like Keira Knightley and I nearly tip myself into the canal when I spin in my saddle to look at a particularly fetching swan.*

Surprisingly, in the days that follow, I don't feel a scrap of 'Did I squander an eligible man?' regret, which has always been my greatest fear up until now. Always the reason I kept plugging away at it, flogging the horse until it's dead, making absolutely sure it's not a go-er, wringing every last squidge of possibility out of it, trying to resurrect it with those 'beeeeeee-kerchung' defibrillators until I'm absolutely sure it's done, gone, dead as a dodo. I've spent years avoiding the 'What if?' remorse of letting a man go.

Falling in love with a city is much safer. I'm smitten by Bruges and, like a person, it may change or get bigger, but unlike a person, it will never leave or cheat. I read that Joan Didion felt this way about New York. 'I do not mean "love" in any colloquial way,' she said. 'I mean that I was in love with the city, the way you love the first person who ever touches you and you never love anyone quite that way again.'

My life plan has finally become bigger than just landing a leading man. I've decided my greatest fear is now not squandering a man-shaped opportunity; my greatest fear is not living my life to its full potential.

I then spend a total of seven months living in Bruges. I love so much about the Flemish lifestyle. How everything in the city is within a 15-minute bike ride. Bikes are basically like leg-extensions to the Flemish. I see a girl cycling at 20 miles an hour, look no hands!, smoking a cigarette and sending a text at the same time. Road rage towards cyclists simply does not exist in Bruges.

I love how literal they are (in Flemish, a kettle is a 'water cooker', croissants are 'morning cookies', a lawnmower is a 'grass machine' and a hosepipe is a 'water snake'). I love how on Halloween they all get their freak on by dressing up and walking deep into the pitch-black woods on a 'witch hike', where actors in horror make-up leap out and scare the bejesus out of them. I love how Flemish architecture is a thrown together hotch-potch of both the most beautiful architecture ever, adjacent to the most beastly (hence the smash-hit book *Ugly Belgian Houses*).

I love how neat Belgium is. Y'know how Poirot carries around a little comb with which to tidy his moustache? Yep, that's bang on. You haven't seen folding until you've seen a Flemish laundry cupboard. It is a thing to behold. Labels, razor-sharp folds, ironed pillowcases. I have no idea how they find the time.

My Flemish boyfriend doesn't have one ginormous change jar in which to up-end his pocket. Oh no. He has five change jars, sorted into amount denominations. I have a *Sleeping with the Enemy* flashback when I open his kitchen cupboard to see jars and tins in perfect face-front squadrons like saluting soldiers. I wonder if I should start practising my swimming quicksmart.

And it's not just the people who are neat. The countryside is perfectly geometrical. Half-a-mile of trees with ruler-straight tops. Bushes are perfect orbs. Hedges are ruthlessly pruned. Even when the leaves turn shimmergold in autumn, they seem to be cleared up before they hit the ground. The Flemish must come to Britain and think we are fantastically messy. They must think our trees are downright irresponsible; that our bushes are a disgrace.

I love the rare moments of Gothic grandeur in their lexicon, like the poetry of calling heavy rainclouds 'thundertowers' and holes for prisoners in castles 'the well of oblivion.' How they declare pointless endeavours as 'like taking water to the sea'. How a busy square is one in which you 'have to walk across the hats'.

Equally, I love how deadpan they are: I point at a field and say, 'Awww, look at the cute baby cows!' My Flemish boyfriend glances and says, 'Those are for eating'. Or the time I hold out an apple and say, 'In England, we call this nature's toothbrush' and he replies, 'In Belgium, we call it an apple'.

I go from wobbly to assured on my bike, as I bomb past the rotating windmills. I marvel at the Madonna and child made entirely from white chocolate (Why? Because they can) in the Chocolate Museum. I hang out with the singing nuns in the Beguinage, basically a gated village for single or widowed women, and read about how men are still not allowed in after 9pm. I stand in the square and beam as a Fifties flash-mob starts jiving and twirling around me, wearing neckerchiefs, swirly skirts and belts 'n' braces.

At Christmas time, I wander into a super-cute chocolate shop and find the server singing along to Rage Against the Machine, 'Fuck you, I won't do what you tell me, fuck you I won't do what you TELL MEEEEE', while arranging smiley chocolate Santas. Their second Santa, Sinterklaas delivers his presents by boat on 5 December; the naughty children get bundled into a sack and taken to Spain for a year to be taught how to behave. Spain is like finishing school for obstreperous Flemish children.

So, yeah, you may have noticed the casual mention of a boyfriend. I don't remain single in Bruges. After a couple of months I start dating again, how everyone starts dating nowadays, by downloading an app and uploading pictures of myself that show I am sporty (diving shot, tick), fun (silly shot of me wearing a bear hat, tick), refined (dressed for dinner shot, tick) and well-travelled (Yosemite shot, tick).

I RE-ENTER THE DATING ATMOSPHERE
Before meeting my boyfriend, I date a Flemish policeman, who is outrageously Viking-esque handsome. He is like a man hewn from living rock. I fail to twig that the Zoolander-style Instagram shots of him topless, pointing at far-off things in order to show off his lats, or glats, or whatevertheyare, and the fact he hashtags them #shredded, can possibly mean he is vain AF.

I am too blinded by his extraordinary looks to clock that it's probably a bit weird that he's talking about building me a room in the house he's planning, where I can overlook the river and write (Noah Notebook, is that you?) after one date. I sit there, spellbound, if vaguely uncomfortable, as he serenades me down the phone with his guitar and Bon Iver. Some dates on, the moment we sleep together, he freezes over. The serenading and house-architecting stop, abruptly. Just like a Viking, he'd come to conquer.

So when I meet Tom, I am looking for kindness, personality and wit, as well as physical chemistry. A friend first, and a lover second. I get it.

Meanwhile, I burrow deeper into the duvet with my new love, Bruges. I hang out in a basement bar with 80s' music and darts, accessed through a hidden hobbit-esque doorway.

I entertain a constant stream of family and friends at the weekends, but midweek is spent entirely alone. In Bruges, I learn to love my own company, to find myself to be a worthwhile person to hang out with.

LANGUAGE CLANGERS

I try to learn Flemish, much to everyone's amusement. The way I say 'Bon Appetit' in Flemish sounds more like 'cockroach'. Welcome, dinner guests. Cockroach! Please do enjoy your meal! I announce in polite company that I am frigid, when I mean to say I'm cold.

Tom and I don't share a mother tongue, which leads to many comical misunderstandings. I text Tom saying I feel frisky. Tom texts back saying he can help me with that, and comes round with a bottle of lemonade, thinking I mean 'thirsty'. Then, there were these conversations:

Tom: 'What are these called?' *Points at a freckle on my arm*

Me: 'Freckles.'

Tom: 'Oh, like the cartoons who live on the rock?'

Me: 'Come again?'

Tom: 'Y'know, Fraggle Rock.'

Or when I ask Tom what he has in his fridge for lunch.

Tom: 'Some tsunami salad. And crap. Crap is delicious.'

Me, ignoring the tsunami salad for now: 'What do you mean by crap?'

Tom: 'They're like spiders except they live on the beach and walk sideways.'

I watch sunset overlooking the canal that curves around the Beguinage like a hug. The swans congregate to be fed by a restaurant at sunset. It's heart-poundingly spectacular. A tiny love-locks bridge is tucked away there, if you know where to look. I look at the new locks and root for 'Mr and Mrs Crosby. Married'.

I remember that when I was in Paris with Seb, I scolded him for not having the forethought to plan both a surprise trip to Paris for my birthday, *and* pack a padlock for us to attach. Sound the 'unreasonable!' klaxon.

I feel zero need to attach a padlock myself with Tom. We are just casual right now; Bruges is my husband, while he is merely the hot gardener I'm having a fling with.

LESSONS I RE-LEARNED:
1. When men/women say they're going to build you a room in a house after one date, they're definitely just trying to get laid.

2. The Waiting Place is no place to live.

Single can often feel like toe-tapping waiting, constant craving, or feverish searching. But when we're in the waiting room, or casting our searchlight on the horizon, we're not living our lives, as they are, to the full.

I still find myself at the Waiting Place occasionally; at the road-scanning, slightly-frowning, watch-checking bus stop. But the difference is, I now know when I'm doing it, when I'm living in suspended animation. Nobody wants to live at a bus stop. So I shake the toe-tapping trance off, get up and leave. I remember what Seamus Heaney says so beautifully, below. And I go to the living place instead.

'The way we are living, timorous or bold, will have been our life.'

– SEAMUS HEANEY

THE ONE WHERE MY BOYFRIEND SLEEPS WITH SOMEONE THAT'S NOT ME

Tom, the Flemish one with the 'crap' in the fridge, who liked my 'fraggles', ended up cheating on me. When we were just about to celebrate our year's anniversary, and had just half-moved in together, having mapped out a plan whereby I would spend half of my time in England and half of it in Ghent with him.

I was devastated. I truly thought that we were incredibly happy. It knocked me sideways for a good month or so. I even entertained some sadistic fantasies about stealing his super cute cat when I went back to pick up my stuff.

But, there was smoke before the fire. I just chose to ignore it. I remember Tom explaining why he'd cheated on both of his long-term exes. Both times, it was their fault. The first made him feel suffocated, while the second stopped having sex with him.

I knew this was a red flag, that he'd placed the blame for his infidelities squarely at their door, and wriggled from beneath the responsibility himself. But I stored this conversation in a file in my mind marked 'ignore', because I wanted to continue to date him.

Interestingly, I didn't tell any of my friends about that brain-file, which is always a sure sign that something is amiss. I reasoned that since we were having so much great sex, I was safe.

If anything, in the lead up to the cheating he grew more clingy. He asked me if I could stop spending two weekends a month in London, and only be away from Belgium for one ('I miss you too much when you're gone'). A few days before the infidelity, I told him I was going back to London for two weekends. I'd defied him, and I recall his face shutting like a lift door.

While I was in England, he texted another girl, someone who he'd met in a nightclub a few weeks earlier, to invite her around for a shag. For some reason, the most heartbreaking detail of this, the one I couldn't get past, was that my PJs were under the pillow while they were doing it.

On the day he was unfaithful, he begged me to Facetime him ('I need to see you'), but I was in the midst of a social hat-trick of a day and had no time. Maybe he told himself it was my fault that he cheated, since I wasn't there like he'd asked me to be.

But it wasn't my fault. It's never anybody's fault, *other than the one who cheated*. If a person wants to cheat, they will cheat, no matter how much you Facetime them, and no matter how much you are shagging.

One crucial thing I did differently, after Tom's infidelity revelation – after perhaps two days of futile back-and-forth between us, which only served to make me feel more wretched – was to cut him off. I realized that continuing to communicate with him was not the way to heal.

I told him we were going to have to cease all contact, which he resisted. I exported our chats out of my phone, deleted his number, blocked him on all social media, and I finally started to mend.

A month on, once I'd gotten some perspective, and pieced my smashed self into a workable mosaic, I said to a friend that it was still a great relationship, probably my best so far, despite the soul-shattering end. 95 per cent good.

'But he cheated on you?' she cried in protest.

'So what? That doesn't undo all the good,' I said.

She wasn't the only one who said this, when I told them about my 95 per cent good theory. Everyone said this. I think my loved ones were worried that I was moving towards getting back with Tom. I would never do that, I have too much self-respect now.

But his infidelity did not change everything that came before it. By focusing on the 5 per cent at the end I would be cheating myself out of the recollection of all that was great and right about it too. It would be like dismissing a film as rubbish just because the last ten minutes are disappointing, even though the rest was spectacular. Instead of dwelling on the bitter end, I chose to also remember the blissfully lazy Sundays of chicken sandwiches and horror films, the walks along the starlit Bruges canals, the bike rides past windmills.

You're not going to spontaneously combust into flames of need if you dare to remember the good times. As my on-the-money mate Jen says,

'You know when people say "Your ex is an ex for a reason"? Well, yeah, that's true. What's also true is that they were your girlfriend/boyfriend for a reason too, you dingbat.'

LESSONS I RE-LEARNED:

1. When a person is unfaithful, it's everything to do with them, and nothing to do with you, or your relationship.

2. If somebody thinks cheating was OK with their ex, they're going to think cheating is OK with you. There's a vast canyon of difference between 'I cheated and here's why it wasn't my fault' and 'I cheated and now I don't ever want to do that again'.

3. A bitter end does not undo all the beauty that came before it.

4. You can't begin to heal until you cease all communication. Using communication with your ex to try to mend yourself is exactly like drinking wine to cure a hangover. Using the thing that hurt you, to try and heal you. Put the thing down.

THE ONE WHERE I REALIZE THAT THERE'S NO SUCH THING AS A FAILED RELATIONSHIP

That's when I realize that society has it all wrong. Just because a union doesn't end with the switching of rings and the releasing of doves and hand-painted names on stones to denote where your mates sit at dinner, it doesn't mean it was a failure. Or that it wasn't love. Or that it wasn't fun. Or that it wasn't an enormously rewarding learning curve.

Many of you will have found this book in your hand, having recently bounced painfully out of a relationship. Society may 'There, there' pat your hand as if this was a failure, given your relationship ended, but I'm here to tell you, *that's not true.*

Marriage-for-life became a societal norm during a time when we were lucky if we lived until we were 40, and there were only six people in the village to pick from rather than six million on Tinder, and you needed to sleep next to a warm body at night to live through 'til morning. Marriage was a necessity and given we didn't live long, it was probably pretty easy to marry young and stay married.

Now that our life expectations are a colossal 40 years more than that, maybe the idea of a partner-for-life is as defunct as a job-for-life? Who knows. Maybe it's more realistic to just search for a 'partner-for-right-now'?

I don't know about you, but I've changed galactically in the past ten years…in the past five years…in the past year even. As a cocksure and incredibly naive 17 year old, I planned to be married by 25. 'I'll be married by 25, first kid at 28, second at 30.' Bish bash bosh.

When I was 25, I was in a relationship that was founded on our shared love of getting obliterated, eating kebabs and smoking roll-ups, so if I'd married him, I probably would have had a few organ transplants by now.

Now that we have many long-term partners over our lifetime, it's inevitable that most of these will end. Serial monogamy has replaced the forever-relationship as the new norm. Forever-relationships are very few and far between these days.

Similarly, a divorce does not equal a failure, and anyone who thinks it does is to be completely ignored. Did you make some beautiful children? Or have eight good years out of eleven? Well then, that's a winner overall.

Think about it. We don't rubber stamp fizzled-out friendships (which are 'for a reason, a season, or a lifetime', as the saying goes) as 'FAILED' just because we move further apart, or we no longer work in the same office, or we simply stop hanging out. We don't say friendships were a waste of time, unless they end in a joint mortgage and platonic eternity rings.

It's time to re-define ended relationships as chapters in the spellbinding saga of your life, not entire standalone books. Some chapters will be longer than others, some will be light and frothy, others will be dark and stormy, some will be lustful and lascivious, others will be powered by cocoa, films and early nights. But *all* of them are fascinating and all of them aid in the development of the protagonist: ourselves.

I've had six long-term relationships (if you count long term as being a year+) and have grown from being an absolute gibbering imbecile, a gormless bull crashing around a china shop, to what I am now: a decent amateur. But still learning. Always learning.

I now know never to look at my personal bests on a league table next to athletes. Comparison is a soul-killer. As long as I'm progressing, getting better with each relationship, I'm happy. In my last few relationships I have mastered: barely arguing, not snooping and amicable endings with no name-calling. These are personal bests for me and I am proud of them. What are your personal bests? What progress have you made?

Each relationship has taught me the indispensable lessons that follow below. I wager that if you think hard about each of yours, you will find the same. Let's start with Tom, my most recent serious boyfriend, and work backwards.

TOM
A RELATIONSHIP DOES NOT HAVE TO INCLUDE RAISED VOICES
Tom and I had two disagreements in the time we were together. Both of them were the blandest arguments I've ever had. Anyone watching us

from afar would have thought we were discussing whether the other had fed the cat, or whether Skips or Monster Munch are the superior crisp.

We had conflicts of opinion, sure we did, but they didn't escalate, given we were both entirely willing to agree to disagree. 'Let's agree to disagree' is a magic phrase. I always thought harmony would be humdrum, but it really wasn't. It was nice that we just *got on*.

It was a real planet-realigning realization for me, that relationships don't have to feature sharp-words-at-dawn showdowns.

CRISES BIRTH CREATIVITY

There's nothing like a calamity to get creativity flowing. I took that anguish from his infidelity and alchemized it into rocket fuel. Our split was like the Big Bang for my career.

The security of us being ripped from beneath me lit a fire in my belly, gave me a gigantic kick up the bum, and put a quickness in my career step. Heartbreak is an energy source. You can harness it to do things you never thought possible.

RALPH

I CAN'T DATE SOMEONE WHO USES THE FLOOR AS A BIN

The first time I saw Ralph's bedroom at his mother's I swear my eyes popped out of my head and my jaw hit the floor with a thunk, like a cartoon character. It was like he'd kept everything he'd ever owned.

In actual fact, he had. I once cleared it out, because I couldn't stand it, and chucked four bin bags of 'definitely rubbish' without even having to consult him on their trash/treasure status.

When we moved in together, I thought I could train him, change him, but no. If somebody is an Olympian level of messy, they'll never change: they are so messy they could represent their country. They're so good at it, they will never be bad at it.

I would literally find empty food wrappers and receipts on the floor of our flat. He claimed they'd fallen out of his pocket, but hmmm, the alarming regularity of this made me doubt this claim. The truth was, he would just throw rubbish on the floor for me to pick up.

Now, a decent level of tidiness and a shared approach to housework is a must for me.

A LOVE OF DOGS AND THE COUNTRYSIDE IS A MUST

For some women, it's dinner at Nobu that flicks their switch; for me, it's a walk in the Devil's Punch Bowl with a couple of cute terriers. This was one of the things that really worked about us.

SEB

BORROWING MONEY FROM YOUR PARTNER IS NOT A GOOD IDEA

I used to shake Seb down for a loan every month without fail. I was so intent on spending all of my disposable income on sauvignon blanc, Vogue menthols, fried chicken and 2am taxis, that I could never make my pay stretch. He always obliged.

But it started causing strain between us. I'd started expecting him to sub me. Gimme.

I now never mix relationships and loans. My parents have the dubious honour of providing any 0 per cent loans I now need.

I LOVE A NERD

I'd always thought that my type was a skateboarder, or a surfer with beachy hair and a gnarly edge, but actually, what really lights me up is knowledge, wit and, even, bookishness.

Seb and I would lie in bed; given I had trouble sleeping (due to my alcohol addiction and mounting raft of anxieties as a result), I would say 'Tell me boring things about outer space/photography/evolution/that Dawkins book you're reading'. He would then tell me at great length about our galaxy, and how the sun is one of 200 billion stars. I would pretend to be stultified, when I was actually electrified.

His soft words would allow me to slip into the black sea of sleep, still my sail, catch the wind and head for the moon.

'Some people have one partner for life, but most don't – and each of our loves is crucial and unique.'

– REBECCA TRAISTER, ALL THE SINGLE LADIES

THE ONE WHERE I DATE A DOG-WHISTLE POLITICIAN

'YOU'RE BEAUTIFUL TO ME'
NOVEMBER 2016

I'm two months deep into a tinderbox relationship with Rob. One of those 'Just add people!' insta-relationships, where you become an immediate couple. Rob and I have future-mapped; we're going to live in a really cool converted shipping container filled with woodsy, rustic furniture he's made with his bare hands and have a big family while we both freelance from home (not sure where we're going to put said children, given we'll be living in a shipping container, but y'know, details). I wasn't sure about the kids, but he talked me into it by agreeing to actually do 50 per cent of the work.

I'm starting to realize that Rob is oh-so-subtly putting me down. The time I put a coat on and he ordered, 'No, take that off. It's OK for dog-walking, but not for dinner'. Or the time we sat across from each other in the cafe at the Natural History Museum and he said, 'Has anyone ever told you you're beautiful?' I was stumped as to how to answer. Ummm, of course they had – frankly. But if I said 'Yes', that sounded arrogant. So I just said 'Thank you'. And he chased it with 'Well, you are to me anyway'. Which felt...weird.

Today, he's decided to tell me about somebody he once went out with who 'was the most beautiful girl I've ever been with'. I didn't ask him what she looked like, or anything about her at all actually. When I say that I'm not sure I want to know about that, he says, 'But you're beautiful to me, and you are much more beautiful than her on the inside'.

Then he tells me that he doesn't believe people can be truly creative unless they use drugs (knowing full well that my job is creative, and that I don't do any drugs including alcohol).

Ohhhh, I know what's going on. Suddenly, as I'm showering, the truth rains down on me. I'm dating a dog-whistle politician. What is dog-whistle politics? Let me tell you. ~~I read about it in The New Yorker~~ *I learned about it while watching Scandal.*

Dog-whistle politics are where a message looks or seems

straightforward, non-offensive, innocent, but it packs a coded punch; it feels off, amiss, wrong to a subset of people. Like a dog whistle, not everyone can hear it, but it's there. That's how I felt.

I felt that he was a surreptitious self-esteem squasher, but my examples were trivial and throwaway, as if I might have misunderstood. Like if I challenged him on it, he'd be all like 'Who me?' and I'd feel like an overreacting fool.

You've probably dated a Rob too. They're men and women who start off telling you that you are the best ever, the bee's knees, awesome-on-toast, and then over time they start to lob you backhanders. Things that seem like compliments, but leave you slightly smarting. A seemingly well-intentioned ball chucked a bit too hard, aimed at your face rather than your chest.

This time, I didn't continue to date him. This time, I trusted my instincts, cut our date short, and ended our insta-relationship later that day. I didn't feel anything other than relief.

My gut is normally spot-on these days. Now that I don't do any drinking, I'm better at thinking. And at listening to the Spidey senses that babies and toddlers seem to have about people's characters ('Waaaaah! Get this heinous person away from me! WAHHHHHH').

The tingle as to whether somebody's good/bad seems to be mystical, but it's just science: us picking up on thousands of different micro-gestures and ever-so-subtle voice intonations.

LESSONS I RE-LEARNED:
1. Tinderbox relationships are bad news
Future-mapping with Rob was madness. I had a box of cream crackers in my cupboard that I'd known for longer than him. And tins of food I'd known for years longer. But when I'm deep in a tinderbox, I don't see it. I just think we're 'meant to be'.

Tinderbox relationships are fast to whoosh! up into flame, but also quick to burn out. Quick to turn to ash. One minute you're all warm and toasty; the next you've been plunged into shivery darkness.

2. If you're ever with someone who gradually makes you feel smaller, whose praise has a sting in the tail, who has you doubting yourself, then you bail ASAP. You just *do one*. Because what is a two right now, will inch up and become a four, and then a six, as the months and years roll by.

They make themselves feel bigger by standing on you. And I don't know about you, but I don't want to be stood on, ever again.

THE ONE WHERE I JUST WANT TO WIN

I once had an 'Eureka!' moment when my friend Holly said something akin to, 'I didn't really want *him*. I just wanted to *win*'.

I was like: 'That's it! That's what I do! I treat dating like a competitive sport'.

I really, really like winning. I come from an ultra-competitive family. I was taught to play cards at the age of four. I'm in it to win it. I pretend to be OK with losing, but really, I loathe losing.

I want to win.

All genders are conditioned into 'winning' partners, but I would say women in particular are under such colossal pressure to get a ring on it, that we often lose sight of whether we actually want what we're winning. 'I don't think I even wanted to live with Rick,' writes Amy Schumer in *The Girl with the Lower Back Tattoo*, 'but I wanted him to want to live with me. Being a woman is so fun!'

When we talk to our friends about how things are going with a new boy/girlfriend, we'll list the 'wins'. Well, he/she wants to be exclusive, he/she asked me to meet the family. Ooh, good signs, our friends will say. Ding, ding, ding! Smashing it. I do this, all the twatting time. I catch myself, mid-win-list. Ohhhh.

We've got our eye on the prize, our sights on the finish line, our head in the game, without really thinking about whether we even want to run the actual race, let alone finish it and collect the trophy.

Here's a little story that sums it up nicely.

I TRY TO CAPTURE A MAN IN A GLASS
MARCH 2017

José and I are tangled up in a post-coital afterglow. We've had eight dates. Eight brilliant dates, in which he's made me laugh so much I've cried (by imitating a slightly camp salsa teacher and impersonating those people who ask constant, unknowable questions during films: 'Who's that?...Ohmygod, why is she going in there?...Where are we now?....What's in that chest that he keeps looking at?').

The first time we had sex, I lit loads of candles. 'I feel like you're going to sacrifice me,' he said. We've been on long walks alongside the battleship-grey Thames, we've grocery shopped/cooked together, and we've messaged each other a very moderate 500 times a day.

He's going travelling for six months next month. Something that I knew right from the get-go. It even said so on his dating profile. Swipes right! 'Him, please, app.' I think I'm looking for a long-term relationship, but out of my dozens of matches on the app, I chose to go on a date with the guy who's about to leave the country. Standard me. Choosing the man least likely to want a relationship.

'So, what are we going to do when you're travelling?' I ask tentatively, as he kisses the archipelago of freckles on my back. 'Ummm, well you can come out and see me?' he murmurs, sleepily.

Five minutes later, I've managed to get him to agree to me flying out every month or so. Win. I venture to win another point, I fix my gaze on the hoop, I shoot to score.

'So, are we exclusive? You're not going to be shagging other girls while you're away?'

He literally squirms away. I am the metaphorical giant with a glass and he is the beetle I am trying to trap.

'Can't we just see what happens?' he asks. 'I don't want to shag anyone else right now, nor am I. But I'm more of a date-to-date kinda guy. I'm really into you and I want to see you again, for sure, but I don't know how I'm going to feel in two or three months' time.'

WHAT?! That is not good enough for me. No way José! How dare he not be sure. He knows me by now. He should know. I lie there simmering with rage, like a steaming pot with a clattering lid on a stove, and I eventually leave at 6am.

I text him saying we should have a break in contact for a while. He says that's cool and that he found our conversation intense. It slays our playfulness. It punctures our banter. We then half-heartedly message for another couple of weeks, trying and failing to find a time to meet up, until he starts ignoring me when he goes on a ski trip.

He then reappears a week later, as if nothing has happened –

'Hey cutie, how's it going? Is everything still my fault?' (I hear this nothingness and re-emerge is called 'submarining' in the twenty-tens dating landscape.) I feel a brief buzz of triumph (I've 'won' the fizzle-out now, since he messaged last) and ignore him. We don't see each other again, romantically. (We're now friends.)

A fortnight later, after my fervour to 'win' has departed, I realize with a jolt that I didn't know if I wanted what I was even suggesting. Did I really want to be in an exclusive relationship with a man who was out of the country for six months? Nope. Did I really want to fly to wherever-he-was every month? Nope. It would have been a bloody nightmare.

Was what he was suggesting sensible? Living in the moment and taking each date as it comes, given we'd only known each other for the grand total of...six weeks? Yes.

I actually now use his 'Do I like them and want to see them again?' here-and-now philosophy for all fledgling relationships. Rather than trying to second-guess the future, I just try to take it a day, maximum a week at a time. José has become my accidental dating guru. Yes way, José.

Mindfulness is all about living in the moment, seeing what is happening right then and there, rather than future-tripping and freaking yourself the fack out about what *might happen*. And that helps me stay sane. So I guess this is mindful dating.

I still feel the urge to 'win' and collect a specimen. 'Get under my glass, man! Stop wriggling! No flying away for you!' But now I ask myself, I really soul search, as to whether I want to be under that glass with them. Do I? Am I ready? Or do I just want the satisfaction of having them as a trophy? Do I just want the victory of peering in at them.

Once I peel away the confusing layers of ego and pride, digging deep for the truth, I usually excavate a surprise. Most of the time, the answer is no. Usually, I do want them, but only for right now. I might be ready for sexual exclusivity, but not for boyfriend/girlfriend monikers. I might be ready for boyfriend/girlfriend labels, but not ready to move in. Normally, I'm pushing for commitment beyond what I actually want myself, in my bid to 'win'.

LESSONS I RE-LEARNED

1. To stop hovering around people with an upside-down glass, and chill the heck out.

2. That, often, something that seems so important in the moment will be laughable a fortnight later. If in doubt, do nothing. My snap romantic decisions are like rubbishy instant coffee; I now let decisions percolate.

THE ONE WHERE I WANT TO GET MARRIED, EVEN THOUGH I DON'T WANT TO MARRY ANYONE

Open scene: I am about to go on holiday with a man I have met twice, and I don't think that's weird. I think it's romantic, wild and spontaneous. *Carpe diem!* YOLO! I'm part of a growing social trend – 'Holidating'. I know, because I read about it in a magazine.

So, to give you the back story, I met this man ten years beforehand in Amsterdam, when I spent 48 hours with him, during which we were both mostly lashed. Then I met up with him in London many years later, when we had an off-our-faces liaison, during which I can't remember anything past midnight.

We have kept in touch ever since, and our communications have been peppered with ~~him trying to sleep with me some more~~ a tantalizing 'what if?' curiosity. A couple of weeks ago we decided over Facebook at 11pm (because that's when the sagest decisions are made) that since we're finally both single at the same time, and ~~he has always wanted to sleep with me again~~ we have always 'wondered about each other', that he will fly from San Francisco to meet me in Ireland for a road trip.

My friends and family look slightly startled when I tell them, apart from my mum, because she's an unrepentant love addict.

THIS IS ROMANTIC.

NOVEMBER 2017*
This is idiotic.

Standing at the airport, or more accurately walking around in circles to nix my nerves, I have realized that I am spinning out and wearing spirals into the carpet because I barely know this guy. I have the sum total of two-and-a-half-days knowledge of him, much of which I was blackout drunk for. And I am about to spend a whole week with him.

He emerges from the gate grinning – taller and more handsome than I remember. Woof. He seems sane enough. He doesn't appear to have a

* Names, details and dates have been changed to protect anonymity.

suitcase of knives with which to carve me up. OK, let's do this.

We are acting like an established couple within two hours, holding hands as we go for a long walk along the precipitous cliff that curves from Cushendall Beach to the tumbledown medieval Layd Church, where capsized gravestones jag out of the grass like sunken ship's masts. You can imagine wannabe witches doing naked dances by moonlight, The Craft style.

I might have done a naked dance here, for all I remember, given there have been many times in Cushendall when I have drank poitín (pronounced 'potcheen') Irish moonshine made from potatoes, obviously, because we love POTATOES.

That night we talk to another couple who have just got married. My instant-boyfriend says he's never been married, but y'know, now he's met me. Everyone turns to me and laughs. Half of me digs it (the love addict), half of me thinks it's bizarre (the part that's starting to wise up).

We're staying in a B&B run by a no-nonsense, funny, wise woman I call my 'second Mammy', Ann. She starts off the evening saying, 'He's great! Very dynamic! Clearly besotted with you' and ends it grimacing, saying, 'He's a bit much isn't he? I mean, saying he loves you already?' (The 'love ya' was delivered with all of the depth and showbiz tooth twinkle of a gameshow host, more for the crowd in the pub rather than me.)

Still, I'm chuffed to bits that this big, hot, charismatic American appears to want to marry me already. He also happens to be a millionaire and thus contravenes the familial joke that 'Catherine can sniff out the poorest man in any room'.

I insist on splitting everything, in fact I end up paying for more, because I want him to know I'm not interested in his money; which I'm genuinely not. Although, I confess, I am relieved that I will no longer have to get one of those 'pension' things.

I'm more interested in what he appears to be offering me emotionally, which is lifetime commitment on a silver platter. 'I love your brain,' he says later that night, as we cuddle. 'That's what will keep me engaged when we're 80 and sitting on a little park bench.'

He talks about Our Future constantly, over the next three days. How he's going to take me to Louisiana to eat the best chicken wings ever. How we should sign up to a couple's massage course. How he's going to teach me to ski.

Doubts creep in when we have this conversation. 'So what did you tell your mates about coming away with me?' I ask. 'Did they not think it a bit odd? My mates thought I was a basketcase.'

He smiles. 'Oh, I just told them that it was your dream to scatter your dad's ashes around the four corners of Ireland...and that I was coming along to help you realize that dream.' Huh? He actually painted himself as some kind of ash-scattering knight in a rental car?

Then there was the time we passed a lovely, smiley couple and said 'afternoon' in that chorus sing-song 'We're all in couples and secretly smug' way." He could have done a lot better,' he snickered, once we'd passed them. 'Do you always judge people entirely on their looks?' I ask, half-teasing. 'Well yeah, don't you?' he replies, utterly serious.

He tells me about the time he went to a yacht party (or 'pardy') and realized he was the best-looking guy, whereas his girlfriend was the worst-looking girl. Apparently, that's when he knew it was over. I literally don't know what to say in response to this. My mouth is hanging open, aghast. I resist the urge to check for hidden cameras, because I have the sneaking feeling I'm on a 'Pranked!' TV show.

I have to ask him to stop constantly whingeing about the rain, 'because it's Ireland, and it rains here, so please, just deal with it'. I tell him that the Irish have 11 'levels' of rain, all the way from 'spitting', to 'rotten', to 'bucketing', through to the apocalyptic – 'hammering'. And that this is merely 'spitting'.

Basically, I'm beginning to actively dislike him, but I fight it, because he represents person-shaped commitment. Marriage man, here from San Francisco to save me!

I'm beginning to suspect he might be a sociopath, after him telling me that he had to 'learn how to feel compassion' as a teenager, because he didn't understand it. But I silence my doubts, because I want to move to San Francisco in a big whirligig of sensational romance! And get married atop Half Dome in Yosemite and then settle into a painted lady on Twin Peaks, and go to SoulCycle daily and for 'hikes' (here in the UK, we just walk, it's so bland).

I'm beginning to fear he might be a player, given I come back from the loo – twice – to find him giving attractive women his card (supposedly for work; I don't see him give any men his card). But I squash those fears because I want to take him up on his offer to go and live part of the year at his place in Paris.

He directly discusses when we will get married, over a lunch in a lodge at the bottom of a waterfall. I flush scarlet. He's tapped into an old secret desire of mine, or a not-so-secret one, which makes me feel naked, but this conversation also makes me feel intensely uncomfortable. It's way too soon. Like planning a threesome before we've even held hands. (This is new for me, this way too soon reflex. 2013-me would have sent out a 'Save the Date'.)

Three days into the holiday during which he's underwhelmed by every wonder Northern Ireland has to offer (The Dark Hedges, the Giant's Causeway, Glenariff Waterfall Park, Glenveagh castle), I'd rather peel my face off than spend more time with him. I'm starting to snap, roll my eyes, scrunch up my nose, yawn when he tells me he went to Harvard for the trillionth time.

I suggest we spend the evening apart 'to get some alone time'. I go for a run and reflect on my conflicting emotions of push–pull, commit–kill, want–dislike. My head feels like a swirl of irreconcilable oil and water. Meanwhile, he huffs off to the pub, clearly unhappy about 'alone time', calls his ex-girlfriend and they decide to get back together.

He tells me about their reconciliation the next day, after a lunch where I come back from the loo to see him giving yet another woman his card. He tells me that he actually spent the week with her just before flying to Ireland. I think I feel more sorry for her, than me. She thinks he's been on a poignant ash-scattering trip, rather than a ~~let's-shag-as-much-as-possible~~ 'let's see if this has legs' jaunt.

I'm crushed, at his revelation. What about the couple's massage course? What about the hiking? Who's going to teach me to ski now?

'Maybe it's just not the right time for us,' he says. 'Maybe we can give it another go later down the line.'

My newfound self-respect stands up inside me and stamps its foot. 'Um, that's a no from me,' I say. 'This door is now closed.'

He tries to get me to come on the next leg of our trip, Dublin, regardless. I emphatically refuse. 'Well, you can always change your mind on the way,' he says, generously.'"I won't,' I immediately say.

As we drive the final hour before we part, he is clearly wholly unaffected by what has just gone down: our weird fake-up after four days of being an insta-couple; this incredibly tense car ride. He is singing show-tunes at the top of his voice as if he's on the stage. I feel like the Phantom of the bleedin' Opera is giving me a lift to Coleraine. I am now convinced he is a sociopath who is unable to feel normal emotions. I can't wait to get out of this car.

In the days that follow I heal from my sudden 'No more Louisiana chicken wings' shock by helping my second Mammy with her B&B. I sit alongside basking seals on the rocks of Rathlin Island, who side-eye me at first and then snooze once they've established I'm about as much of a threat as a piece of seaweed. I scrub bathroom after bathroom. I sit by the fire and hear death-defying tales from the rock-climbers staying there.

I hang with Ann and her lovely family next to the warmth of the Aga, cuddling their sheepdogs, feeling like part of them, even though I'm technically not. This is how it feels to be loved. It's gentle, slow and accepting; not unsettling, in-yer-face and like being picked up – and inevitably dumped down – by a tornado.

I search for answers to what just happened online, and alight upon the very real possibility I just road-tripped with a casebook narcissist. The hallmarks of which are: OTT love-bombing and then an abrupt about-face, when they drop and devalue you. It doesn't say anything about melodramatic show-tune singing, but I feel sure that is also a classic sign.

I explore why I wanted to marry somebody I don't want to marry. What is up with that? He was doing my head in, so why would I want to sign up for a lifetime of somebody doing my head in? A lifetime of somebody I wouldn't even choose to be friends with?

Congratulations! You win a lifetime with somebody who you can't stand! Your prize is 50 years of him calling the magic of Ireland 'disappointing', or turning his nose up at hearty pub food and grumpily trying to find a Michelin-starred restaurant in Donegal on Yelp, or telling you for the fifth time what his company's yearly turnover is.

Wanting to marry him was like wanting to be the director of a company, deciding to work there forevermore, when I don't even like their mission statement, or the staff, or the coffee, or the building, or the commute, or any-godforsaken-thing.

I've now realized people – me included – do this all the time. We want to marry people we don't actually want to marry. Or want to 'get married', even though we don't want to marry anyone.

I recently sat around a birthday dinner table with three highly eligible single women, also in their late thirties and all hugely successful. We were talking about how Sadie has recently joined Soho House and the Groucho Club. 'They're full of eligible men,' says Isabella, rubbing her hands together with glee. 'We're going to go husband hunting there.' I imagine them in tribal make-up, brandishing spears, tiptoeing soundlessly through the plush carpet of the Groucho.

I volunteer, 'Can't we just focus on being happy and living life rather than hunting down husbands?'

'NO!' says Isabella. 'I've been happy and lived life and now I want to GET MARRIED.'

I mean, I get it. I've been there, hence all of the above. I am still there, sometimes, but it is bananas. There we sat, a hedge-fund manager, a fashion buyer, an author and a TV presenter, talking about husband hunting. Can you imagine an equivalent group of men talking about 'wife hunting'? Nah.

LESSONS I RE-LEARNED:
1. Tinderbox relationships are bad news
(OK, yes, I realize I have now re-learned this a few times in the past dozen pages. I know, I know, hush now, you don't need to keep going on about it...let's change the subject, please?...Holy smokes, is that a squirrel surfing? *Points and runs away*)

2. Wanting to get married for the sake of getting married is insane
Surely we want to get married because we've met a person we never want to live without. We're in a relationship we never want to leave. The

one follows the other. Yet we want the marriage before we've even met the person.

It's bizarre, abstract and it makes no sense. So, personally, I've resolved to stop it, as best as I can.

THE ONE WHERE I FEEL LIKE THE MOST SINGLE PERSON ON THE PLANET

JANUARY 2018

DAY ONE

I hold my mum's hand as we drive to our hotel, bumping past dogs that trot down the road on a mission (I hear The Littlest Hobo soundtrack in my head: 'There's a voice that keeps on calling me, Down the road, that's where I'll always beeeee').

Why are foreign dogs so road-wise, whereas British dogs are big dunderheads that will bounce into the road given any opportunity? British dogs would definitely never survive in the wild; they have the outdoorsy skills of Mr Bean compared to these dogs, who are the canine equivalents of Bear Grylls.

We see a rose-red sign for 'Romeo's plumbers'. I point it out. 'Sounds like you'd get more than you bargained for,' I say. 'You might, I think I'd be safe,' says my sixtysomething mum, and we burst into wicked laughter.

I feel very good about this decision. I could have gone to Bali to see a sort-of-ex and flirt with him and his mate for a week, but I've chosen to come away with Mum to Antigua instead. This is what I really need. Total R and R. Mum and I have exactly the same sunbathe, eat, read, repeat vision for a holiday. Plus, I love her with all my might. So, she trumps some hot guy these days.

DAY TWO

I've been here 24 hours and have gradually deflated. Pfffffft. I've decided that there is nowhere you feel more single than in a resort hotel geared towards couples.

I've already had to correct three people with, 'Oh no, I'm not here with my husband'. 'Why not?!' they ask, astonished, as if I've forgotten him and ought to turn on my heel to go get him sharpish. 'Because I'm not married.' Silence. They scrabble around for something else to say.

I go down to the shore to watch the sunset. The sun, bashful about its beauty, hides behind motionless lavender clouds that look like an aerial city. A dolphin loops in the bay, a crab scuttles shiftily, as if a shoplifter on a getaway, while a mongoose pounces from hiding place to hiding place on the lawn.

Couples walk down the beach past me. I look at them. If only I had someone to share this with.

DAY THREE
Today the sea is rowdy, a commotion of white horses thundering towards us, causing tourists to squeal and grab their belongings before the bounty-hunting waves claim them.

My mind feels just as tumultuous. People keep asking me why I'm single, why so lonely, where my husband is, and I'm feeling prickly as fuck.

To be fair, most of these enquiries are from local men trying to pick me up, but I'm rehearsing defiant slingbacks like 'I'm not lonely, I'm alone, there's a difference', or 'Where's my husband, where's your wife?'

I'm feeling sore about my single status, amid this ocean of couples. Even the nervous emerald-and-amethyst turtle doves hop around in pairs.

But, this is all in my head. I'm not alone, I'm with my mum, who I chose to come here with. I know that, rationally, but beneath my intellectual reasoning my wild-eyed subconscious is doing a great impression of a sloshed Bridget Jones singing 'All by Myself'.

DAY FOUR
Where Mum and I have chosen to sunbathe on holiday speaks volumes about our extrovert vs introvert status. She has always made a valiant effort to talk to everyone on whatever island we're on (I once said to her at an airport – 'Look! There's some people you haven't talked to yet, there's still time, go get 'em tiger').

She chooses to set up shop on the busiest thoroughfare there is, beside the pool that everyone walks past to go to breakfast, lunch and dinner. Shooting fish in a barrel, she is. Whereas I walk down the beach, past the people playing volleyball, past the huts selling crocheted tie-dyed bikinis, and set myself up behind a bush. I'm practically wearing a bit of tree on my head as a hat, like a birdwatcher.

That night, we meet a lovely sixtysomething couple with those gleaming, perfect American teeth that we Brits look at with wonder. How do they get those? What do they do?!

They don't attempt to pin down my marital status immediately, as if they need to tick a box on a clipboard survey (Name? Marital status?). I later ask Mum, 'Did they ask about my love life while I was in the toilets?' Nope, she says.

So a big-up to Gerry and Suzy from Wisconsin. They restored my faith in the notion that my romantic status is not the most interesting thing about me.

DAY FIVE

The next morning I wake up still tangled in a dream. Unable to tell what's real and unreal. I dreamt of my Have It All pin-up. We probably all have one. You started on a level-ish playing field, but they Got It All at the right age. Late twenties they landed the big job, had the dream wedding with peacocks strutting around a country house garden, and had two beautiful children, a girl and a boy.

I wake, tangled up in her and immediately feel lonely, sad and left behind. Early morning is not the most rational time.

One of my best mates, a psychotherapist, once told me that this just-woken-up time is when positive visualization works best, because the gates are the most open between the conscious and subconscious mind.

I used this slice of limbo between dreamland and real-land when I was in the run-up to doing live TV, something I was terrified of. It seemed to work, as even though I had an overwhelming urge just before going on set to RUN, run for the doors and never stop running, I took a deep breath and stepped onto the set instead.

It's imperative that I challenge this in-between-sleep-and-waking belief that I will never Have It All like her and that I am less-than as a result. I don't want this less-than notion to seep into my subconscious. Do I even want 'It All'?

Firstly, I ask myself: where has this come from? Undoubtedly being surrounded by a crowd that is 90 per cent in a couple. But I have been on holiday with boyfriends before and known that even though we present as 'couple, tick, sorted', they are not the guy, this does not *have legs, this is only a holding bay of a relationship.*

Am I seeing things straight, or skewiff? Do all of these couples look blissful? I really look at them, while I am having a little conversation with a green and silver finch that is trying to pinch my orange juice. About half look happy.

Lastly, is it true? Am I single by necessity, or single by choice? As much as I forget it on a regular basis, the reality is I have actually ended the last three entanglements I've been in.

I feel better, having sorted out my tangled victim storyline. I am not a victim, I have chosen to be single.

I dive into the tremulous honeycomb of rainbows at the bottom of the pool and feel the inadequacy wash away. My sanity rushes back in as I slice through the water.

I'm sure Got It All woman looks at my life and wishes she had aspects of it. An ability to go and live in a different country just because I fancy it. The freedom to sleep until 9am if I please. The lack of stress about boilers breaking down, or basement floods, or whatever reality comes with owning a house.

What I don't have in baby-powdered cuddles, a house to decorate, and the security of a life partner, she doesn't have in freedom and lack of responsibility. Each lifestyle comes with its pros and cons.

DAY SIX
The sea looks as if it's lit from within, as if there are a thousand duck-egg blue lightbulbs lined along the bottom. The tide is incoming. The hopeful waves stretch further up the beach each time, their fingers reaching up through the ripples of sand to try and grab the grassy land. Then they're pulled back, defeated by the almighty suck and pull of the moon. But they come at it again; with even more determination and force.

I admire their indefatigable reach. It strikes me that the way the tide comes in is the same way that anyone gets anything done, whether it's getting sober, studying for a degree, building a shed, or teaching their brains to feel happy single.

DAY SEVEN
I see a woman at lunch without a partner. Ooh! I ask myself what I

think of her. Do I think she's sad, dejected and unwanted, as I imagine people must think of me? Nope. She looks happy, calm, independent.

Then, a man comes up behind her and kisses her on the forehead. Of course. I laugh darkly.

I cast around the restaurant and notice that nobody is appraising me. I realize that it's narcissistic to imagine that anyone is particularly looking at me, or forming an opinion as to why I'm single, or why I'm on holiday with my mum.

I think back to one of those moments I had that altered how I see the world irrevocably. Y'know how when someone stares at you, you assume they're thinking the worst? One time after a swim, I emerged from the sauna. A woman was sat outside and stared at me in a lingering way, literally sweeping me from my top to my toes.

'She is looking at me because I'm repellant with wet hair and no make-up!' I thought. 'I am so disgusting that I'm a public spectacle!'

And then she opened her mouth and said, 'Wow, look at you! What a figure! How long do I need to stay in the sauna to come out looking like that?'

It so perfectly demonstrated how we project negative assumptions that have no basis in actual truth (as the saying goes, 'Assumptions make an ass of u and me'. Or something).

A lot of the time, when people are staring at you, they're likely thinking 'I like his hat' or 'She has nice hair' or suchlike. When you stare at people on public transport, why is it? Is it because you find them to be so vile that you can't tear your eyes away? Or that you find something about them compelling, whether it's their expression, or the way they're mixing double leopard print, or the way their face animates as they tell that story. Exactly. I rest my case.

'Maybe they think we're together, maybe that's what they're trying to figure out, maybe that's why they're so nosey,' Mum says, about the people with the single/married clipboard. 'Maybe they think we're lesbian lovers. In which case, I've done very well for myself. I must be rich.'

Now, whenever my 'They think I'm a single loser!' paranoia powers up,

I think, 'Oh hi, narcissism! Yes, you look pretty today. Now leave me alone'. Narcissism is essentially human, we all have it, but that doesn't mean we need to let it convince us that everybody at the restaurant is staring at our table-for-one. Because they're likely not. They're probably just sizing up my sundae as a potential dessert option.

There's a liberation to be found in realizing that I'm not as important to others as I think I am. In realizing that nobody actually really cares that much that I'm single.

LESSONS I RE-LEARNED:

1. The world can sometimes be obsessed with relationship status, yes. But I make this far bigger, in my head, than it actually is. I imagine people are staring at me, when they're casing my chocolate sundae.

   Plus, if I can forgive myself for awarding too much significance to my love life in the past, then I can forgive the wider world too. They've heard the same how-we-met stories, watched the same films and been trained in the same way.

2. There are perks to both ways of life, single and attached. We both look over the fence at each other's grass and long to roll around in it.

THE ONE WHERE I HATE VALENTINE'S DAY

14 FEBRUARY 2018

I see a luminously happy mid-twenties couple, lamp-lit from within by their love, taking a selfie in front of what I presume is their first place together. I want to push them into the road.

OK, maybe not into the actual road, I'm not a psychopath. But I certainly want to push them into that ornamental pond in their front garden, so that they get their preppy pea coats, black-rimmed glasses and artfully scruffy hair wet.

I am so angry at love today. Valentine's Day can do one. Why do they get to be in love and moving in together, while I'm still seeking, still searching, still single? The unfairness pricks me like a spindle of doom in a fairytale.

But then I remember something that stops me dead. I have been them. I have been this couple.

I've lived with two long-term boyfriends and, both times, we were that inner-lamp-lit couple, taking pictures of our first tenancy agreement, snicking boxes open excitedly, tumbling into the bed, closing the door against the world and feeling like that was it, we were done, we were in, we Knew. The hunt was over, for us.

Nobody can ever Know. That's the thing. The brutal, savage, exquisite agony of love. You never Know that somebody is yours for ever. That not-knowing is what drives people to the farthest reaches of sanity and into the shadowlands of insane behaviour, whereby they install tracking devices on cars, hire private detectives, or burst into their office past a bemused secretary expecting to find him/her pants-down. 'A-ha! I knew it!' Triumphant in their own wretchedness.

We'd all be doing ourselves the biggest favour ever if we just let go of the need to Know. Isn't today, for now, right here, good enough? It's going to have to be, because that's all we really have. I know that's the most inconvenient truth. It's ghastly and I hate it. But accepting it is how we stay sane.

Accepting that even a year's minimum tenancy agreement does not guarantee a year; that a marriage contract can be undone, and that this happens four times out of ten. Accepting that even a baby that is a miraculous fusion of your cells, a gorgeous entwine of your DNA, a composite of your nose and their eyes, your peculiar little toe and their widow's peak, does not guarantee anything. Everything can be undone, in the love realm. There is no such thing as a guaranteed ever-after.

I look at the couple again and feel some sorrow for them. They probably don't know this yet. They're too young to know it. They have the unshakeable naivety, the boundless optimism, the death-do-us-part hope of youth. That comfortable cocksureness could be chipped away over the years, a little may fall into the sea with every raging storm of an argument.

Only, I hope it doesn't. I hope they've got it right and it stays and endures and exalts. I wish them eternal agreement over the washing-up, a lifetime of serene rather than snippy car journeys, a forevermore of mutually satisfying sex.

Did I just talk myself out of hating the happy couple? It seems so. Huh. I mentally draw a heart around them, wish them all the luck in the world, and go on about my day.

LATER THE SAME DAY: *I realize something. I have never not been disappointed on Valentine's Day, even when I was in a relationship and received all of the heart-shaped, rose-scented, red-sparkly hoopla. Something about today brings out my inner twelve-year-old, the kid who was always gutted when the postman whistled on by. Or when a card appeared in my school bag, which I breathlessly tore into, only to find my mum's unmistakeably elegant hand saying 'Guess who?' (I know who! LE SIGH.)*

Why is Valentine's Day such an almighty let down? Because it feels like a 'Who's the most loved' show-pony-trottin', high-falutin parade of one-upmanship. There's always someone in the office who gets ostentatious blot-out-the-sun flowers, or a platoon of aggressively red balloons, or a hard and glittering Tiffany engagement ring.

I always feel cheated, somehow. Not because of who I'm with, or what they give me, but because of the pomp and artifice of the day. Even happy couples sit through overblown Valentine's dinners feeling a little like players on a stage. I've done it. Everyone's done it.

I know that today's single sorrow was just a blip, a downward swoop that will curve back up.

LESSONS I RE-LEARNED:
1. Valentine's Day is a big fat let-down, even when you're in a couple.

2. It's not Them vs Us, only Us.

On the day of Prince Harry and Meghan's wedding I was at a party talking about the wedding with four married women, one in the process of separating from her husband. 'I sat in my car and watched it all on my phone,' said the newly split. 'Watched them say all that bullshit to one another about loving and honouring for ever.'

I was shocked. But all of the married women gave knowing nods. They even said, 'I know, right?!'

It made me realize that it's not Them vs Us, only Us. Everyone struggles with this hankering for something more, even the married; even the happily married. And why? Because we've been told over and over and over that it needs to be magical and mystical and 'You complete me' breathless, like in *Jerry Maguire*.

Let's root for, rather than resent couples, because we're all in this together.

13 THINGS I HAVE FINALLY STOPPED DOING

However, despite all the Dory moments, there have been some wins. In the shape of things I've finally cut out, at long last. Here they are.

1. CHECKING OUT HIS/HER EX ON INSTAGRAM

Therein madness lies. When does this ever end in anything but paranoia and insecurity? I have never been reassured by 'checking out the ex'. I always find something about her that is better, whether it's her eyelashes, waistline or career.

Now, if I feel even remotely tempted, I preserve my sanity by blocking said ex. Then I forget what their handle was within two seconds and the option of ever stalking them is handily wiped out forever.

2. LOOKING FOR THOSE TWO BLUE TICKS...

...that say that somebody has read my WhatsApp. Followed by hatching a dragon egg of doom, whereby I will never hear from them again, because they read it three hours ago! (Yes, I also used to swipe to see when they read it.)

I'd happily strap those two blue ticks to a rocket and send them off into a black hole, because they are horrible for our mental health.

(In reality, I just ask my Millennial friend to show me how to turn them off.)

3. USING THE PHRASE 'LEFT ON THE SHELF'

This should be banned, forevermore, unless we're talking about corned beef, or canned carrots, or beans'n'pork sausages, or some other minging tinned good that nobody should ever buy.

Similarly, 'over the hill' is something that should only be used for directions, while 'washed up' should only ever allude to dishes.

4. NOT ACCEPTING HELP

Let's face it, there are things about being single that suck, and mean we have to do double the work.

This includes hosting family for a weekend. A couple would normally split tasks, but given it's just me, I have to: clean the flat, wash bed linen, make beds, shop for all the meals, make the meals, clean up after the meals. That is a motherload of work for one person. Yet, when my family offer to help chop, clean, strip beds, I wearily say, 'No, no, you're *my guest*' like a martyr.

Nowadays, I say, 'Yes please. Thank you'.

5. CLICKING TO SEE IF THEY'RE ONLINE
Then spiralling off into a fictional storyline as to why they are online and not messaging me back. And OMG, obviously if they are online and not messaging me, that means they are online and messaging ANOTHER WOMAN. Which is just crackers.

6. NOT ASKING FOR THE BED I NEED
Single people are often infantilized. I have heard stories of single friends being made to sleep in places a couple would *never* be asked to sleep: beds shaped like race cars, on sofas in living rooms, even on the floor next to a child's bed (since when do children usurp adults in bed terms?). Single people need privacy and a grown-up bed just as much as an adult couple do. If there really is no room at the inn for a different bed, and I'm not down with the sleeping sitch, then I consider booking a B&B.

It's like Karley Sciortino said in her piece for *Vogue*, 'How did I become the last single person in my friendship group?': 'Seeing my friends usually means being the one single person amid a mob of couples, who treat me either like hired entertainment ('tell us a funny Tinder story, clown!') or like their problem child.' Karley writes about a getaway to a shared house with her couple friends. 'There are three bedrooms and one pull-out couch, and suddenly this year I keep being demoted to the couch, so that the couples can have "privacy". Excuse me, but do single people not need privacy?' #coupleprivilege

7. GETTING MIFFED THAT I HAVEN'T GOT A PLUS ONE
For the wedding. There's zero point in shaking my fist at the sky and cursing the wedding-arranging establishment. Nowadays, I. Let. It. Go.

8. DOUBLE-MESSAGING
Their/my phone is not 'playing up'. They got my message. They have not forgotten how to read. They don't need a 'nudge'. If they don't reply, they can jog on. Rejection is the universe's protection.

9. SENDING 'I SAW THIS AND I THOUGHT OF YOU' MESSAGES

I didn't see this and think of them. I thought of them, repeatedly, and *found this*, in order to have an excuse to message them and crank them into communication.*

10. ASKING MY FRIENDS TO INTERPRET CHAINS OF TEXT MESSAGES

Friends who have never met the man in question. 'What do you think IT MEANS?' I would ask them. They haven't the foggiest. The person most likely to know what it means is – myself.

11. THIS THOUGHT: 'I'M JUST GOING TO CHECK HE'S OK'

I don't need to check he's OK. My message will not save him from a hostage situation. He will not message me back saying, 'No, no I'm not! Which is why I haven't messaged you back, I'm so sorry! I'm strapped to a chair in Azerbaijan! Some bastards kidnapped me while I was skipping home from our date, twirling round lampposts like Cary Grant and singing 'Isn't she lovely'. Now they want £25 before they'll fly me home. Would you mind pinging it over? Then we can continue our path to marriage'.

Luckily, £25 is exactly what I have in my account. I transfer it and finally, *he's OK*.

12. THINKING THAT THE PERSON WHO SENDS THE LAST MESSAGE 'WINS'

(I know. I know. They kinda do. But I am trying to become an actual grown-up.)

13. SAYING THAT I 'HARDLY EVER LIKE ANYONE'

I would say to friends, wide-eyed with earnestness, 'I know he's [insert reason man is inappropriate, inadvisable or unavailable] but I *really* like him, and I hardly ever like anyone!' and they would sigh ever-so-slightly and say, 'Cath, sweetheart, you've said that to me three times in the past year about three different guys'.

Yeah. OK. Good point.

---

* Let's reminisce! A decade ago, this used to manifest itself in me 'accidentally' sending said man group texts wishing him Happy Easter or somesuch nonsense, or 'Oops!' inviting him to my house party. In the early 2010s, it was the Facebook 'poke', often employed after a bottle of wine and midnight.

VII: THERAPY OPENS DOORS IN MY HEAD

I DISCOVER NEW ROOMS

But still, even after all my tending of single joy and re-learning of lessons, there are three things I keep smacking up against, that I don't know how to move past. *Smack*, 'I really must get rid of that thing', *smack*, 'Why the devil is this still in the way?!', *SMACK* 'OK, for heaven's sake, I get the hint!'

1. I am the walking definition of Daddy Issues, and I believe I unconsciously go for men who bear more than a passing resemblance to my late father.

I've read, many times, that a less-than-ideal relationship with a parent can impact your future relationships, particularly when it concerns women and their fathers.

Linda Nielsen, a professor of psychology, told the *Telegraph*, 'If you go into a grocery store when you're hungry, you'll come out with junk food,' she said. 'You just grab whatever's on the shelf that makes you feel good right now. When women don't grow up affirmed and acknowledged by their fathers, they're like hungry shoppers. They generally make bad choices.'

Fabulous. If anyone's a hungry shopper due to feeling a lack of paternal affirmation*, it's me.

2. I am repeatedly attracted to men who are slightly indifferent towards me, despite all of my knowledge around Reward Uncertainty (see page 43). If somebody's super into me, *I think there must be something wrong with them.* I actually do. *Facepalm*

3. I know that I am still hovering at around a seven if single joy is a spectrum of one to ten. I don't understand why I can't push it up to nine or ten.

So yeah, I need therapy. Here goes.

Like everyone, my dad was a scramble of good and bad. He could be lovely too. I remember him often winking, pointing and clicking his tongue at me, and saying, 'You're some kid'.

I GO FOR AN EXPRESS THERAPY WORKSHOP

I seek out the services of Hilda Burke, a psychotherapist who I have worked with before and know to be excellent. She tells me that due to several factors, these three sessions won't be 'real therapy'. For starters, I'm doing it for a book and hopefully for reader benefit, rather than exclusively for my own benefit. Secondly, she knows she'll be quoted, so this is a self-conscious process on both our parts. Thirdly, we really don't have long to work with, so she compares this to an 'express workshop' rather than true therapy.

She says we'll be delving into issues that would normally take months, even years, for clients to get to. It's a bit like we're on a caving expedition, but rather than doing a day of training above ground and working our way into the depths of the Earth gradually, over numerous caving sessions, we're going to go right down into the deepest, darkest nooks and crannies, crawling through tunnels we can't stand up in, and abseiling down vast underground cliffs.

This is accelerated, expedited, a sudden plunge. Because of this, she checks if I'm OK throughout the sessions and stresses that I don't need to tell her everything, or go full-disclosure, given we are going so fast.

THE SESSIONS

Something I did not expect is the dread I felt beforehand. I felt like I was going to cry the moment I stepped into her lovely artsy studio, replete with a fluffy cat that is basically a circle with eyes. I thought I loved talking about my emotions, I think of myself as highly psychologically aware; I expected to take this in my stride. Bahaha. Not so much. I tell her about the dread and she says it's very common.

Another surprise was that before I went to see her, I felt like I'd got things sussed. That I'd joined all the dots, created a picture. But she directed me towards some doors in my mind that I wasn't even aware were there, let alone had the wherewithal to prise open. She also illuminated some corners of well-trodden rooms I thought I knew backwards and inside out, showing me objects I'd never seen before.

THE ROMANTIC PARENTAL MODEL

Hilda asks me what I learned about romantic relationships from observing my parents. I say: that conflict is normal, the onus is on the woman to keep the man's interest, sex is the one way women have power over men, and being single is horribly sad.

I had no idea that I'd learned those four things until now, but it makes absolute sense, given those four pillars have very much informed my romantic relationships until recently. My entanglements have been held up by the four walls of arguments, my fear of him losing interest, a focus on sex and an unwillingness to let even toxic relationships go.

She also asks me what I felt was missing from my childhood and I reply instantly: 'Stability and security'. Why? We moved around a lot, moving house six times before I was 18, including a huge move from Northern Ireland to England. I went to five different schools, and I observed the breakdown of three major relationships before 18 too: that of my mum and dad (when I was 10) and their subsequent long-term partners.

Moving around taught me invaluable lessons, such as how to flex to new people and places, how to make friends, and how to start again, but at the time, I just wanted to stay *still*.

POLAR-OPPOSITE REACTIONS

I tell Hilda that my brother and I reacted to this tumultuous upbringing in polar-opposite ways. We have a running family joke that my brother went into a bank aged 12 with a pile of money and asked to set up a bank account, only to be turned away for being too young. He has always craved – and created – security. He joined the RAF, an undeniably structured and disciplined sort of life, and trained as a pilot. He met his lovely wife aged 24 and was married by the time he was 29. They now have two kids and own a big house.

Whereas I have done the exact opposite. I have recreated the tumult of my childhood by throwing my money into the air like it's confetti, moving rental properties six times in my twenties (to be fair, sometimes this was beyond my control, because – renting), and never having a relationship last longer than three years. Hilda says that she's observed that men often find it easier to break the pattern of a familial dynamic, unlike women. Huh.

WLTM AN EMOTIONALLY UNAVAILABLE PARTNER

I tell Hilda that save two exceptions, I have a repetitive pattern of being attracted to, and getting involved with, men who are like my father:

charming, attractive, dashing, but ultimately emotionally unavailable. And usually, they have an eye for the ladies. They're interested in me, but not in committing; often to anyone, not just me. It's like I'm a human metal detector for the most commitment-phobic man in any room. Bzzzz. 'Found him!'

Given what I've told Hilda about my father and my first stepfather (from the ages of 11 to 15), she concludes that I am looking for men who, 'feel familiar, and feel like home, even when home is not necessarily a desirable thing'. She asks me if there's a pattern as to when I'm not interested in a suitor. I say that keenness repels me. Hilda says that it's hardly surprising that keenness, acceptance and approval are turn-offs, because I never experienced that from either father figure in my formative years. Therefore it's unfamiliar, and even threatening.

As a result, when a partner is a super-keen 80–100 per cent into me, even if I liked them at first, I will find things wrong with them in order to unhook myself. Whereas when a man is 60–79 per cent keen, that's when I'm hooked. That's when I become the emoji with heart-shaped eyes. Anything less than 60 and my self-respect kicks in and I bail, but that 21–40 per cent lack is like romantic crack to me.

I've always seen my attraction to men who resemble my father as an attempt for me to heal that paternal wound, and find the devotion I was seeking from him and never found. Hilda sees it a different way. 'You're seeking out people to re-wound you,' she says. It gives me a jolt. It strikes me as apt that 'partner' is an anagram of 'parent', given the blueprint that we unconsciously take into adulthood.

When she asks what I desire from the ideal partner, I answer in a heartbeat, 'Stability and security'. I only realize hours later that these are the exact two things I said were 'missing' from my childhood. I also realize with a twist of irony that these things frighten me and turn me off, when I actually encounter them.

I also surprise myself by saying that I want this hypothetical relationship to, 'be founded more in friendship than in sex'. What's that I say? Holy cow. I did not know I wanted that! I've always maintained that sex is the thing that separates relationships from friendships, thus have had it thrown up on a pedestal as exceedingly important. Hilda keeps making truth bombs fall from my mouth. It's unsettling, scary and important.

TRUTH BOMBS

We talk through Tom's infidelity and I uncover something I had no idea I believed. That I blame myself. Having told Hilda that him suddenly cheating was an extra harsh karate kick in the teeth given I felt 'very secure and settled' in that relationship, I find myself saying that perhaps it was my fault, that I was responsible, given I got *so relaxed* I stopped wearing make-up regularly and started wearing trackie bottoms rather than dresses.

'Maybe I let myself go,' I say, before catching myself in an 'Ohhhh'. Hilda points out that this sounds like language my late father would have used, right out of the lexicon of the 1950s–70s Irish patriarchy, when he was raised.

I had no clue that I felt responsible for this. Intellectually, I know this is poppycock, but, emotionally, I clearly have something to work through. Which probably dates back to that thing I 'learned' as a child: that women are responsible for keeping the man's attention.

Hilda says that the reason there's a cognitive dissonance, a push-pull, a contradiction, in many of our beliefs, is because learned childhood beliefs often live in the unconscious. We don't even know they're there. 'The subconscious is just beneath your consciousness, it's in the periphery of your vision, it's something that you see moving out of your corner of your eye,' she explains. 'Whereas your unconscious is behind you, in your blind spot. You don't know it's there, even if it's very close to you.'

In my conscious mind, I know that I am definitely not to blame for a partner's infidelity, ever, but there is a contradictory belief running around in my mental blind spot, one that I didn't even realize existed until now.

We talk about my father's repetitive pattern of leaving women shortly after they turned 40 and trading them in for a younger model in her early thirties. He did this four times in total, finally alighting upon a wife just a few years older than me. I talk about how my dad once told me that women start to decline at 25 and how he used phrases like 'washed up' and 'over the hill' for women in their forties.

Because of this, I'd always had 40 ringed in my mental head calendar as 'SHIT!' and believed I had to do all of my man-attracting before then, before my main currency (my looks) dwindled and became redundant. I mean, writing this down, this is clearly utterly ridiculous, but that misogynistic notion lived in my head for many years. Hilda says it's no wonder this has had a profound effect on me, given my dad didn't just say this, he lived it out, over and over.

Hilda also picks up on the fact that my dad was a late baby, an 'accident' and felt unloved and unwanted by his fortysomething mother. Oh. It makes me realize that maybe his aversion, avoidance and dismissal of fortysomething women was nothing to do with the women, and everything to do with his own residual childhood issues. I feel a pang of sympathy for him. It's not all about me. Everyone has their very own backpack of rocks, which they hoist throughout their lives.

I also keep mentioning the age 45, as in, 'I'm more than happy now to wait 'til 45 or beyond to meet whoever he is'. Hilda asks me why 45, and I realize that this is the age that my mum met my now-stepdad (who is wonderful beyond measure and accepts/adores me unconditionally).

I realize that even though I am definitely happy being single right now, I am still very attached to the idea that eventually *I need to meet someone*. I've just expanded the time limit I've given myself. Rather than having 40 loom over me as the age the magic falters and my coach turns into a pumpkin, and I have to go home to sweep chimneys or something, I've extended it by five-to-15 years. Aargh.

DATING SABBATICALS

I proudly tell Hilda about the dating sabbaticals I've embarked upon, the whole year, the numerous little stints since then. I tell her that I go on them when I feel the panic start to grip me, when I can feel myself switch into phone-watching and waiting mode, when love addiction starts to dig its claws in once more.

I expect her to be impressed, but instead she says, 'So, it's a bit like pouring the vodka bottle out?' Ahem. Maybe. Perhaps the solution is learning how to date in moderation, rather than absolute abstinence? It makes me think.

She asks me what my hopes are for the book, what I want readers to gain. 'I want them to feel like they're complete as a single, that they're not missing another half, that they're not a failure because they're single.'

She asks me where I sit on that scale, if it were one-to-ten? How convinced of that I am myself? I answer that I'm a seven. 'I know it and believe it absolutely in my conscious mind, but I think the remaining three lives on in my unconscious mind,' I say. 'Which is why I'm here.'

THE SINGLE CONTENTMENT SCALE

Hilda then asks me the most important question of the entire session. 'What's stopping you from sliding to ten on the single contentment scale?', she enquires. 'What do you feel like you'll be missing out on, by going the whole way?'

She says that people hang onto their addictions, whether they be eating disorders, alcohol, sex, gambling or shopping, because a belief still persists that if they give them up, they'll miss out on something. 'With alcohol for instance, for you, it was the perceived fun,' she says. 'So, what is it this time?'

What losses are kicking around? I realize that even though I'm not sure I actually want biological kids, I believe I'll have to let go of the option of having them. Given my mum is giddy with excitement every time I'm dating someone, I'll also have to let go of pleasing her.

Finally, I locate a FOMOOM (fear of missing out on men). I feel like if I relax too much into singledom, it'll be like allowing myself to be sucked into a squashy sofa. That I'll be unable to get up again. That somebody will walk on by and I'll be so relaxed, eating Doritos and watching *Santa Clarita Diet*, that I won't notice them. I realize that I feel like I have to sit slightly upright, a little braced, a touch tense, in case I need to spring into action. All of this is news to me. I had no idea I thought it, or felt it.

So, if I fully reconcile myself to the idea of not having kids naturally, to the prospect of potentially disappointing my mum, and slay the notion that sitting in a squashy sofa means you can't see people beyond it, then I figure I'll have made huge progress. And the pièce de résistance? Truly making my peace with the notion of a partner-less future, walking right into that, through it and around it.

FAIRGROUND ATTRACTION

Finally, there's one more truth bomb to come. Hilda asks me how I felt when I took that year off dating. My shoulders drop about four inches, I glow from within, sigh, and say, 'Amazing. So chilled'.

She asks me why, and I say that I didn't feel I had to try, wait, watch. When I'm dating and it's going well, I feel a real high, but the dark side of the moon is thus. When it's not going well, when I'm not getting what I want from them, I feel hungry, bereft, incomplete. I feel more incomplete when I'm single-and-dating, than when I'm single-and-not-dating.

Basically, being single-and-not-dating feels like walking around a fairground and eating candy floss and laughing with my mates, while single-and-dating feels like strapping myself into one of those 90-foot rides that pulls you up slowly with a foreboding chug-a-chug-a-chug, then drops you down abruptly, swings you about, shakes you around, all of which you have absolutely no control over. Not dating is predictable, grounding and lovely, while dating is up, down and all around.

My mood when single-and-not-dating isn't tethered to another person's whims, feelings or texting punctuality. I realize I actually prefer not dating. My head silently explodes.

Now, there have definitely been times when my coupled-up contentment has been equal to my single contentment, but those have been deep into the relationship, probably over six months in, when I reach that 'Ahhhh' stage whereby I genuinely feel anchored, solid, secure. I can count those years (from my fifteen years in constant relationships) on one hand.

That leaves more than ten years when I haven't felt like that. The important distinction? I wasn't *happier* in the relationships, even during the 'Ahhhh' secure stage, than I was being single.

This is like a floodlight being switched on in my head. I'm not saying I'll never date again, of course I will, but it will be a means to an end, I will attempt to learn to do it moderately (more on this later), and this single/coupled happiness split-screen has made me realize that I don't need a husband in my future to see a happy one.

This opening of the 'single forever' room in my head is a revelation. I'd always had it barricaded shut as a no-go before. I'll be honest – I still prefer the 'eventually meet someone' room, but I'm starting to walk around and sit in the 'single forever' room. It's very peaceful there, there are no whiskers to clear out of the sink, or halved bed space, or in-laws to ingratiate myself to.

I realize I like it there. In fact, I could even live there.

MY THERAPY TAKEAWAYS

ON MIMICKING OUR PARENTS' ROMANTIC MODEL
'We all repeat patterns, but becoming conscious of that is the key to freeing yourself of it,' says Hilda. 'Once you know what you're doing and why, you start to feel like you have a choice to unlock yourself from that. You can say to yourself, "OK, so this is the kind of partner I'm drawn to, this is how I'm acting and here's where it came from". Then the next time you meet someone like that, you may still be attracted to them, but you'll have more awareness of that pattern repetition, rather than just blindly going along with it.'

We don't always mimic, says Hilda. 'When we create romantic relationships that are the exact opposite of our parents', that can be unhealthy too. It's about making your own choices, irrespective of what your parents did.'

ON HOW TO ENJOY BEING SINGLE
'I'll often say to clients who feel that being single is a miserable waiting stage, "Let's say you do meet the person within the time frame you want,"' Hilda says. '"Imagine that you have two years before meeting them. How can you look at this time, this two years, as a golden opportunity. How can you appreciate this time?"'.

'What I find is that often, the clients are actually attached to seeing singledom as a kind of purgatory,' she continues. 'I can be met with a lot of resistance, as if they feel like if they let go of their single discontentment, let go of the notion of a coupled-up state as superior, if they enjoy single *too much*, they'll never make it into a couple. Unless they retain that lack, that gap, that longing, they'll lose the ability to change it.'

I identify with this strongly. It's a bit like my core self belief that I'm 'lazy'. There is so much evidence to the contrary, but I'm scared of letting go of this belief. I tie it to my wrist as if it's a helium balloon that may float off forever. Why? I feel like it motivates me to get off my arse and do stuff. I feel as if, without it, I will never do anything again. My 'laziness' will become permanent, unless I'm constantly trying to disprove it.

ON WHY WE SEEK PARTNERS
WHO ARE LIKE OUR PARENTS

'We gravitate towards the familiar, even if that was a parent who wasn't your biggest fan,' Hilda says. 'We think that now we're adults, we'll be able to turn it around, and convince them (or rather their latest incarnation – the partner we've chosen) that we really *are* great. It's an attempt to give the dynamic a different ending, but it often just results in us being re-wounded again and again.'

ON NOT PUNISHING PEOPLE
WE'VE ACTIVELY CHOSEN

'So, if we had a critical, emotionally withholding parent, we'll often look for a partner with the same traits,' reveals Hilda. 'Then, when we find we can't change the ending, and that we still can't transform the withholding into adoration, we'll try to change *them*.' They poke parts of us that are already bruised, and arguments are a result.

'But, the wound was already there to begin with. It pre-dates your partner,' says Hilda. 'Our partner's negative traits are what we actually looked for.' Maybe you're magnetized by partners who you need to show all your tricks to, in order to win them over, she suggests. 'You chose them *because* they're hard to impress. Then, later, this becomes the thing you try to change about them. Accepting ownership for having chosen them is important.'

ON WHY APPROVAL-SEEKING IS ADDICTIVE

'If a parent's love felt conditional, it can create an unconscious template whereby the only desirable partners are those who need chasing. We recognize that feeling, of approval being a movable target that we can never quite reach, and re-seek it in adulthood,' she says. 'It's a very addictive feeling.'

It's not as if these partners, the ones that need chasing, are giving us *nothing*. 'They're feeding us just enough attention, chucking us a few snacks to keep us going,' says Hilda. 'Ultimately, we're following the breadcrumbs they are laying down, but we never get to the gingerbread house.'

Those who are 'too keen', who offer us the exact GPS location of – and keys to – the gingerbread house, don't recreate that wanting, waiting, anticipating feeling that was laid down in our earliest years.

ON TROLLS THAT HAUNT US

It's very common to be haunted by critical parental voices, just as I am haunted by my dad's 'spinster' narrative. 'When we dismiss the inner troll immediately, without hearing it out, it generally doesn't work,' Hilda says. They come back, repeatedly.

'Often I'll ask a client to use two chairs, in order to give the negative voice a full hearing, and to respond,' she says. 'You keep switching chairs, to denote your voice vs your troll's. Once you let the troll say everything it wants, it eventually gets tired and talked down. Your stronger, more positive self-talk wins.'

Hilda cites the case of Chelsea Clinton, who recently got trolled by someone who compared her to both a donkey and a horse. In response she tweeted, 'Thank you James! Donkeys are known for their independence, intelligence & persistence and horses for their speed, perceptiveness & memory. I'm flattered by the compliment, thank you!' And just like that, she cut her troll down to size with grace and intelligence. We can do the same with ours.

• For more on Hilda's work, go to www.hildaburke.co.uk

A CONVERSATION WITH THE IRISHMAN IN MY HEAD

I decide to call out my misogynistic troll, as Hilda suggested, and have a conversation with him. To let him blether and scold and blast me. To square up to him and say 'Take your best shot', and actively block his jabs, rather than bolting from the boxing ring.

Given he's Irish, let's go totally clichéd and ridiculous, and call him Paddy. *Quelle surprise* (not): Paddy was born in the 1950s and cemented his beliefs in the 1970s...just like my father. Oh what a shocker; he also has a Ballymena accent, just like my father.

Paddy: 'What about ye, Catherine? Any danger of you getting married any time soon?'

Me: 'Paddy, I wish you'd stop going on about this. I've told you before, there is no sign. And I'm having a brilliant time anyway, I'm living in Barcelona. And did I tell you about the book deals? I'm just about to start my third book!'

Paddy: 'Pet, a job won't keep you warm at night, so it won't.'

Me: 'I'm pretty sure it will, given it makes me something called *money*, which buys a roof over my head, bedsocks, central heating and goose-down duvets.'

Paddy: 'Och, you career girls are all the same, you leave it way too late, and then nobody wants you! The graveyards of Belfast are full of single career women like you, who died all alone!'

Me: 'I'm pretty sure the graveyards are also full of married women too, given marriage does not give you the superpower of eternal life.'

Paddy: 'You're too clever for your own good, you. No wonder you'll die alone, bit of a smartarse aren't ye?'

Me: 'OK, so I hate to be even more of a smartarse, but getting married is not insurance against "dying alone". 60 per cent of Brits aged over 85 are widows. It's very sad, but true.'

Paddy: 'Well even so, before that somebody loved them. Single people lead very lonely, loveless lives, so they do.'

Me: 'Ummm, but dozens of people love me. I am very close to my family. I get love on a daily basis.'

Paddy: 'Hang on, talking of family, hadn't you better get on that sharpish? When are you 35? After that it's all over, y'know.'

Me: 'Well, I'm actually 38, Paddy.'

Paddy: 'Hells bells! Sweetheart, you best get yourself married and pregnant pronto. I don't even know if you can get pregnant at that advanced age! The hospital will call you a "geriatric mother"'.

Me: 'Actually Paddy, a 2004 study found that 82 per cent of women aged 35 to 39 conceive within a year of trying. Among the younger age group, those aged 27–34, the success rate was 86 per cent. So, this suggests there's only a four per cent drop in chances of success, between those aged 27 and those aged 39.'

Paddy: 'You're a gas! That can't be true. I read about the 35 thing. After that there's no chance, you flamin' eejit.'

Me: 'Birth rates of women over 40 have now overtaken those of women under 20.'

Paddy: 'Please tell me you do intend to have children in the very near future?'

Me: 'To be honest, Paddy, I'm not sure. I might if I meet the right person and it's the right situation. If not, I don't feel I'll be incomplete in any way. There are a lot of perks to a childfree lifestyle.'

Paddy: 'But who will look after you when you're wearing nappies, tell me that? It's all grand now, you're gallivanting around Spain, but what about when your hip is banjaxed and you can't walk?'

Me: 'I hate to tell you this Paddy, but I'm pretty sure that a lot of people who have been stuffed into retirement homes actually have kids. And are spending the proceeds from the sales of their bungalows in Eastbourne on said retirement-home fees.

'I don't know any elderly people kicking back in a luxurious penthouse granny flat with a rooftop pool, being looked after by an adult child who doesn't need to work and can therefore stay home and do whatever their doting parent desires.'

Paddy: 'Right you be. Well, here's a good one. I read that women over 40 have more chance of getting killed by a terrorist than getting married!'

Me: 'Oh Paddy. Twenty years after *Newsweek* published that particular "fact" (and panicked thousands of women into an aisle stampede), they finally published an apology and a retraction. In fact, the cover headline of the follow-up story said it all.

"20 years ago Newsweek *predicted a single, 40-year-old woman had a better chance of being killed by a terrorist than getting married.*

"Why we were wrong..."

'The piece revealed data that showed US women over 40 actually had more than a 40 per cent chance of getting hitched.'

Paddy: 'OK then...but regardless, nobody will want you soon enough. Your looks are fading! You'll be left on the shelf.'

Me: 'There is so much wrong with that, I'm not sure where to start. Firstly, I have a lot more to offer than my looks. And "left on the shelf" implies that I am a consumable item that you can buy from a shop, and any man with money can buy me. There is no shelf. And I am not on it. Any more than single men are rescue dogs in a pen, hoping to be picked.'

Paddy: 'But honeybunch, how the feck are you going to find someone now? All your peers must be married.'

Me: 'They're really not, Paddy. Over half of Brits my age are single. Things have changed a lot since 1970s Ireland. We don't live in small towns or villages with very limited options. We don't have to marry the person from the next street along, for lack of choice. Also, we now have something called "dating apps" that give you access to thousands of single people. It's like having thousands of single people's phone numbers in your pocket.'

Paddy: 'Jesus, Mary and Joseph. Sounds like the devil's work to me. Well, even if you do find someone and have a babby, there's nothing sadder than an old mother, aye.'

Me: 'Oh Paddy. When do you think I should have had a child?'

Paddy: 'In your twenties! Of course! We had our first, Nuala, when my wife had just turned 20. You best skedaddle and find yourself a man quick smart.'

Me: 'Paddy, if I'd had a child in my twenties, I probably would have gone to jail for leaving it in a car outside a nightclub.'

Paddy: 'What are you on about, you headcase?!'

Me: 'I used to be a total hellraiser, Paddy. I could barely look after myself in my twenties. Now that I don't drink, ever, I probably could be a fit mother, but I can also have a childfree life that is incredibly happy too.'

Paddy: 'Hang on a minute there sweetheart, did you just say that you DON'T DRINK? Boys a dear. I've never heard tell of such preposterousness. Have a wee dram with me now. It'd be rude not to!'

Me: 'Paddy, I'm really sorry, but we're done here. Cheerio now.'

THE VERDICT: That was really cathartic. Having a conversation with my hidden misogynistic troll really exposed the fact that many of the things he yells at me are works of fiction from a bygone era, which have long since been disproven.

It's funny, once I brought him out of the shadows, he became less menacing. Less malevolent. It took away a lot of the unknown, murky power he previously had. I don't need to take Paddy's opinions on board any more than I would listen to someone who believes that women should be seen and not heard, or that men don't 'buy the cow when they can get the milk for free'.

It's also softened me up a little towards him. Paddy may be carrying around archaic beliefs and misconceptions, but I can forgive him for that somewhat, given he grew up in such a dramatically different social landscape.

That forgiveness wasn't easy to come by, mind. It's like Cheryl Strayed says about forgiveness not being the pretty boy in the bar; it's the old fat guy you have to haul up the hill. Forgiveness is an activity, not an emotional state you miraculously happen upon.

Nonetheless, even though he's forgiven, I'll be telling him to wind his neck in the next time he peeks his flat cap over the parapet.

ATTACHMENT STYLES AND WHY THEY'RE LIFE-CHANGERS

After our therapy sessions, Hilda sends me a link to a book called *Attached* by neuroscientist Amir Levine and psychologist Rachel Heller. 'Huh, that's weird,' I think. 'She's the third person within a month to say that I should read this.'

The third totally independent person. The universe* may as well have bewitched the book into movement and had it waddle over from the bookstore to gently slap me around the face, or dropped it through my skylight via a drone from some celestial version of Amazon.

Suffice to say, I finally got the hint and *read the flipping book.*

And, they were absolutely right. It was a life-changing read for me. It was like that revelatory reveal, the finale of a crime drama where you find out who the killer is, and everything starts to make sense. 'Ahhh, that's why he...and that's why she...and that's what it meant when...!' I mean, there are a few red herrings you have to ignore, but mostly, the narrative suddenly shifts from an annoying puzzle, with multiple random sticky-out bits, into something which clunks and slots neatly into place.

It turns out that my love-addicted ways are not me being a needy nutcase, after all. It turns out there is a NAME for my particular brand of crazy, people. Which is just tremendous news. I also discover that a fifth of the population also has what I have (many of whom I suspect will now be reading this book. Hi pals). I'm not insane, I'm just an anxious attacher. Whew.

Anxious-attached people often experience dating as soaring highs and crashing lows; both euphoric and devastating. 'Anxious-attached children get distressed when their mother leaves a room, because they don't know if they're coming back,' explains Hilda. 'When the mother does come back, the children often don't demonstrate any relief or joy, as they're distrustful that their mother will stick around. They lack

I am a heathen who doesn't believe in the universe puppeteering anything: I believe life is random, if sometimes serendipitous. But if the universe was some heavenly deity doling out book recommendations, I strongly believe she'd be Maya Angelou sitting on a cloud in a white nightgown.

confidence in the bond between them.'

This dynamic replays itself in adult relationships, Hilda says. 'If a suitor delays in calling them, the anxious-attached person will think, "Maybe they'll never call me again", whereas a secure-attached person will think, "They'll call me at some point" and get on with work and life in the meantime. A secure-attached person is surprised by abandonment, whereas an anxious-attached person expects it.'

Anxious-attached people often dynamite relationships prematurely, she adds. 'Say if a person doesn't get in touch within 24 hours of the date, they might block their number. Whereas a securely-attached person would think, "I've only met him/her twice, they contacted me within two days of the date, and it's nice to hear from them". Anxious-attached people can often have unrealistically high expectations of suitors, whereas secure-attached people have more grounded expectations.'

Oh, and there's more. I am an anxious attacher who is overwhelmingly attracted to people called 'avoidant attachers'. Yup. Honestly, reading the description of avoidant attachers was like reading a list of ingredients on a cereal box named 'Cath's exes' containing a jumble of miniscule men (no added sugar).

It turns out that avoidants and anxious types are irresistibly attracted to each other at large; it's not just me and my exes. All over the globe, this same disenchanting push–pull, yes–no, 'I want'–'I avoid' love story is being played out, like the ultimate anti-fairytale, over and over again.

I wrote 5,000 words about what I learned from reading *Attached* but I couldn't fit them into this book. So, I've popped them onto my blog. There's a quiz on there, so that you can figure out what attachment style you are. See the 'Attachment Styles' blog on www.unexpectedjoy.co.uk

And, I thunderously recommend you also read *Attached*. It is hands-down the most illuminating and sense-making book I have ever read on relationship psychology. Don't make me ask Maya to send a celestial drone to your house.

WHY PLAY-ACTING IS POINTLESS

Play-acting is tiresome. It's why millions of women thought 'YES', when they read the now legendary 'Cool Girl' passage in Gillian Flynn's *Gone Girl*.

Cool Girl is every guy's dream. She eats hamburgers whole and still rocks skinny jeans; she likes football, is up for a threesome and plays video games for four hours; she's hot and understanding in equal measure. We can only pretend to be a Cool Girl for so long, before the illusion is pierced.

In the film of *Gone Girl*, the Cool Girl 'I wax-stripped my pussy raw' soliloquy is delivered as Rosamund Pike sheds Cool Girl like a snake shrugs off a dead skin. She eyes herself defiantly in the mirror while simultaneously smoking and dying her hair brown. She gaily tosses donuts, unflattering reading glasses and shapeless tank tops into a supermarket trolley.

I mean, she's a psychopath, but in that moment, I identified with her *hard*.

GAME-PLAYING MANUALS DON'T WORK

As Dolly Alderton neatly says in *Everything I know about love*, 'You should never take any advice from a sassy, self-help school of thought that makes the man the donkey and you the carrot'. People are not donkeys. People are not carrots.

There's an Irish saying that goes, 'A man chases a woman – until she catches him'. I heard it numerous times in my childhood. It neatly sums up all of this twaddle that women are taught. That we have to let a man do all the running, while secretly devising a Machiavellian plot to ensnare him. That we have to put on a 'whatever' front, while casting spells using strands of their hair and tucking secret 'wedding-inspo' books under our beds.

'Dating manuals' are generally bare-faced enablers for love addiction. They cash in on the anguish, and do nothing to treat the source. They take that 'incomplete single' misery, exploit it, and email you dangling a seven-day course for 'just £59.95!', once you've finished devouring the e-book, sadly looking for solutions to your ailment of singledom.

They mostly fall into two camps. How to feign indifference in order to pique interest (*The Rules, Why Men Love Bitches*), and how to morph into someone you're not in order to be 'more attractive' (*The Game* and *Act Like a Lady, Think Like a Man*).

They have smack-you-in-the-kisser titles like *Why You're Not Married Yet*, or *Solving Single: how to get the ring, not the run around*. One tells you to, 'serve your husband' (*Why You're Not Married Yet*), while another tells you, 'He simply won't respect a woman who automatically goes into overdrive to please him' (*Why Men Love Bitches*). One tells you to make them pay for dinner; another tells you that you need to demonstrate that you're financially independent.

They tend to be insultingly reductive of half of the population, slinging them into a pigeonhole. Women are chucked in the 'desperate, needy' category, while men are depicted as the enemy, who will throw you down like a discarded Xbox if you dare show reciprocation.

One recent dating-manual publishing sensation is Rachel Greenwald, who is to feminism what Godzilla was to New York skyscrapers. She is the author of *The Program: fifteen steps to finding a husband after 30* and *Find a Husband after 35 (using what I learned at Harvard Business School)*. Both of which I would gladly burn.

She tells the reader to market herself like a product, to *always* wear push-up bras, and to put her husband-search above her job, friends, pet, every-damn-thing. Lines like, 'Don't use too much hairspray. Men like hair that is soft to touch, not hair that feels like cardboard' and 'No bright red please – you are a future wife, not a hooker', make me suspect she is a 1970s Stepford wifebot working on an antique typewriter, using time-travel post to mail her manuscript to the Noughties.

Greenwald also tells the reader to drop any friends or family who don't support her 'quest for a mate'. She goes on to fearmonger: 'Remember, after 35, it's "Marriage 911". This *is* an emergency!'

I'm not a violent person, but I sincerely want to bop Rachel Greenwald on the nose.

None of these ridiculous books gets to the heart of the matter. Reprogramming the belief that we are 'less than' without a relationship, and therefore need to read nonsense like this in order to snag one.

If you are truly content single and know that you will still be happy whether Dan/Pam-who-you've-met-twice calls or not, you won't have to feign anything. If you have a buzzy social calendar, you won't have to fake being busy. If you are financially independent, you won't have to pretend to be.

WHAT THE EXPERTS SAY

These dating books are big business, given they ker-ching millions out of people's misery. I dug around and couldn't find one actual psychological expert who thinks these books are a good idea. The authors of *Attached*, for instance (a neuroscientist and a psychologist), can't abide them.

Esther Perel, who is probably the world's most respected relationship psychotherapist, and whose TED talks have garnered 20 million views, wrote recently: 'Being "chill" or "cool" is not a sign of emotional maturity or intelligence...It leads you to act fake and pretend that your partner's hurtful actions don't bother you – which deprives your relationship of true closeness and connection.' She goes on to say, 'If you begin a relationship on the presumption that you have everything figured out, you are setting yourself up for stress later on. Your bond will be built on unrealistic expectations, and your partner may be resentful once you reveal your true self.'

Psychologist Jennifer L Taitz points out that winning a game is not the same as creating a loving relationship. 'Winning and loving are at odds, since strategizing, as prescribed in many books, is often cunning and inauthentic.' What does she advise instead? 'Honesty and vulnerability.' These books may get you more bites or second dates, but they won't create anything long-lasting. 'Capturing someone's attention – and creating real closeness – are such different pursuits.'

'Game-playing is exciting in the short term, but it doesn't get you what you're after in the long term,' agrees neuroscientist and author of *The Upward Spiral*, Dr Alex Korb. 'You don't have to pretend you're something you're not. But being *real* doesn't mean you have to roll out all your faults either. Present your best side. It's simply good marketing.'

So, be yourself, and be honest about what you want. That's not to say that you should show up to your first date in a wedding dress/morning suit, but authenticity is the best foundation for any healthy relationship.

You're not a performing seal. If you need to perform tricks to keep his/her attention, you never really had it to begin with. Imagine how exhausting that would be long term. You're starting an intimate, supportive relationship, not joining the circus.

I ACCIDENTALLY STEP INTO *THE GAME*

The bestselling dating manual aimed at men is called *The Game*. Here, I have a story that will hopefully show men: this baloney doesn't work.

SEPTEMBER 2005

I am working for Cosmopolitan magazine and I will literally go to the launch of a paperclip if it offers free drinks. Tonight, my buddy and I are heading to the press shindig for a book called The Game, which we don't give a flying fuck about, but there's an open bar all night, so – wahey! Get in my face, free drinks.

When we get there, we clock a high concentration of unusually alert men. Several of them are wearing odd things, like a red blazer, or a yellow hat. Weird. Anyway. We get two drinks each to get us started.

An attractive man approaches me and starts chatting. OK, nice. But he will only talk to me over his shoulder. Whenever I try to get around to the front of him, he moves, so that we're doing this peculiar circular arrangement, like an Edwardian courting dance. When I'm mid-sentence, answering a question he has asked me, he blurts, 'Hang on, I have to go and talk to someone'. I'm left, mouth open, wondering what the hell just happened.

Next up, we get caught in a shoal of men. One of them says to me, 'It's really hot over here, shall we go by the window'. Er, it's not hot. But I follow him, puzzled. When it's polite to, I ping back to my friend.

Attractive circular-Edwardian-dance man comes back, but I've been put off by his sudden departure, and give him a cold shoulder. Then, a hush stills the room. 'It's Mystery,' I hear men whisper in awe.

He looks like a less hairy Russell Brand – crossed with Criss Angel. He comes over to us and starts talking determinedly to my friend, while totally ignoring my attempts to muscle in on the conversation. 'What's her deal?!' he says to my mate, swatting at me as if I'm a fly.

Eventually, he swivels to look at me. We then have a very odd exchange whereby he does some magic tricks, films me, and then asks, 'Can I trust you?' 'Of course,' I reply, baffled. He hands me a plastic bag and asks me to look after it for him, dashing off. I peek inside. Comedy glasses and wigs.

My friend and I are keen to go somewhere else. So after half an hour, when Mystery isn't back, I pop over to the author of The Game, *Neil Strauss, a very nice man who I've met earlier, and hand the very-important-bag-of-disguises to him.*

Neil Strauss looks at the bag as if it's the funniest thing on the planet, and roars with laughter. He literally doubles over. 'It didn't work,' he says, through tears of amusement. 'What didn't work?' I ask. 'Mystery gave you this bag to keep you here. And it didn't work.'

So, there you go. I was *super easy* to pick up back then, and yet a roomful of supposedly trained 'Pick Up Artists' failed.

I've since found out that all of the tactics used on me are strategies cited in the book, such as 'peacocking', 'active disinterest', 'isolating the target', 'negging'. And finally, some sort of plastic-bag-placeholder strategy that I didn't see in the book.

Why didn't any of these hoodwinks work on me? Because it didn't have to be so complicated. All they had to do was fetch me numerous drinks (because those were the kind of drinks I liked, back then), and be interested in me.

I rest my case. Games don't work.

VIII: WHO ARE SINGLE PEOPLE, ANYWAY?

FACTMONGERING SOME COMMON MYTHS AWAY

MYTH
Single people are lonely

REALITY
They have more friends

A new partner pushes out two close friends on average, says research from Oxford University. So the coupled-up have less friends in their inner circle than singles.

Research shows that single people are the opposite of lonely, says psychologist Bella DePaulo. 'It's the single people who have more friends.' She riffs that married people may have 'The One' but single people have 'The Ones'.

Meanwhile, a study that surveyed 16,000 Germans found that people who live alone are actually *less* lonely. Which doesn't surprise me. In the past, I've let my friendships and family bonds slip when I've been cocooned in a relationship. Single, and particularly when living alone, I am actually more sociable.

MYTH
Single people are selfish

REALITY
They're more giving to their community

In the 'You're selfish' section of Tracy McMillan's book *Why You're Not Married…Yet*, she really has a pop at the so-called self-absorption of single people. We think about our thighs, our outfits! 'You think about your career, or if you don't have one, you think about becoming a yoga teacher', she writes. How very dare we. There we go again, *thinking about our careers*.

Actually, Tracy, several studies have shown that single people are more giving to their social network and town than their married counterparts. A 2011 US report showed that 84 per cent of single women and 67 per cent of single men help their parents, as opposed to 68 per cent of married women and 38 per cent of married men.

'It's the single people who are doing more than married people to stay in touch with their siblings,' says DePaulo. 'It's the single people who are more often tending to their parents, exchanging help with their neighbours, contributing to the life of their towns and cities. In contrast, when couples move in together or get married, they tend to be more insular.'

MYTH
Single people are layabouts

REALITY
They're fitter than married people

An American study found that single people spend, on average, 48 more minutes a week exercising than marrieds. The married people weighed a ballpark of five pounds more than singles.

Moreover, many studies show that singles enjoy better overall health than marrieds. For instance, one 16-year-long survey of 11,000 Swiss women and men found that those who married reported slightly worse general health.

Occasionally 'Married people live longer!' articles do the rounds, but critics of these studies have pointed out that, oftentimes, widowed people were counted as single. And the tragic propensity for a widow to die soon after their spouse could be skewing the figures.

Indeed, it seems that for women in particular, it could be a better health bet to never marry. An Australian study of more than 10,000 seventysomething women found that lifelong, childfree singles were less likely to smoke, had fewer illness and a healthier BMI compared to their married/divorced counterparts.

MYTH
Single people are breathlessly hunting The One

REALITY
Only 30 per cent are

Nope. We're not all frantically trying to un-single. Some 70 per cent of singles in the UK say they haven't tried to find a partner in the past year; among women, this rose to 75 per cent.

Maybe because we're too busy trying new things – and wanderlusting.

Some 82 per cent of singles questioned said that being single gave them 'an opportunity to try new life experiences' and 89 per cent said that travelling alone 'boosted their confidence'.

MYTH
Single women are ruthless sperm-hunters

REALITY
Get over yourselves, men who think this

The myth that all 30+ women are trying to ensnare whoever-they're-sleeping-with into an 'accidental' pregnancy does my HEAD in. I recently had a fun physically oriented fling with someone who was fixated on the idea that I was going to fall pregnant 'by mistake' and 'trap him'.

On and on *and on* he went. I told him several times I had no desire to get pregnant, but it didn't shut him up. Until I sent him this text one day, as a riposte, just to give him a notion of how this feels.

'Dear [name obscured]. I need to say something and I don't want you to take it the wrong way.

I am beginning to suspect, given the frequency and ferocity with which you are having sex with me, that you are trying to impregnate me in order to trap me into a lifelong relationship and gain a share of my no-doubt-significant future earnings.

As a result, I am having a second IUD implanted in order to blow up any designs you may have upon my womb.

I hope you are not offended by my frankness.'

It's probably the best text I've ever sent. And yes, I do text with full words, paragraph breaks and correct grammar. Doesn't everyone?

MYTH
Single women are sad, single men are happy

REALITY
Single women are generally happier than single men

A *Single Lifestyles* survey by Mintel found that 61 per cent of single women are happy being single vs 49 per cent of single men. Which just goes to show what a myth it is, that men don't want relationships. A US study found that 63 per cent of men currently having casual sex would actually prefer a romantic relationship.

MYTH
Successful, clever women don't get married

REALITY
That trend is now reversing

Up until recently, higher-earning and higher-educated women were least likely to get married, but now that trend is reversing, as illuminating data shows that Alpha women are teaming up with Beta males. 'The University of Barcelona recently pored over census data from 56 countries, spanning 1968 to 2009,' says Rebecca Traister in *All the Single Ladies*. 'And determined that marriage patterns are, in fact, adjusting to the higher numbers of women attaining higher education, with more women marrying more men with lower education levels.'

MYTH
Single people are picky

REALITY
They're picky

This is the only one of the beliefs that circulates about single people that is actually true. We are choosy. We are picky. Yep, you've got us on that one. It's a fair cop, guv.

It's like Neith Boyce, a novelist, *Vogue* columnist and refusenik of marriage, wrote back in the early 1900s: 'There are available suitors...if one is not particular'. Man, that's good. I want to cross-stitch that onto a floral cushion *right now*.

I mean, isn't it wise to be choosy? It's like Tim Urban says on the marvellous waitbutwhy.com: 'When you choose a life partner, you're choosing a lot of things, including your parenting partner...your eating companion for about 20,000 meals, your travel companion for about 100 vacations...and someone whose day you'll hear about 18,000 times'.

Right? So, picky is good.

SINGLE SPOKESPEOPLE

Not all of the figureheads that follow are still single, but most of them are. One is a fictional character: don't care. The reason they're here is that they've spoken up about the positivity of the single experience, and the wonky perception of singleness.

I don't believe in a them vs us divide. If one of my single heroes gets married, I don't feel disappointed in them, I don't score a line through their name. I think, 'Good for you'.

Finding the joy in being single, is not about scorning marriage or the married, any more than finding the joy in being married should be about deriding singles or shooting them pitiful looks.

Incidentally, dear reader: I looked for celebrity men for this chapter. I wanted half men, half women. Turns out celebrity men don't provide quotes about being single. Interesting, right? Why? Perhaps because interviewers don't really ask them. Who knows. All I know is that I couldn't find the freakin' quotes, despite spending hours hunting.

CAMERON DIAZ
'There are many soulmates. My soul has a lot of different facets and it needs a lot of different men. Friends, too. Friends can be soulmates.'

CHER
'Mother told me a couple of years ago, "Sweetheart, settle down and marry a rich man." I said, "Mom, I am a rich man"'.

DREW BARRYMORE
'It's ironic that we rush through being "single" as if it's some disease or malady.'

JANE AUSTEN'S EMMA
'I always deserve the best treatment because I never put up with any other.'

MARIANNE POWER, AUTHOR OF HELP ME! ONE WOMAN'S QUEST TO FIND OUT IF SELF-HELP REALLY CAN CHANGE HER LIFE
'All my life I've felt like a failure because I wasn't getting married or having boyfriends like other people – but maybe I wasn't doing that because that's just not what's meant for me. I like my freedom and I

really like to be on my own. When I think of what I want in the future I think of travelling and fun. I want to have great sex and romances but the idea of settling down makes me feel trapped.'

AMY SCHUMER, IN THE GIRL WITH THE LOWER BACK TATTOO
'Then one day, out of nowhere, the fear I had of growing old unmarried just faded...I'd hear stories of happy second marriages, or tales of people not meeting until they were in their fifties or sixties, and feel calm about the whole thing. I was settling nicely into my thirties. I was dating a little but was not at all as consumed with it as I had been in my teens and twenties. The days of *He didn't call me today and it's three pm – what does that mean?!* were truly behind me. I realized that nothing was missing.'

KATY PERRY
'I've learned I'm in a very modern fairytale, but I also know I don't need the Prince Charming to have a happy ending. I can make the happy ending myself.'

JANUARY JONES
'Do I want a partner? Maybe. But I don't feel unhappy or lonely. It would have to be someone so amazing that I would want to make room. Someone who would contribute to my happiness and not take away from it.'

SALMA HAYEK
'It's nice to have a relationship, but women have become addicted. You can have a relationship with God. With nature. With dogs. With yourself. And yes, you can also have a relationship with a man, but if it's going to be a shitty one, it's better to have a relationship with your flowers.'

TAYLOR SWIFT
'Being alone is not the same as being lonely. I like to do things that glorify being alone. I buy a candle that smells pretty, turn down the lights and make a playlist of low-key songs. If you don't act like you've been hit by the plague when you're alone on a Friday night, and just see it as a chance to have fun by yourself, it's not a bad day.'

JENNIFER LAWRENCE

'I'm not a lonely person. I never feel lonely…It's not a sad thing to be alone. I think what I was trying to get across was that I don't feel a lack of something not being in a relationship. I don't feel like there is an emotional void to be filled.'

STEVIE NICKS, FLEETWOOD MAC

'I don't feel alone. I feel very un-alone. I feel very sparkly and excited about everything. I know women who are going, like, "I don't want to grow old alone". And I'm like, "See, that doesn't scare me…" I'll always be surrounded by people.'

DIANE KEATON

'I remember when I was young I honestly believed in some ridiculous way that you would find someone who would be the person you lived with until you died. I don't think that because I'm not married it's made my life any less. That old maid myth is garbage.'

TINA FEY

'According to author Sylvia Hewlett, career women shouldn't wait to have babies, because our fertility takes a steep drop-off after age 27. And Sylvia's right; I *definitely* should have had a baby when I was 27, living in Chicago over a biker bar, pulling down a cool $12,000 a year. That would have worked out great.'

TRACY EMIN, ON MARRYING A BIG STONE SHE REALLY LOVES FROM HER GARDEN IN FRANCE

'It was about me thinking differently, not resting on my laurels, not thinking that I was a failure that I didn't have what other people had…I never met the right person to have children with. I never met my soulmate. Maybe I'll meet them. Do you know what? I'm so happy because I didn't make a mistake, did I? And I have another 30 years ahead and anything could happen. I'm not closing myself off, I'm just not opening myself up to disaster, that's all. I love my own company, I really enjoy it.'

GLORIA STEINEM

'We are becoming the men we wanted to marry.'

IX: THE 'HAPPILY-EVER-AFTER' MARRIAGE MYTH

IS MARRIAGE EASY STREET, REALLY?

What's that noise? Is that all the divorcees who are reading this laughing their heads off? Oh hi! *Waves* You know the truth. You know it's not easy street.

However, honestly, I swear to Maya Angelou, there are plenty of never-been-married people who truly believe that once they get married, they will be able to put their metaphorical and financial feet up. I know! But they really do.

I occasionally slip into being one of them. I was recently saying to my married friend Jen that 'I feel like if I had a partner, life would be easier, we'd share the food shopping, share the cooking, share the household chores, share the bill-paying'.

She encouraged me to think back to the two times I have cohabited with partners. 'Was it really easier?' she asked. 'Because even though my husband is great, I found living on my own easier.' (And then Jen asked me what I miss most about being in a relationship, and I said 'giving affection' and started stroking her thigh and her hair, while she looked slightly scared.)

Well, gee whiz. Knock me down with a feather. Jen was totally right. It wasn't easier. At all. Even when I did live with a boyfriend who pulled his weight (the first one), it didn't lessen my work, the life-min merely doubled and was split. When I lived with a boyfriend who treated me like a domestic slave (the second), my work became much greater, because I was picking up after him, doing his washing, and so on.

My fantasies about marital easy street bear no resemblance to the reality of cohabitation I have experienced. I rhapsodize about the foot rubs my mythical husband would give me, but those never materialized in my years of cohabiting, and what's more, I don't even like foot rubs.

But if you had looked at the social media representation of me with either serious boyfriend, you would have seen a different story. You would have seen the rose-glow version. #nofilter my ass. The pink-cheeked us having climbed a mountain, us on apparently hilarious dog walks, us hosting cosy dinner parties. You didn't see the bitter arguments over why there's no milk, or the stony-silenced meals, or the tense car trips, or the nights in separate sleeping quarters.

This is why comparing the reality of your situation to somebody's Facebook representation is truly like splicing your behind-the-scenes bloopers with their glossy best-bits showreel.

We don't see *any* of the negatives on couples' social media. Which is why it's so easy to romanticize coupledom. It's smugged all over social media. I've done it myself.

And yet, no one evens up the score, by saying how happy they are single. Or, I haven't seen them do so, anyhow. Single joy is not visible in my feed, and believe me, I put my hours in on the socials.

'I have noticed that we think that whatever we *don't have* will make us happy,' says psychotherapist Hilda Burke. 'I've worked with a number of single, successful women in their mid-to-late thirties, who want a partner and a baby, feel their clock ticking, and harbour a fantasy that their life will be so much easier *if only* they had a husband. After a session with a woman in this predicament, I'll often see a couple straight afterwards and hear one of the partners expressing their fantasy that *if only* they were single again, their life would be happy and uncomplicated.'

Intrigued, I asked some friends of mine to tell me what marriage is really like. (Note that all of these friends are *happily married*, so this is inevitably skewed towards the positive. I didn't ask the fractious couples about this, because...*grits teeth and grimaces*.)

WENDY SAYS: Here's the truth: marriage is hard work. While I'm under no illusions that divorce can be even harder, I don't think I was psychologically prepared for the constant graft and compromise marriage involves.

OK, it's great to pool two incomes and buy a nice house. But it also means you have to live with his giant TV and regularly defend the right to keep your shoes because he thinks they're clutter. You wipe the crumbs off the kitchen counter that he never, ever sees, while he watches sport on that giant TV and wilfully ignores you cleaning up after him again. You have to put the bins out at least half as often as he does or you're a bad feminist.

Work-wise, if you do a job that is equal to his in terms of income, you do it without wifely niceties such as dinner on the table or walking in to a weekend of carefully curated social activities. If he earns significantly more than you, then yes, it does open you up to privileges like posh restaurants and long-haul holidays, but he will always make it known that he is the one who worked for it. You'll miss the evenings you came home from work late without having to talk when you walked in the door. You'll miss eating cereal for dinner. You'll have someone to share your problems with, but he will tell you how to solve them. You'll take on his troubles and be baffled by his inability to drink less/let go of his phone/say the right thing to his parents. He will be more frustrated by your problems than his own.

So, marriage is not easy street. I could write an equal-sized essay on the benefits of marriage, and therein lies the whole truth: marriage is hard work, but when it does work, it's worth it.

NINA SAYS: I keep my marriage happy by keeping it as 'single' as I possibly can, to minimize niggles.

1. There's absolutely no aphrodisiac like time apart. Missing each other feels good – whether it's nights out spent separately, work trips away or going against the conventions of what a marriage 'should' look like and spending Christmas apart, like we do. Give each other space, quiet moments, solo time.

2. Buy the biggest bed you can afford. The dream is to feel like you're still sleeping alone.

3. Never argue hungry. Never attempt a DIY project without snacks. 99 per cent of arguments don't happen when both people are full.

4 If you couldn't be bothered to cook when single and lived on Deliveroos, you're unlikely to suddenly become a top chef once married. Continue to live on Deliveroos and cut yourself some slack.

5 Get a cleaner. Treat your marital home like a flat-share – get an impartial professional in who LIKES cleaning.

A weird thing about marriage is that your partner will suddenly throw complete shade at your way of doing certain things – loading the dishwasher, how soon after eating a meal that you clear the plates away, why you have no idea where the five different pensions you've had from previous employers are. And you'll have NO rationale or comeback for why you do it that way/have done that other than, 'It just is'.

Marriage is a tremendous, eye-opening, secret-outing sharing of assets. Everything gets put in one pot, rather than 'your money' and 'their money'. And it can be brilliant, financially: the pooling of resources can allow big purchases that individually you might never have achieved. But you need to be very aligned on your spending goals and habits, particularly if one partner out-earns the other, or one has debts.

FLORENCE SAYS: I've just got home to discover that – during the hottest heatwave I've ever known – my husband has left the freezer door open. So, not only has all the fish in the freezer had to go in the bin but also the ice lolly I've been fantasizing about all afternoon. Oh, and there's the soggy floor he hasn't 'noticed'. Apparently I am 'nagging' for getting home after a crap day, stepping in dirty fish juice and telling him off for being careless.

If you are expecting moving in with a man to be like getting an on-call handyman/financial adviser/sex beast/spider slayer, I have to disappoint you. These days, very few men can multitask to that degree.

In my house, I am the fuse fixer. If the boiler breaks, I'm on it. I manage all the bank accounts and bills. I deal with the mortgage, talk to plumbers and have to leave him scripts if electricians come around and I can't be there.

Here are the upsides: it is lovely to live with your best friend, have cuddles on tap, someone to make your dinner (I'm rubbish; he's great), reassure you that you look nice (when you know you don't) and book holidays with.

But he hates my taste in TV and we have a rule we can't both be in the kitchen at the same time or there would be a divorce.

When he goes away, I miss him madly. When he comes back, I pine for the boy-mess-free life I briefly had.

Now I feel guilty...He has just come in and apologized about the freezer. Apparently, it was an accident caused by him trying to make me a nice cold smoothie for when I got in from work. He has given me this information with his big blue eyes. Maybe living with boys isn't so bad after all.

JEN SAYS: Getting married is a cakewalk. I organized the whole thing myself within a few months without breaking a sweat. I got my dress in the first shop we went in. I was like, 'This is the badger!' My mum was gutted.

Being happily married is another story.

We all know that almost half of all marriages end in divorce, so obviously getting hitched is no guarantee of lasting love. Yet, sometimes people think that if they just got married, they'd also get a happily-ever-after voucher, and of course that's codswallop.

Being married is not all hearts and flowers. In fact, it rarely is. Mostly it's wet towels on the floor and toenail clippings in the bed. Any happy relationship takes work. It takes commitment and maintenance. Patience and tolerance. Compromise and negotiation. Sacrifice and perseverance.

Buddying up with someone might benefit you financially, or it might not. It could financially ruin you instead. You might fall in love with someone who does all the cooking and cleaning, and brings you breakfast in bed with the morning papers. Or you might wind up with a lazybum who doubles your workload and forgets your birthday.

I got married three years ago, while still in my thirties, to a guy I'd been with for three years. (All the threes are just a coincidence.) I got married mainly for the party and to see if anything did actually change. Nothing significant changed.

I love my husband immensely, but I loved him just as much before our wedding. The ceremony didn't make our relationship any stronger. *We* make our relationship stronger.

My life wasn't empty before I met him. It was just different. Mostly, I love being married. But I also mostly loved being single too. One situation isn't inherently better than the other. There are pros and cons. As with anything – it is what you make of it, so try to make the absolute most of whatever you have, while you still have it.

AND THEY LIVED HAPPILY-FOR-A-BIT

There's a persistent myth afoot in society, a consistent delusion, that married people are happier than single people.

Which leads to this conversation.

1. Well-meaning married person tries to cure my singleness by: (delete as appropriate) telling me to be less choosy, spend less time on my career, stay still and stop flitting off to other countries, or go out with their mate (who I don't want to go out with).

2. I smile, thank them, and tell them I'm just fine.

3. They cock their head with sympathy and say, 'I just want to see you happy'.

If I had a pound for every time I've had this conversation, I'd have...OK, only around £9. But still. That's nearly a tenner. I don't know any single person who hasn't had this 'I just want to see you happy' conversation, repeatedly.

However, research shows that this 'married people are loads happier' thing is not true. I'm afraid that there is absolutely zero proof of that society-wide delusion. I looked. Sorry, Marriage Myth Committee, your claims are sandcastles in the sky.

What is true, however, is that both couples and singles believe that a significant other makes them happier. A 2012 survey of 20,000 adults conducted in 24 countries found that 45 per cent of the singles think that finding a partner would make them happier. While nearly two-thirds of married couples and people with a significant other say their partner is the most important source of happiness in their lives.

In fact, the 'they lived happily-ever-after' trope would more accurately read 'they lived happily-for-a-bit'.

Just like when I went to get my teeth whitened, and ended up getting my 'teeth samed' by some cowboy dentist who laughed all the way to the bank, married people wind up with the *same* happiness, once the confetti has settled.

Bella DePaulo, a former professor of psychology at the University of California, uses graphs to show this same-same effect, in her TEDx talk, *What no one ever told you about people who are single.*

A bunch of college students were asked to predict their future happiness, single or married. As expected, their predictions of marital happiness were astronomical, shooting-star-level, euphorically high. Way below on the graph a sad little line showed their dismal projections of single happiness levels.

DePaulo then rolls out the hard data of long-term single happiness: which is much higher than the students predicted. Then, she shows what actually happens when people get married, the real data, rather than the fairyland-imagined data. There is indeed a 'small increase', a little happiness bump, just before and after the wedding, lasting roughly a year either side.

But then, something unexpected happens. Their happiness levels *resume to the happiness levels they had as a single*. See? Same-same. Happiness-saming. Maybe the anticipation, delight and aftermath of a wedding just makes people happy, rather than the actual marriage.

The biggest study of married vs single happiness ever done, which looked at more than 24,000 people over 15 years, also found that the happiness bump before and after marriage was tiny. 'It showed that on average, marriage increases your happiness by one per cent,' says psychologist Jennifer L Taitz.

THE FEAR OF THE ALTERNATIVE

We are so brainwashed by the 'happier together' myth that once we're in a relationship, we clutch it like a life raft. A terrifying study surveyed 20,000 adults and found that a quarter of coupled-up people said that *nothing would make them happier* than finding another partner. A quarter! Ticked that.

These people should clearly be single. Which makes me really, really sad. Fear of singledom keeps so many people stuck.

So, in summation, single is not better than being married, but it's not worse either, save that two-year wedding bump. Single people are not less happy, big picture wise. Tapping up existential joy has very little do with whether there's a ring on your finger.

'Happiness in marriage is entirely a matter of chance.'

— *JANE AUSTEN*

FAMOUS WOMEN WHO MARRIED LATE

A US study found that if you wait until after 25 to get married, your marriage is much more likely to survive. In Britain, the amount of women getting married in their late thirties/early forties has doubled in the past decade.

Charlotte Brontë, who married aged 38, wrote this in a letter to a friend after her marriage: 'I know more of the realities of life than I once did. I think many false ideas are propagated...For my part I can only say with deeper sincerity and fuller significance – what I always said in theory – Wait…'.

Helen Mirren didn't marry until she was 51. 'I married Taylor a lot later in my life and it's worked out great...always give your partner the freedom and support to achieve their ambitions.'

Mariella Frostrup recently said that she is, 'relieved I didn't meet my husband until I was nearly 40', because with expected lifespans now extending, she has 'reduced that daunting time span to a slightly more manageable duration'.

Julianna Margulies didn't marry until 41. 'I feel very grateful that I had the courage to say no when I did and say yes when I could, that I waited to find the right mate and to have this little family.'

Elizabeth Gilbert writes in *Committed: A Love Story*: 'I had jumped into my first marriage, at the totally unfinished age of 25, much the same way that a Labrador jumps into a swimming pool – with exactly that much preparation and foresight. Back when I was 25, I was so irresponsible that I probably should not have been allowed to choose my own toothpaste, much less my own future'.

That marriage ended after six years.

She later wrote, 'Marriage is not a game for the young. Wait as long as you humanly can to get married, and your odds of staying with one partner forever will increase dramatically. If you wait until you are, say, 35 years old to get married, your odds of success are pretty terrific.'

REASONS I PROBABLY SHOULDN'T GET MARRIED

1. I AM PRONE TO PROFOUND DOMESTIC DISENCHANTMENT

Despite being very happy with Tom, I would experience this intense sadness whenever I sat down for a workaday dinner with him, after moving in. It was an 'Is this it?' ennui. I would feel like crying. Like my heart was being squeezed by a fist. And I didn't know why. Now I think I do.

It was the sensation that my world was shrinking, the walls were closing in, like in a trippy dream. That the horizon was no longer accessible. I'd secured him, I was living with him, so this was the dream right?

Except, now I was feeling this enveloping sorrow at the thought of this being the rest of my life. Me + him + dinner forevermore. Like a kid who spends all their pocket money hooking ducks at the fair and then when they finally have the coveted teddy bear is like, 'Oh, do I even want this?'

Later that night, we would curl around each other and fit like nesting bowls, and I would dismiss the profound disenchantment. But then it would happen again. And again.

I had it with another boyfriend I lived with too: Ralph. And I've figured out why. Neither Tom nor Ralph were travellers. They didn't give a monkey's about leaving Belgium/England. Neither wanted to live anywhere but where we were currently living. Which made me restless as hell. I think I have gypsy blood.

2. I'D RATHER BE DELILAH

D'you remember the 'You're a spinster!' speech my dad delivered to me, when I was 33? During it, he lobbed something at me about 'You're going to wind up like Delilah Dingalong!' (totally just made up that name, to protect this person's identity).

I remember this coming back to me again and again, long after that shouting match. See, the thing was, when I compared the lives of Delilah Dingalong (my dad's ex) and her counterpart (my dad's current wife) I much preferred Delilah's life. She frequently ate buns in bed, spent evenings reading books by candlelight, owned five dogs and two horses, and lived in a rural idyll the likes of which would feature on a

'Magical Ireland' tourist board advert.

In contrast, my dad's wife was basically his domestic slave: cooking, cleaning, washing, going to the gym obsessively (because otherwise he'd tease her about getting fat), playing video games with him, dressing up like a doll when they went out for dinner.

Given the choice, I didn't want to be slave wife, I wanted to be buns-in-bed Delilah.

3. I LOVE BEING ALONE

'Alone' and 'lonely' are very different things. Alone is a place I go where I can truly relax, exhale, and do whatever the heck I want. I need to be alone to work; unless it's quiet, I can't hear what I need to write. I very rarely feel 'lonely'. I can do three solid days of that, until I start to crave company, and am liable to draw a face on a volleyball and call it Wilson.

Meanwhile, some of my most excruciatingly lonely times have been in relationships where I feel unheard, uncherished, unappreciated. You can be lonely in a roomful of people. In a bed with someone 6cm away. In a wedding gown about to get married. 'Lonely' is a state of mind, while 'alone' is merely circumstantial.

In most of my happiest childhood memories, I was alone. We would go to this remote cottage in Donegal, halfway up a mountain. It had no electricity, so we ate by candlelight and cut turf to burn for warmth. There was no running water, so we'd wash in the waterfall. We read books and played gin rummy and slept in an enormous timber bunk bed ('Bagsy the top bunk'), underneath a skylight crammed with stars. It was heaven.

My brother and I would sprint out of the door at 8am and only come back to eat; dirty, happy and with lungfuls of fresh air. We would play at being 'kings and queens' of our kingdom of sheep and then, while my brother swashbuckled with twig light sabres and constructed elaborate *Star Wars* storylines, I would sneak off and play with the millions of pin-head-sized baby frogs on a bog dotted with buttercups, a bog that would try to steal your welly given half a chance. Or slip-slide down the mountain to go and see Daisy, the farmer's donkey, who I was besotted with.

And then I grew up and was taught that being alone was sad, and togetherness was where the happy was.

4. I PREFER LIVING ALONE

I never have to answer a text or phonecall asking me, 'What's for dinner?' as if I am somehow in charge of dinner. Who made me the Mayoress of Dinner? I don't recall running for that office.

I also really like only having to wrangle my own mess. Having been raised by a crumb-fearing mother ('What are all these CRUMBS?' was probably the most oft-spoken phrase of my childhood), I am now more fastidious than your average bear about my surroundings. I end up doing housework that's not mine because it bleeps in the corner like a Pokémon, flashing, waiting to be caught. I need to attend to it, otherwise it does my head in.

It's so restful to come home, shut the door and have my own little nook. With no one to tell me that there are too many candles or cushions, or indeed, to tell you that there are too many Xboxes and samurai swords, or vinyls and bike parts, or vintage travel posters and pasta makers, or whatever your bag is.

Alain de Botton says that some people are simply not naturally assembled for cohabiting, and I suspect I might be one of them.

5. MARRIAGE MIGHT KIBOSH THE THINGS I WANT TO DO

There are three things I've done in the past few years that have been the absolute pinnacles of my existence on planet Earth so far. They were: living in Bruges, writing my first book and my current situation – living in Barcelona.

Had I been married, I'm really not sure any of those things would have happened. Would I have been able to bugger off to another country? Would I have been able to go through spells of writing for 12 hours a day, if I'd been coupled? Doubtful. But I have. And I've enjoyed every minute.

I would have had to...compromise. Take my partner's feelings into account. Let them read the manuscript of *The Unexpected Joy of Being Sober* and listen to feedback as to whether they were cool with my revealing details of drunken one-night stands. Not go and live in a different country for seven months, if they didn't want me to.

I mean, I could have gone to Bruges for three weeks maybe, or I could have written a watered-down, less raw book, but man-oh-man, that would have been annoying when what I wanted was to grab each endeavour by the scruff of the neck. Single, I have been able to make my own decisions without considering anyone else's feelings.

Paulo Coelho once wrote, 'Stress, anxiety and depression are caused when we are living to please others.'

I please myself. I decide when I want to leave a party, I decide what I want to do this weekend and who I want to see, without having to consult *anyone else*. It's wondrous.

6. I'M TEAM PUPPY RATHER THAN TEAM BABY

Give me a puppy and I will coo and take a million pictures and try to kidnap it. Give me a baby and I'll hold it fearfully, in the manner of cradling an atomic bomb, for as long as is polite, and then hand it back.

Toddlers? Heck yes. You can make cushion forts and do magic tricks where you just chuck things behind your back, or conjure coins from behind your ear, and they think you're frickin' magical. Toddlers are a riot.

But babies? I just don't get it. I'm not clucky, I'm not into it, I don't lose my mind over miniature Converse like other women. If I found a superb partner and we had money enough to pay people to take the child off us, and I had space to do my own thing for a few hours a day, maybe I could be a mother, but otherwise, probably not.

Today I was watching a super-cute kid swim on her back, like a wriggly seal, and I thought how cool it would be to look at her and think, 'I made that'. But then I realized that when your heart detaches from your body and starts walking around, or swimming around like a slippery seal, that must be both profound and incredibly alarming. Because what if something happened to that seal? I'm not sure I could hack it.

7. THE THOUGHT OF FINANCE-MERGING FREAKS ME THE FACK OUT

When I was a twentysomething imbecile (not a pop at all twentysomethings; only myself), I thought that getting married would be like getting a credit card that you'd never have to pay off. 'Free money! What's his is mine, right? And he can have access to alllll my Rimmel make-up with broken lids. Sweet!'

Yet again, I was labouring under an assumption that when I got married, I would become a different person. Just like when I wanted a 'big wedding' and forgot that the idea of dancing in front of a hundred people would likely cause me to have a heart attack.

In the past five years, I have always chosen to split costs clean down the middle despite what my partner earns. There's been the odd occasion where a boyfriend has bought me an expensive dress as a treat, but when that happened, I didn't like feeling beholden to him.

Marrying someone minted and merging our finances might indeed enable me to live in a huge house, or to holiday in Aspen, and he might be able to spoil me with spa days, but those spa days would come with strings and guilt, in my head.

I used to think I wanted a higher-earning spouse so that I could loll around on a chaise longue in a silk dressing gown eating sugared almonds all day, but the reality is, even if I had that option, I would want to work and pay my way. Writing lights me up like a lantern; after a few days of non-working, I start to feel full of shadows.

Ali Wong's *Baby Cobra* Netflix show became phenomenally popular not only because she's a comic genius but also because she actually said what a million women were thinking: that she got knocked up because she didn't 'want to work no more'.

A friend of a friend once told me that she got pregnant because she wanted a 'rest' from her demanding job (all the mothers reading this laugh forever at the idea of motherhood being a 'rest').

Many single women fantasize about lying at home, caressing a swollen belly, no longer needing to work. I'm sure many single men also fantasize about marrying an heiress and being able to play *Grand Theft Auto* all day.

But do you really want that? Imagine having to ask your partner for money. Or buying a pair of shoes and having to answer to them about the purchase. I can't even! I would hate that.

I'm so used to having my own mismanaged money. As much as twentysomething me thought she wanted a walking cash machine, thirtysomething me knows that in reality, I wouldn't want to use it.

I've also watched a few of my friends go through the agonizing division of assets that a divorce brings.

I don't know what it will look like, if I ever marry, but I do now know that finance-merging is not always joyous. Plus, I've dated a millionaire, and he was an egomaniac. Careful what you wish for, amigos.

REASONS TO GET MARRIED

1. BECAUSE YOU DON'T WANT TO DIE ALONE.

I hate to break it to you, but they may well die on you. Leaving you to die alone.

This is also not a decent reason to have children. Retirement homes are crammed with people who had kids to look after them into their dotage. Imagine how maddening that would be, if you spent 18, nay more like 30 years, raising them, and then they stuffed you into 'Happy Valley' as soon as you started needing nappies.*

2. FOR FINANCIAL SECURITY

Marriage absolutely has the potential to take you up a notch wealth-wise. But it also has the potential to take you to the cleaners. What if your partner loses their job, you know you'll have to support them, plus you, on one salary, right? What if they turn out to be a total financial fuckwit, who runs up loads of credit card debt? And if it all goes tits up, as 42 per cent of British marriages tragically do, divorce is eye-wateringly expensive. The average divorce costs £70,000.

3. BECAUSE SOCIETY EXPECTS YOU TO

If the only reason you want to get married is so that you can feel like an authorized grown-up, a licensed person, an approved human, then definitely don't.

I realized this recently: one of my favourite things about being in relationships is that I can say, 'Oh no, I HAVE a boyfriend'. Or walk down the street with him and feel endorsed by his adoring gaze.

Doing things merely because society expects them of you is a surefire way to wind up on your death bed saying 'I wish I'd...'. Joan Didion once said: 'To free us from the expectations of others, to give us back to ourselves – there lies the great, singular power of self-respect.'

---

* On the flipside, if that did happen, I'd finally be able to make fine use of my A-Level memorization of King Lear's wild-eyed speech, 'How sharper than a serpent's tooth it is to have a thankless child!'

To hell with what society thinks; give yourself back to *yourself*.

4. BECAUSE YOU LOVE THEM TO BITS...

And can't imagine ever wanting to be without them. This is the only reason that is actually wise. The only reason we'll keep.

If you would marry them even if you couldn't tell anyone else, ever; if you would marry them if you couldn't wear a ring; if you had to get married in an empty room wearing a bin-bag, and you still *would*. Then that's a great litmus test that you *should*.

If I ever meet someone where this applies, I probably will marry them.

X: COLOUR YOURSELF IN COMPLETELY

AN UNFINISHED PICTURE

'Nothing will work unless you do.'

– MAYA ANGELOU

I remember bemoaning my lack of another half to my mate Kate, who is basically Yoda, and she said to me: 'But Cath, two incomplete people don't make a healthy relationship. Two *complete* people do.' The subtext was like a bucket of cold water over a drunk person.

I was indeed incomplete. I realized that I was like a picture that had only been coloured in halfway. I hadn't bothered to colour in several sections, because I'd thought that someone else would come along, and we would merge and overlap, and their colours would shade in my blank bits.

I think many of us do this. The man who hasn't learned to cook or wash his own clothes; the woman who thinks that her Future Husband will curb her snowballing shopping addiction; the person who believes that they will become tidier once they live with someone else; the one who wants to go travelling, once they meet someone to do it with; the person who tells themselves they'll get fit once they have a running partner.

We consciously or unconsciously don't complete ourselves. Is it any wonder we then feel incomplete?

Confronting the fact I was like a half-finished picture was tough, but a crucial step in my love addiction rehab.

OLD ATTITUDE: **'I will learn to drive once I'm settled in the country/ planning kids'**

NEW ATTITUDE: **'I will learn to drive *now*'**

When I turned 18, my mum and stepdad gave me £500 and said, 'We strongly suggest you spend this on learning to drive'. So I spent it on clubbing, tiny dresses, cider and Embassy Number 1. That money kept me in hangovers for over a year. Score.

Then I moved to London aged 23 and never felt the need for a car. Nor the desire, given you weren't allowed to get sh*tfaced while driving, and slugging from a wine bottle while kerbcrawling for hot men was frowned upon.

But now I don't drink at all, and I don't need to buy micro outfits from Pineapple for clubbing, and I don't tether life goals to, 'I'll do that once I meet *him*' so I am finally learning to drive. Which feels incredibly satisfying. I mean, I'm terrible at it, I tried to go down a cycle lane yesterday in order to slavishly follow a sat nav, and I try to get into the wrong side of the car constantly, but I'll improve.

OLD ATTITUDE: 'I will get my future boyfriend to put that picture up'

NEW ATTITUDE: 'I will do it myself'

There is no such thing as 'blue' or 'pink' tasks, only tasks. And I've recently realized that you really don't require a penis to hang a picture, or back up your files, or assemble flatpack furniture. All you actually need is a brain, some tools that ideally aren't miniature and pink, and maybe YouTube. Similarly, you don't need a vagina to sew on a button or iron something; or boobs to make a casserole; or oestrogen to make a house 'homey'.

It was empowering to discover that in order to emancipate my strawberry jam from a jar whose lid was clearly screwed on by some *Terminator*-strong factory-bot, all I need is a rubber band, rather than a man.

Maybe this is blindingly obvious to you, and has been since year dot, but, for me, it was a revelation. Tasks don't have colours.

OLD ATTITUDE: 'Meeting them will start me saving'

NEW ATTITUDE: 'I will look after Future Me'

Throughout my life, I have been haunted by my own personal four horsemen of the apocalypse: anxiety, drinking, love addiction and money.

The first two are now in my rear-view mirror, mere dots in the road behind, and I am currently taming the third right here in these pages. But the fourth, money, is still something that scares the bejesus out of me.

There's a scene in the *Lord of the Rings* films where the hobbits are being pursued by a merciless Ringwraith and they hide in a hollow underneath a tree's roots, bricking themselves.

That's basically how I feel about money. 'Hide! Be quiet! If I don't make a sound, it won't find me!' While the menacing money horse stamps and scrapes and whinnies above me.

Alongside that terror, lives my cavalier attitude to money, whereby I'm like, 'WOOHOO. Fun coupons! Let's spend it! Oh, it's all gone. Aargh.' And repeat, ad infinitum.

I'm basically like Leonardo DiCaprio in *The Wolf of Wall Street*, who shouts from his moored yacht: 'Hey, you guys, look what I found in my pocket!' and then peels off notes and throws them to the strangers beneath, like seeds to birds.

My stepdad and I have a running joke, whereby a few days after payday he'll say to me, 'Have you managed to get rid of all your money yet?' And I'll say, 'Not yet, but NEARLY.' He then replies, 'You can do it, I believe in you.'

So, fun coupons. Money burning a hole in my pocket. Except I'm not a multi-millionaire, in fact I earn about a quarter of what most of my friends (lawyers and accountants...and more lawyers and accountants) do. So, y'know, that's not really working out for me. However, I did manage to go on about four holidays last year, if you include mini-breaks, so I'm clearly far from destitute.

Chasing the horizon and taking pictures of rainbows is what I love, but pictures of rainbows aren't recognized by the bank as legal tender. I own lots of books, but unless I want to fashion a fairytale house out of my books and live in them in the manner of the little old lady who lived in a shoe, I need an alternative plan to keep Future Me in roofing, peppermint tea and yoga classes.

I'm 38 and have only just cleared my ever-present debt and started saving. I previously always thought that my future beau would take my financial fuckwittery into hand, and we would save together, and that would be that problem fixed. *Dusts hands*

Now I've realized that it's down to me. It's on me. It's up to me. I owe it to Future Me. Just like nobody else could fix my drinking problem other than me, nobody can fix my money problem other than me.

DISCLAIMER: THE SINGLE FINANCIAL STRUGGLE IS REAL

Having said all of that, it's worth pointing out that the single financial struggle is very real, rather than imaginary. In Britain, singles pay on average £1,800 a year more on household expenses than couples. Another study estimated that the average single spends an extra £266,000 on living costs over their lifetime.

We also pay nearly double what couples do on holiday, given we can't split the share of a room. These extra living expenses mean that couples have on average £6,000 in savings, while singles only have £2,000.

The majority of singles say that if they were suddenly jobless, their savings would be gobbled up within a fortnight. (I don't know how they can spend £2,000 in two weeks, but hey ho.) And that is a scary place to be. A fortnight from potential homelessness? Yikes.

People who get married and stay married have 77 per cent more net worth per person than single people, said research by Ohio State University. Just 36 per cent of singles in the UK say they feel financially secure, compared to 52 per cent of those who are in a relationship.

So yeah, it's real, you're not imagining it.

However, on the flipside, singles earn a lot more. Like, a LOT. A US report called 'Knot Yet' found that highly educated women who delay marriage until their thirties earn on average $18,000 a year more than a woman who married in her twenties.

OLD ATTITUDE: 'I will buy property when I meet *them*'

NEW ATTITUDE: 'I will try to buy ASAP'

Similarly, I'd always told myself that there was no point even trying to buy property while single. And I'm far from alone. A third of renting, single Brits think they have no chance of buying, until they meet a partner.

Mortgages are something to enter into as a pair, I thought. But that means I have been chucking money down the rent-chute for my entire adult life. It makes no sense. So now I am pointing myself towards buying alone.

It's always been a popular strategy (particularly among women) to go into cohabiting or marriage with an emergency running-away fund: 'In event of split, smash glass.' But now, people are beginning to upgrade from a secret savings account (or a 'knipple' in Yiddish) to a break-up bolthole. They're beginning to buy and maintain their own separate property, should things go south. Friends of mine have told me that they will always maintain their own property, no matter what betrothal or babies lie ahead, as an insurance fund. Property is power.

It makes absolute sense and is something everyone should perhaps shoot for, whether male or female, richer or poorer. Even if you can only afford a tiny flat in the provinces or a parking space in London (me, probably, when I eventually apply for a mortgage and get laughed at), it's still better than the rent-chute.

You may need to use the shared ownership government scheme, or you may need to beg your family to go in with you. Joint mortgages don't necessarily spring from being in a couple. You can team up with anyone.

It's the property version of a panic room, having your own break-up bolthole. A joint mortgage that starts out feeling like a golden handshake can later morph to become steel handcuffs. I know couples who have had to live together for months and months after splitting, while waiting for their house to sell, since neither of them could afford both the mortgage repayments *and* rent.

BUT HOLD UP: YOU'RE NOT AN ISLAND

However, this colouring-in lark doesn't mean you have to do everything alone. You are not Atlas, who carried the world on his back. It can feel juvenile asking your parents for a loan, or asking your brother to help you move house, but it's not. You're merely doing what married people do all the time: asking for help.

I once said to my stepdad that as a single person, I sometimes feel like there's nobody to lean on when the shit hits the fan. 'But you do have someone,' he said. 'You have us. *Lean in.*'

It changed how I see everything. So now, I lean in, and not in a Sheryl Sandberg way. In an... 'and e-x-h-a-l-e' way.

THE GETTING-SHIT-DONE LULLABY

So, when I started making inroads into driving, beginner's DIY, saving and looking to buy, my oneomania calmed down and went to sleep, as if I'd sung it a lullaby. The ability to stand alone, to provide for myself, appeared to be part of the antidote to my man-vacancy panic.

We shelve all of the aforementioned Adulting, thinking we'll sort it later. Which merely puts more unseen pressure on ourselves to couple. This time created entirely by ourselves. We can't point fingers at films, fairytales or society on this one.

I think our urge for a relationship is tangled up, and sometimes confused, like a ball of mixed strands of wool, with our urge to have security and a pot of gold at the end of the working rainbow.

It felt insanely good, doing all the Adulting. I felt calmer. Because I'd started creating my own security, rather than looking for it on *Hinge*. My aim now is to colour myself in all the dang way. Every corner, every tricky bit, every inch of sky. I highly recommend it. After all, if you're complete without them, a partner becomes a choice rather than a necessity.

'If we did all the things we are capable of, we would literally astound ourselves.'

– *Thomas Edison*

XI: HOW TO DATE
IN MODERATION

RESPONSIBLE DATING

OK, so, realistically, we're not going to forsake people we fancy altogether, locking our legs shut forevermore, or hanging up our lucky pants for all eternity.

Y'know those little tags in drink adverts/labels on booze that say 'Drink Responsibly' (personally: never did, never will, *never gonna happen*. Also, I hate those labels because they oh-so-subtly place the blame on the person, rather than the booze, if they wind up wasted: 'We told you to drink responsibly! You mis-used our luxury product!').

I digress. We're not talking about drinking, we're talking about dating, and unlike 'Drink Responsibly', 'Date Responsibly' is a lot more achievable. We've just never been taught how to do it. Especially in the new way-too-much-information digital realm.

When I told a friend of mine about writing this book, she said, 'But you've been dating, so you're not happily single'. Wha? Whoa there, missy. Hold your horses.

Of course I am. I've dated plenty of totally decent catches who I've chosen not to be with, because the whole point is: I only want to settle with the one I can't *not settle* with. (And if that means I never settle at all, then that's A-OK with me nowadays.)

There are not a mere two tick-boxes to choose from:

☐ Happily single and not dating

☐ Unhappily single and dating

No. The world is not black/white. There are not two doors behind which you can live. There are a million doors to choose from. Happily single and seeking a meaningful relationship can co-exist. They are not mutually exclusive.

But we now know that we can be just as happy without a relationship, so unless you catch yourself a remarkable fish, perhaps throw them back into the dating pool: 'So long, friend.'

The door I have chosen to live behind now is, 'Happily single and sometimes dating, if I feel like it'. My baseline is happy, no matter what the outcome. If a guy cancels a date these days, I'm pretty relieved rather than 'Wahhhh'. There are perks to a cancelled date. I don't have to spend an hour applying make-up and doing my hair (which realistically, I am never going to stop doing pre-date), so I can go to yoga and get my sweat on instead.

If something falls apart after a couple of months, I'm deflated for a few days for sure, but then I bounce back up to baseline happy. That, dear reader, is a revelation for me.

I decided to teach myself how to live in this 'dating but not that overly invested' place through a lot of reading, a lot of expert insight, and a lot of trial and error. Now I *can* date without losing my mind. Without my marbles skittering all over the floor, and shooting into irretrievable darkness beneath the fridge.

Here are the tools I used. Who knows, maybe they'll help you too. To 'moderdate'* with perspective, humour and bounceback self-esteem. To see dating as fun, rather than a chore. To stop feeling like you've strapped yourself into a theme park ride that tosses you mercilessly about like a giant juggling with a mouse.

To hang out with a guy without finding yourself going into 'private' mode on your computer and stalking his LinkedIn at midnight. To get to know a gal without just-so-happening to go to her favourite cafe, 'because you like it there'. (No you don't. Leave.)

If you're ready, come live with me behind the 'Happily single and occasionally dating' door. It's a really lovely place to be.

REFRAMING THEM AS A PERSON, NOT A POTENTIAL SPOUSE

We are meeting a person, a potential friend, not a potential future husband/wife. This is not an arranged marriage meet. We don't *have to marry them*. Or *get them to want to marry us*. We don't even have to fancy them, or get them to fancy us. If it just so happens that this person later becomes a potential partner, then great, but if not, no biggie.

My friend Laurie recently said, 'Why is it that I never get nervous about

* I know moderdate doesn't quite work, but we're just going to run with it, K?

meeting potential friends? I don't worry whether they'll like me, I just think if it's meant to happen, it'll happen. I went for a coffee with a woman last week and while it was lovely, there was no friend spark, and I didn't take that remotely personally, nor did she. We just didn't...fit. So why is it that when I meet a man for a date, and the same misfit thing happens, it cuts me to the core and I think there's something inherently wrong with me?'

Right?! I am the same as Laurie. I can take it as a personal affront, a sign I'm broken, a message I'm unlovable, whenever somebody doesn't want to date me. But that's because I've framed the dates in my head as Potential Future Husband.

So, now I practise seeing dates as just meeting a potential new friend for a coffee/walk/whatever. It helps shrink the enormity of it, cutting it down to a much more manageable size. If it's a non-starter, it's nothing to do with me/them being inadequate, it's simply that we didn't *fit*.

DODGING THE LATER-IN-LIFE PRESSURE

The early-twentysomething who didn't give a flying fig whether it led to a second date can morph into a tense-thirtysomething who feels like this is their final punt at locking down a partner.

When we're dating in our thirties and beyond, it feels like the stakes are higher. Like pushing all our casino chips onto one number of the roulette wheel. It's nerve-wracking AF. Aargh. *Looks away as the ball clatters into its slot*

But it's only that way because we let it feel that way. Re-think it. You're pushing a 'week' chip rather than an 'entire life' chip onto the number. There's no giant egg timer with an alarmingly fast cascade of sand.

Well, there is, but it likely has four decades of sand in it, not three years' worth. We're not going to cease to be attractive, or interesting, or datable, just because we turn a certain age.

PLENTY OF HEADSPACE

Also, remember the advice from Hilda on page 169. If it helps you to think, 'I have five more years before I panic', if that gives you some headspace, some breathing room, then do that. *There is no 'right' way to do this.*

It's like how some people say, 'I'm not drinking this year' rather than, 'I'm never drinking again'. Do what helps you. Make up your own rules. If *not settling* is more important to you than fitting neatly into society's expectations, remember that you've chosen that.

FROM ANXIOUS TO EXHILARATED

Despite all of my perspective-adjusting, dates are still as nerve-wracking as hurtling down a black ski run, especially when you don't drink. One of the best pieces of advice I've ever had on this was from my friend Sam Purser-Barriff, a psychotherapist, who suggested that I sidestep from anxiety to excitement.

'Tell yourself you're excited, exhilarated, buzzing about going on this date, rather than stressed,' she said. 'The thing is, when your heart is pounding, your palms are sweating and your mind is racing, dialling down to calm is practically impossible. It's too far to go. Whereas sidestepping from nervous to excited, from overwrought to energized, is much less of a way to travel.'

Flipping over to excitement will actually help you nail the date. 'The stress hormone cortisol is a symptom of anxiety, but also excitement,' Dr Ian Robertson, a neuroscientist, told the *Telegraph*. 'The same hormone affects you differently only depending on the context that your mind imposes upon it. If you are anxious, cortisol will impede performance, but if you are excited, we know that it boosts performance,' said the author of *The Stress Test: How Pressure Can Make You Stronger and Sharper*.

Now, when my knees are practically knocking, I don't try to get my body down to zen; I just tell my body that I'm electrified, rather than agitated. It's saved my worried skin more times than I can count.

THE SOCIALLY ANXIOUS SPIRIT ANIMAL

Have you read Philip Pullman's *Northern Lights* trilogy? It's a masterpiece. In it, people have what's called a 'daemon', what some cultures call a 'spirit animal', which speaks volumes as to their character. So, beware if somebody who seems super nice has a snarling hyena as a daemon. Or, somebody might seem cold, but if their daemon is a bouncy labradoodle, it's probably a safe bet that they'll warm up.

My point is, I found that it helped me to turn my anxiety into a daemon;

an extension of myself. Dr Steve Peters suggests a chimp in *The Chimp Paradox*, but personally, my anxiety feels like a trapped bird.

It's probably a blue tit. When I feel it starting to flap and spin inside me, when its little bird heart starts beating like a teeny tiny drum, I talk soothingly to it, just as you would soothe an actual animal.

My friends do this too. My mate Jess describes her socially anxious spirit animal as a rabbit who gets paralyzed in the headlights.

Separating my panic out from myself, and making it a psychological pet, really helps me.

ANXIETY IS MOSTLY INVISIBLE

What you see is not necessarily how I feel. There are very few people in my life who will know when I am nervous about something. About 99.9 per cent of the time, my panic is utterly invisible, and I'm willing to bet that yours mostly is too.

Have you ever applauded a colleague on nailing a presentation and had them say, 'Oh thank you, I was SO NERVOUS'? Or found out that somebody who seems cool as a cucumber suffers from social anxiety too, much to your surprise? Yeah, that. Think about that. You couldn't see their anxiety, so it's likely that they can't see yours either.

Coming back to Jess, she personifies perfectly that socially anxious people can present as socially sparkly, exuberant and effervescent.

You would never know she's anxious, unless you are trained in spotting the micro-signs of anxiety. She's the type to make a group fall about laughing as she talks about how she'd never seen a scone or a radiator before moving to Britain from Australia, or how she thought the school 'coach trip' meant they were being picked up by a full-on-fairytale-worthy carriage drawn by prancing white horses with pink feathered plumes.

If you met me, you'd probably never guess I was socially anxious either. I present as chilled, calm and confident, I'm told. We worriers hide it well, masterfully; we're deft in the art of disguise, given the daily practice we have at doing so.

VISUALIZATIONS BEFORE COFFEE

Remember how we talked about early morning being the best time to do positive visualization (see page 154)? It's when the gates are thought to be the most open between the conscious/subconscious mind. Irrational fears and beliefs live in the subconscious mind and drive phobias, addictions, anxiety, all of that fun stuff.

I also got this tip from my psychotherapist mate, Sam Purser-Barriff. 'During early morning, before we are fully awake, our brain is more susceptible to changing neural pathways,' she told me.

In the few days running up to a date, during the minutes directly after waking up, if you imagine yourself crushing the date with charm and ease, that positivity should start to fall into your, 'But what if they HATE ME' subconscious. Literally changing your date-anticipation neural pathway.

Olympians use positive visualizations all the time, because imagining yourself successfully chucking a ball, or doing a long jump, or whathaveyou, uses the same parts of the brain as actually doing it, which means that your brain is primed for triumph.

But I reserve this visualization tactic for imagining the immediate, definitely-gonna-happen future (the date) going well, rather than time-travelling five years ahead into a hypothetical future that is totally un-guaranteed.

POSTPONING YOUR REPLIES TO THEM

If you, like me, feel that once you've sent a text to someone, they now have the ball, and you have to twirl your racket and bounce around and be alert for the ball coming back, then try this: just hang on to the ball for a while.

If you, like me, find that you enter 'The Waiting Place' whenever you're expecting a response, just sit on your message for a few hours.

Not in a game-playing way, because you already know I don't believe in that string-pulling puppetry; just purely in an 'I'm going to give myself a break and hold onto the ball' kinda way. Not in a 'make them sweat' way, just in a 'make yourself sane' way.

Sit down, have a stretch, stick a half-time orange in your gob, and then return the ball whenever you feel ready.

I'm also a big fan of apps that disable your phone, to give myself a break from the watching, waiting, anticipating. I use *Flipd* on 'light' lock (I'm too scared to do 'full' lock, which literally disables your phone) for a few hours.

The average Brit checks their phone 150 times a day, so it's not just you, or me, everyone's bananas now, but you do get to choose how you react to your phone-fixating.

THE BATSHIT-CRAZY BECHDEL TEST

We've already talked about the Bechdel Test on page 34 and now, instead of just applying this to films, I apply it to my thoughts and conversation. I measure how much I'm thinking/talking about the man-of-the-moment. If it's a disproportionate level, I stamp myself with a batshit-crazy Bechdel Test 'FAIL'.

If I'm spending more than half of my time thinking about, or talking about, objects of romantic desire, then I definitely need to seek out new interests. I need to pick up a newspaper and marvel at advancements in space travel, or learn some Spanish, or call a friend to ask them how *they're* doing.

WHAT WOULD I DO WITH A FRIEND?

I also figure out when I'm thinking like a headcase, by asking myself this one question: 'If a friend did this, how would I behave?' So, if a friend took 12 hours to reply to a text message, would I care?

Would I be wondering if that friend secretly doesn't like me, or has met another, better friend? Would I send a melodramatic message to that friend saying, 'It seems like you're not bothered, so let's just leave it'. *Whips around and walks away*

Nope, nope, nope, NOPE. Applying the 'what would I do with a friend?' model always shows up my crazy. Like those dental tablets that you chew, which turn your plaque neon pink.

THINKING OF MY LOVE LIFE AS AN AFTER-DINNER MINT

As all of my friends would no doubt testify, my love life used to feature as the main course of any conversation we had. I would spend hours boring them senseless about text message exchanges, or making them look at pictures of blokes, or asking them about dilemmas, or regaling them with a blow-by-blow commentary on my latest romantic drama.

Obviously, I still talk to my friends about my dating life, but it's now become an afterthought, rather than the main event. When I have lunch with my mate Kate, she'll often be showing me to the door and say, 'Oh, I forgot to ask you about whatshisname, are you still seeing him?' and we do a very quick debrief as I'm heading out. Just as you crunch an after-dinner mint on your way out of the restaurant.

It does two glorious things. One, it takes the pressure off me, because very few people actually know the whole story of where I'm at dating-wise, rather than it being common knowledge. Two, it makes me a lot more interesting to other people.

Similarly, it used to be my third question of people-I'd-met outside of a work setting. Where do you live, what do you do, and are you seeing anyone.

But now, I've widened my lens beyond that.

I recently lived with a housemate for five months before I finally asked him, 'What's going on with you anyway, any love interests?' It was an aside. We had bigger fish to fry before that.

GIVING MY BRAIN A NEW SWING

My brain is like a trapeze artist. If I only give it one swing, it will stay on that swing. In order to get it off the dating swing, I need to give it another swing to fly to.

It's the reason why, if I'm ruminating over a dating quandary, I feel a million times better if I dive into writing a chapter. Or into helping someone. Or arranging my books into a rainbow formation. You can't just expect your brain to stop unless you gift it a new swing. 'Here you go champ, swing on that for a while.'

Also, I've read in a few places that multiple dating is a good strategy if you're prone to fixating on your current fancy. The idea is you won't get too obsessed/invested in one person and will therefore be more sane. Ummm.

To me, this is like eating cupcakes and angel cake as well as cheesecake, in order to try to quell your infatuation with cheesecake. You're still hooking yourself up to the substance, but just getting it from multiple people, surely?

For me, I'm not built to multiple date, my heart's just not in it, and I also think it's better to give your brain non-dating swings, rather than multiple mini-dating swings provided by half of *Happn*.

NOT DATING LIKE IT'S MY JOB

I was recently watching *The Big Sick*, in which a character says, 'Do you ever want to just get into a relationship so that you can...relax'. Yes. That hits the nail square on the head. Being single can be exhausting, because of that constant feeling of treading water.

But I've only recently realized that we participate in that stress. We choose it. It's not something we have to feel – or do.

We don't have to go on weekly dates if it's draining us. This sucks all the fun out of it and makes it feel like a job hunt or a house search. We don't have to find a partner, unlike an income or a roof. It's an extra, not a necessity.

Scale it down to a monthly event, if that's more your speed. You don't have to get to the end of the men/women on *Inner Circle. You don't have to.* Now, if I don't want to date, I just...don't.

SEEKING A KINDFULNESS LIFT

It can be really tempting, once I'm dating again, to rely on that as my pick-me-up font. But if I do that, I'll soon be back where I started, thinking that romantic connection is the place from whence all happiness springs.

A six-week study of 500 people found something surprising. Being kind to others gives us more of a surge of wellbeing than giving ourselves a treat, such as taking a day off work. In fact, those who treated themselves saw no improvement in their mood.

The study concluded, 'People who are striving to improve their happiness may be tempted to treat themselves to a spa day, a shopping trip, or a sumptuous dessert... they might be more successful if they opt to treat someone else instead.'

I love what Eleanor Roosevelt said: 'Since you get more joy out of giving joy to others, you should put a good deal of thought into the happiness that you are able to give.'

When I feel wretched about something like a dating knockback, I now don't search in a dating app (which was ultimately the vehicle of the knock) for a lift. I'll usually do something for myself to be fair (like go for a massage), but then I'll do something for someone else, like taking my hungover housemate a smoothie in bed, or writing to my niece from 'The Unicorn Queen' (she's real, OK?), or getting keys cut for a friend who's too busy to, or sending a rose plant to the mate who helped me move.

THE TRACTOR PROVERB

Once, I was looking for starry-eyed paternal love from my totally-the-opposite father who had started calling my brother and I his 'adults' and often said he'd never wanted kids. A close relative said, 'There's an Irish proverb about a tractor. It goes: don't go and ask for a tractor from somebody who doesn't have a tractor. There's no point in asking them if you can borrow their tractor, since they don't have one to give.'

Genius, right? I've now applied it to all men. If somebody doesn't own something (a desire for commitment, say, or a plan to have kids), don't go asking them for it. Don't bang on their door and say you need to plough your field, and you need to sow your corn, and they best give you their tractor. Total waste of time. They don't have one! Go find someone who does have a tractor.

It's beautifully simple and has stopped me banging on (or banging, frankly) the wrong doors, many a time.

More importantly, are you absolutely sure you want a tractor right now? Really? Or have you just been told you do?

BEWARE OF THE TINDERBOX RELATIONSHIP

I am liable to find myself in tinderbox relationships, as you know. I now shoot for a slow burn instead, even if my instinct is to throw all the matches on it and turn it into a bonfire from date three.

Mostly, my tinderbox relationships were fuelled by alcohol. Alcohol is flammable, after all.

The drunk rush in, where the sober fear to tread. Sobriety gives you caution and inhibitions, rather than devil-may-care recklessness. This is *a good thing*, although sometimes I do have to remind myself of that, when I'm feeling impatient and craving an instant blaze.

DELAYING SEX FOR AS LONG AS POSSIBLE

I would love to be able to have casual sex, sporting sex, as if hooking up with a squash partner every Saturday for a sweaty knock-around. But I'm not assembled that way.

I know this about myself now.

I also now know about the (unfair, frankly) female oxytocin surge that clouds judgement, and makes us think biker gang overlords or drug dealers* are marriage material, just because they gave us an orgasm once-upon-a-time.

Lust makes us unable to see people clearly, psychologist Robert Epstein told *Elle* magazine. 'Lust is just not enough for what most people want, which is a long-term, stable, happy relationship,' said the author of *Making Love: How People Learn to Love and How You Can Too*. 'It's actually fairly dangerous to have those feelings. Not dangerous in the sense that the person is an axe murderer. Dangerous in that we have studies – well-done lab studies – showing that when people are feeling that way, they're blind to important characteristics of that person.'

These days, I try to delay the sex until I'm sure I'm super into them, and they're super into me, and I see them *clearly*.

HAVING SEX FOR THE FIRST TIME SOBER

It's scientifically proven that alcohol makes you more likely to want to take your clothes off** on a date (even sometimes in public places – just me? Oh). But before you're actually psychologically ready to. If you wake up in the morning and feel like you don't want them to see you naked, whereas last night you tore your clothes off like a gift's wrapping paper, the person to trust out of those two people is Morning You. If you're not ready to be naked with someone sober, you're not ready full stop.

Alcohol also makes you about a billion times more likely to cop off with people you don't actually fancy (and by fancy, I mean their insides as well as their outsides. I pulled smokin' hot men when drunk who were repellent human beings). Finally, although alcohol makes you more

* *My impeccable taste in boyfriends has led me to date not just one, but three, small-time drug dealers in my time. I sure know how to pick 'em.*
** *It's not, but it should be.*

likely to have sex, it is actually proven to deaden your senses, make the sexual act less pleasurable, and put your orgasm further out of reach. Lose, lose, lose.

Even if you're a drinker, I wholeheartedly recommend shooting for sober sex the first time, scary though it is, because it means you a) remember it, b) are infinitely more likely to do it with people you definitely want to do it with, c) can feel the delicious sensation of every square centimetre, d) don't fall off the bed during, or participate in sexual acts you otherwise wouldn't, or start snoring halfway through (again, just me?).

I DON'T HAVE SEX I DON'T WANT

I've now forgiven myself for having slept around during my drinking days. As Cheryl Strayed says, we were all sluts in the Nineties. I just let this slutty period slip over into the Noughties too. Whoops-a-daisy.

I read somewhere that when women are drunk, they hurt themselves by having casual-sex-they-don't-actually-want, whereas drunk men tend to hurt themselves by getting into fist fights. It's not quite as simple as that, because drunk men *also* have sex they don't want, but it did stick in my mind as very true.

Now that I'm five years sober, I'm really choosy about who I have sex with. I know that intimacy is different from sex, but back then I didn't. Two of my friends have been to see sex therapists in the course of their marriages, and both were prescribed hour-long sessions of something called 'fingertipping' to build intimacy. Where they needed to stroke and touch each other, but in a non-sexy way, in a nurturing way, and they weren't allowed to shag afterward. Sex isn't intimacy. I didn't know that in my twenties.

Also, I'm sure I'm not alone here when I say that I have had sex because I feel like it would be rude not to. Feeling that I'd 'led them on'. That I needed to complete the task to dodge being called a 'prick tease'. That their arousal was now my responsibility.

It's the reason 'Cat Person' by Kristen Roupenian, a short story originally published in *The New Yorker*, went astonishingly viral. She summed up, so beautifully, how people often engage in the sexual act because of social mores. The line that most Velcroed in my mind is, 'But the thought of what it would take to stop what she had set in motion was overwhelming'.

It's simple. If you don't want to have sex, don't. It doesn't matter if you're naked, or he or she has the raging horn, or you said earlier that you would have sex, or they're calling you a tease, or whateversuch pressure. Stand up, put your clothes on, and leave, if that's what you need to do. Or if you're at your place, stand up, put your clothes on, and ask *them* to leave.

Now that I don't have sex to please men, the sex I have is no longer like a naked beauty pageant, where I'm trying to gain marks by showing off my baton-twirling or underwear-modelling skills. I have sex to please myself, I enjoy pleasing them in the process, and it's sweaty, messy good fun.

WALKING THE FIRE

This runs counter to my staunch belief in positive psychology, but I've found it helps me way more than the polar opposite. When my standards start being compromised, when I suspect that I might have to let go of him/he's thinking about letting go of me, I take a deep breath and mentally walk right through the worst case scenario, as if entering a virtual reality simulation.

Often it's the dread of what that rustling in the garden could be, that creates the most fear. Once you take a deep breath and floodlight the garden, you see that there's nothing there. (I nearly called the police recently about 'an attacker in the garden'. It turned out to be a particularly noisy hedgehog. When it waddled out of the bushes my heart nearly stopped, and then I laughed my head off.)

We over-estimate how devastating a break-up will be. Harvard research led by Professor Daniel Gilbert asked 500 students to predict how they would feel two months after a split. They predicted far more unhappiness than they actually felt, once the reality landed. Moreover, the happiness levels of those in the study who stayed partnered-up, compared to those who split, *did not differ*.

The fear is often so much bigger than the reality. I was in this fearstruck situation recently with somebody who clearly didn't have a tractor, but I'd been kidding myself that maybe he'd buy one. My dread of The End was looming large. Instead of pushing it away, I walked into it, just as somebody gingerly walks over hot coals on some kooky staff-inspiring retreat.

I imagined it ending. I opened that door, I turned on the light, I took a good long look at the source of my fear. I found that walking the fire was not what I'd expected. Once I'd walked it, I found I felt relief and a resurgence of self-respect. Huh. Who would have thunk it. Once I'd established that I would indeed live if The End came to pass, I felt much more relaxed about the outcome.

That readied me for what happened later that week: a mutual, ridiculously amicable agreement to stop dating. And because I'd already trodden those coals, it literally took me about a day to get over the demise of our two-month fling, whereas a few years ago, it would have taken around a month. I was as gobsmacked as the friends around me, but I really was *fine*.

You might find that when you walk through it hypothetically, it's way less terrifying than you first thought. What you think is an attacker, may just be a hedgehog.

GETTING UNDER SOMEONE TO GET OVER SOMEONE

There's a saying that, 'To get over someone, you need to get under someone else'. I subscribed to this school of thought throughout my twenties and my reaction to a break-up was always, always to arrange a date with someone else.

Now I've realized that's absolutely daft. But, I'm still not immune from falling back into that bad habit. I recently went on a couple of dates with a guy a mere five days after finishing with somebody.

I mean, we had a good time, but did it help me heal? Did it feck. It was the dating equivalent of dropping a hammer on my foot, to distract myself from a bang on the head.

It's enormously tempting to seek out a distract date, a Band-Aid boy/girlfriend, but it merely compounds the misguided notion that we source our happiness from our love lives. The myth we need a romantic charge to keep us puttering along, like an electric car that runs on compliments.

You can be your own power source, rather than needing to plug into other people.

I NEVER CONVINCE SOMEONE TO SPEND TIME WITH ME

Here's what happens when you date someone who's not that bothered. You think that it's something you've done wrong, and that they'll get keener if you can only be funnier, hotter, act less into them, yadda yadda.

Time rolls on, their indifference hardens, your self-esteem softens even more, until it's basically a puddle on the floor made of tears, and you try even harder. Until you are doing all the running around, all of the travelling and all of the diarizing.

NAH. Sod that. You should never need to convince somebody, cajole them, or coax them into spending time with you.

If ever I suspect, now, that somebody is indifferent about me, I simply stop arranging dates. If they're interested, they'll soon make a meet-up happen. If not, I've lost nothing.

BELIEVING THEM WHEN THEY SHOW YOU WHO THEY ARE

One of my go-to mottos is from Maya Angelou: 'When someone shows you who they are, believe them'. It was some advice she personally gave to Oprah (I'd have liked to have been a fly on *that* wall), when Oprah was venting about a man who continually let her down.

Oprah revealed she was 'sitting in a window waiting on him to show up, not even getting on the phone [this was before we had cellphones] because I was afraid that if it was busy for one second that he would call and I would miss the call, not taking out the garbage on the weekends because I might be out the moment that he called, not running the bath water because he might call while I'm running the bath water…and waiting and waiting and waiting'.

I mean, we've all been there, right? I remember taking my iPhone into the loo and weeing while looking at it, rather than risk missing a call from a guy. It's comforting to know that even Oprah phone watches.

Maya's advice to Oprah was simple. He showed her who he was, but Oprah didn't believe him. 'Why must you be shown 29 times before you can see who they really are?' said Maya. 'Why can't you get it the first time?' She adds, 'If a person says to you, "I'm selfish", or "I'm mean", or "I am unkind"…believe them, they know themselves much better than you do.'

This takes me back to the many, many times when I've chosen to ignore somebody telling or showing me who they are. I now pay close attention to what people say and what they do. If a guy says he's not looking for anything serious, I believe him.

There's that saying, 'when you hear hoofbeats, think of horses, not zebras'. Yep. If it sounds like a horse, it probably is a horse.

THE *BIEN DANS SA PEAU* RULE
There the French go, being clever minxes again. In English, this means to feel 'good in your own skin'. When I'm feeling low, or insecure, or ill-at-ease as a human, I simply don't date. Now that I have 'there's no rush, petal' tattooed on the inside of my eyelids, I can take long, lovely dating sabbaticals while I wait until I feel *bien dans sa peau* once more.

My advice would be to only date once you feel like a clever, funny, worthwhile, foxy broad/gent, because it makes the world of difference. Which dovetails nicely into the next point: standards.

MAINTAINING STANDARDS, AT ALL COSTS
It's really, really easy, once you're smitten, to let go of your standards and watch them drift away into the deep blue sea. They're not important, right? This would be way easier without them. *Casts them overboard*

No! You need those! Don't drop them!

I now know what my standards are, what my dealbreakers are, and I never renounce them. It may help to write them down, so that you can't drop them or forget them. Mine are: consistent contact, exclusivity and fidelity, harmony and mutual respect, plus a desire to forge something long term.

Maintaining those standards does mean that I've had to let go of around five men I did like in the past five years. It was tough to chuck them overboard while clutching my standards instead, but absolutely the right decision. I never regret choosing my standards.

Let's finish on a quote from *Scandal*, because, frankly, I have a *Scandal* fixation that I have zero interest in quelling.

'I'm not choosing. I'm not choosing Jake, I'm not choosing Fitz, I choose me. I'm choosing Olivia and right now Olivia is dancing. I'm dancing, Jake, I'm free. Now, you can dance with me or you can get off my dancefloor, I'm fine dancing alone.'

– OLIVIA POPE, SCANDAL

IDEALIZING PEOPLE WE DON'T KNOW

Have you ever gone so deep on text before meeting someone, that it's then weird when you meet them? Me too.

Here's why. A theory of 'Hyperpersonal Interaction' was proposed by Professor Joseph Walther. He found that digital communication has a tendency to turn 'hyperpersonal' fast, even speedier than face-to-face bonding, which is why you find yourself revealing intensely intimate details with someone you haven't even shared a latte with.

His research found that, given we have glaring gaps in our information about that person, we fill in these gaps, in two ways. Firstly, we assume they are more similar to ourselves than we have proof of (if you're honest, you presume that they are too). Secondly, Walther wrote that we, 'construct idealized images' of these partners.

Basically, we fill in the blanks in our knowledge with traits we want them to have. So, we imagine them being super-kind, even though we have no first-hand experience of that. They essentially become a fantasy avatar: half actual person, half a composite you've assembled.

Psychologist Jennifer L Taitz says that this magnification – even invention – of virtues, and minimization of flaws, is a cognitive distortion called the 'Halo Effect'. Interestingly, we're more prone to doing it when people are *smokin'* hot – and we're drinking bucketloads.

'Initially, people tend to positively fill in the blanks when someone is physically attractive (this perception also increases when we are consuming mood-altering substances or convincing ourselves *we need to meet someone already*),' says Taitz. 'It's helpful to notice if you are creating a fantasy that isn't backed by reality and try to pivot and be present in this moment with *what we know*.'

So, what do we *know*. I halt construction of fantasy avatars by compiling two lists. A 'Things I know for sure about them' list, which is often startlingly short. Maybe 1) I fancy him physically; 2) He's great at his job; 3) He wants to hang out with me. And then a 'Things I don't know about them, but have assumed' list, which is always super long.

Often I leap to conclusions based on snatches from social media. I may have surmised that he's thoughtful, respects birthdays and is kind, from one photo of him throwing his dad a surprise birthday dinner.

Then, even if he displays thoughtlessness, or ignores my birthday, or is rude to waiters, I assume that this is the exception to the rule, and that if only he liked me better, he would behave differently.

I used to friend men on Facebook to 'vet them' before even agreeing to a first date. Now I've been known to date someone for months, without even connecting on Facebook. The 'Halo Effect' blinds my judgement.

Ultimately, all that social media tells you about a person is what *they want you to think*.

HEARTBREAK TORMENT? THERE'S AN APP FOR THAT!

Do you want to replay your heartbreak? There's an app for that! Want to download what his ex looked like into your brain? Log on here! Torment can be yours with just a few clicks.

Pre-1994, the only ways we could really torture ourselves was by continually 1471-ing the landline to see if he/she had called. Deep-sighing around our siblings for them to get off the godforsaken phone already, so that we could sit and stare at it.

Then we found grey Nokias in our hot little hands, and discovered the newfound joy/hell of receiving/waiting for text messages. Waking up in the middle of the night to prod it awake, to see if there was a hopeful envelope awaiting you.

That was *nothing* compared to today. Now, we have heart-torture apps aplenty. Want to see your ex's new squeeze in swimwear? Click here! Want to see a video of your current love on holiday with their former paramour? Here it is! Want to read actual conversations they had in comment sections? Here's a drop-down thread!

It's enough to send even the most sane person insane.

THE TEMPTATION TO SNOOP

The digital storehouses we carry around in the shape of our phones, now mean that snooping is difficult to resist. A study found that 34 per cent of British women and 62 per cent of British men now 'mobile snoop'.

It's why the Banksy 'Love Poem' was so off-the-chain perfect. 'Beyond watching eyes/ With sweet and tender kisses...' it begins, so far, so clichéd. Until they awake: 'I found you bathed in morning light/ Quietly studying/ All the messages on my phone.' YEP.

However, people are entitled to their secrets. Did you know that? I didn't. ~~I learned this from Gandhi~~. I learned this from a crime thriller called *Safe*, which I watched largely because I have a crush on Michael C Hall (aka Dexter).

What other people think about us is none of our business. Just because it's *about us*, that does not make it our property. Plus, snooping only ever turns up the bad. Hence the oh-so-true saying that, 'Eavesdroppers never hear any good of themselves'.

Think about it. We say things behind a person's back, which we would never say to the person's face. It's our emotional version of going to the tip. We vent, we rant, we offload, we dispose of.

But the content of those vents, rants and offloads is not the full picture as to how we feel about that person, or what we think of them. Are they? Nope. So, snooping will only ever mean you find yourself rolling around in rubbish.

Snooping will never protect you from an infidelity, either (yes Former Cath, I'm talking to you). My new approach is to trust wholeheartedly, implicitly, even naively, until somebody gives me a very good reason not to. Innocent until proven guilty.

WHY IT'S SO IMPORTANT TO BLOCK EXES
Finally, let's talk about keeping 'tabs' on exes. Nine out of ten of us monitor our exes on Facebook, an anonymous Canadian study found. But it's a sure way to keep yourself stuck in the past.

'Researchers at the University of Miami studied how people adjusted after a break-up', says Jennifer L Taitz, author of *How to Be Single and Happy*. 'They found that the heavy Facebook users did two things. They ruminated more on the split, and found it harder to move on.' She adds that she's never, ever had a patient regret breaking up with an ex on social media.

'Think of the energy and time you have wasted, the books unread, the people unmet, the hobbies untried, the gym unused, as you myopically slip down the solitary Instagram rabbit hole logging whom they've tagged, not to mention the countless hours cross-referencing who has tagged them back.'

– JOANNA COLES, LOVE RULES

ENTER GHOSTING

Another advent of the digital age is ghosting, which hurts like hell. Here's why. 'Ghosting actually reminds me of the famous "still face experiment" from the 1970s, devised by psychologist Edward Tronick and his colleagues,' says Jennifer L Taitz. 'Researchers instructed a mother to first warmly engage with her baby, then to disengage. As you might guess, when warmth is suddenly removed, the child cries inconsolably. Human beings have an innate desire to connect, and it's maddening for someone to get close, then inexplicably pull away.' Yes.

XII: THE SINGLE HAPPY-EVER-AFTER

DEAR ADVANCED ADULTS.
I SEE YOU.

Dear Singles,

Because of the way society is assembled to celebrate couples and commiserate singles, nobody will ever give you a card congratulating you on managing two years of singledom, or arrange a troop of your best mates to go to a cabin in the woods, or buy you a set of Le Creuset pans for getting hitched to a new housemate, or shower you with spa vouchers and miniature clothes whenever you get a puppy.

All of the parades are saved for people doing weddings and babies. Sorry honeys. I know, it's not fair. Your promotion, or first mortgage, or bravery in walking away from a mean marriage goes mostly un-acclaimed, overlooked, while others are thrown parties for getting pregnant. Getting pregnant is utterly joyous, yes, but so is all the stuff the singles do.

When I moved in with my best mate, there wasn't so much as a 'New Home!' card, but when I moved in with Ralph, I was showered with housewarming gifts. Ralph and I enjoyed the special status awarded to couples, whereas Alice and I didn't.

When I got my first book deal, it was the most incredible peak of my life, and while I was indeed besieged by congrats comments, texts and phonecalls (thank you lovelies), I got a total of two gifts and two greeting cards saying 'Congrats! I'm so proud of you'. And I didn't even expect *those*, so I was bloody delighted.

But given a friend was getting married in the same period, and received hundreds of presents, the parallel was not lost on me. It made me stop and go – hang on. Why is my book deal not as celebrated as her wedding?

I'm not saying I should get presents, honestly, I'm not about to direct you to a department store gift list, but there is something wonky about all of this. Think about it. An unattached person buying their first home *single-handedly* will not get the same plaudits, the same social attention, as one getting engaged.

If I sound bitter, I'm honestly not. I'm more puzzled than bitter. I love a wedding, I'll happily play 'sniff the nappy' at a baby shower, and I enjoy buying gifts for both. It's just that we've forgotten how freaky all of this is. How skewiff. How one-sided. How exalted nuptials and birth are, above all other life wins. How it not-so-subtly teaches us that in society's eyes, the pinnacle of our life experience is to locate a partner and procreate.

I really want Charlie Brooker to write a *Black Mirror* depicting a society where singledom is fanfared in the way that coupledom is. That would be a belter. This societal 'And then there were two!' whoopdeedoo not only makes singles feel blue; it also places an invisible cage around the coupled-up, making them fear the big, bad world beyond: singledom.

But, no matter. Society is how it is. Let it get on with it. Now I'll arrive at my point.

I'm rambling at you in this letter to tell you that you're doing an incredible job. Being single is like Advanced Adulting. It's bizarre when society infantilizes singles as overgrown adolescents, or when married people behave like they're somehow on a higher Adulting tier than you, because the fact is, when you're single, you're doing the whole shebang.

The entire kaboodle. Lock, stock and barrel. If anyone should get an Advanced Adulting award, it's the single. As for single mothers? They should get one of those lifetime achievement trophies, a film reel showing their best bits *and* a standing ovation.

'Single people develop mastery,' says psychologist Bella DePaulo. 'Y'know that thing married people do where they split up all the tasks; you deal with the car and the money, I'll handle the meals and the relatives. Well, single people figure out how to do *all of it*.'

You deserve whoops and cards and applause. Give them to yourself. Give them to your single friends. And accept them from me.

I see you. I see that you're a badass.

Catherine

YOU'RE YOUR OWN FUCKING RESTAURANT

There's a restaurant in Barcelona called 'My Fucking Restaurant', which makes me grin every time I cycle past it. I can just imagine how the conversation went. 'Why don't you call it [insert suggestions]?' And the exasperated, defiant reply: 'I'll call it what I like, it's my fucking restaurant!' Ace.

You're your own fucking restaurant. If you don't want to define yourself as 'single' then don't. If you want to say you're 'celibate by choice' or you 'put the spin in spinster', or that you're a 'lone wolf', an 'unshackled siren' or a 'singilante' (like vigilante. No?), then knock yourself out.

Similarly, 'divorcee' is a strange one. Why is it, when you're no longer married, that you continue to be defined by that former marriage, even if it was yonks ago? If you want to say you're 'single' rather than a 'divorcee' then do. You get to choose your own lexicon. Maybe you want to call yourself a 'marriage survivor', or a 'freedom fighter'. Fill your boots. The world pounced on the 'pretentiousness!' of Gwyneth and Chris choosing to say they'd 'uncoupled', but I applauded their choice of how their divorce gets to be defined. It's *their divorce*.

I love how Kate Bolick has reclaimed the term 'spinster' and now uses it with pride. There's a fist-aloft rebellious quality to reclaiming a slur, much in the same way the gay community salvaged 'queer' from the hostility of homophobia, and repurposed it from an insult into a statement of identity.

If we start saying 'I'm a spinster!' ourselves, while grinning, that disarms the word of its negativity, and means they can no longer whisper it behind our backs. It's like upcycling a former torture rack, by sanding it down, making it glow with health, turning it into a writing desk, and painting it a sunny yellow. It has a glorious, grinning, 'screw you!' quality to it.

Personally, I won't be doing that, because 'spinster' reminds me of that shouting-in-the-car debate with my late father, which makes me want to cry. But you do what you like!

And don't forget, you're many, many things. I am single, yes, but I am also a friend, a daughter, a sister, an aunt, an author, a runner, a reader, a cyclist...need I go on? Single is one of many things that I am. I am a dodecahedron, a 30-edged shape (I once thought a 'dodecahedron' was a dinosaur). 'Single' does not define me, any more than 'sober' does. Nor does it define you.

You can see being single as being a straggler, an outlier, a loser in some imaginary race, or you can see it as being a pistol, a rebel, a renegade, a spitfire, a daredevil. I now choose the latter. As Zadie Smith writes, 'I am the sole author of the dictionary that defines me.'

OWN YOUR SINGLENESS

When I was researching this book, and reading reams of stuff about being single, I found myself curling the cover of *How to be Single and Happy* round so that people at the beach couldn't see it. Why, I asked myself? Because a knee-jerk shame about being single was still kicking around. Maybe you're doing the exact same thing with this book, right now.

It made me think about all the times when I have lied about having a boyfriend, often to deflect unwanted attention (as if the only reason I can say no to a man is because I'm 'taken' by another man) or to sidestep the whole 'Why?' boringness.

When I am honest about being relationship-free, I've now realized that I've been saying, 'I'm single' with a sigh, a sad-sack deflate, an apology in my face, a cringe. So now, I've started saying, 'I'm single' with all of the authority and pride that somebody says, 'I'm married'. It's totally changed how people react – and how I feel about it. It also really confuses wannabe street lotharios (you know the ones), who try to chat me up and are now met with a 'No thanks, I'm SINGLE'. They slope off looking baffled.

I am not an ornament that is either on somebody's shelf or available for purchase. I am a person. I am not a dance card with either a tick or an empty box; I am a human being. It's a noticeable mental shift and I love how empowered it feels.

WRITE A LETTER TO
A KID YOU LOVE

We have a responsibility to the children in our lives. A responsibility to impress upon them that life is *so much bigger* than just their love life. Because, as we've already established, they will be told that their love life is paramount, that romantic love is superior to all other kinds, constantly.

I want you to try this exercise. Write a kid-you-love a letter advising them on romantic relationships. For them to read when they're 18. This can be a close relative or a framily (friend family) member; they don't have to be blood-related, as long as you have deep reservoirs of affection for them.

Here's mine, to my niece Charlotte (five, at the time of press) and nephew Liam (nine).

Dear 18-year-old Charlotte/Liam,

I hope you don't, but you might grow up in a world that tells you, subtly and not so subtly, that you are incomplete and somehow broken if you do not have a romantic partner.

I want you to know that this is not true.

Absolutely. Not. True.

Here's what I know to be true. Received wisdom tells you that you give your heart to somebody and they have the power to break it. And that does indeed feel true, when you're in the depths of 'heartbreak'.

However, it's an illusion. You were/are in possession of your heart the whole time.

Here's what I've learned, in my 38 short years on the planet. Your heart is not like a brooch that can pinned on someone, nor is it like a piñata that somebody can smash up with a baseball bat.

Your heart is actually like a colossal, rambling country house. You own this house. Throughout your life, you take in lodgers. Some live there your entire life; some come and go. It's one of those cool, creaky stately homes replete with secret underground tunnels and hidden rooms behind fake bookcases.

There's a whimsical room atop the house that feels more magical than the rest somehow. It's probably set in a tower, a turret with a stained-glass window and curved furniture to fit its round walls. This is where you place the person you are in romantic love with. It's your favourite room in the house, so you award it to them.

The shock comes when the lodger in the tower room suddenly leaves. You forgot they were just a lodger. You forgot they could depart. They may leave under the inky cloak of night. They may leave a mess you have to clean up. Or stuff in storage that you can't bear to chuck, for years afterward. Equally, you may evict them yourself. Which is often almost as hard a process, given it involves painful conversations, and often confrontation.

When the tower room is empty, there's a temptation to sit up there, even long after they've left, howling at the moon about how lonely you are, how unloved. Sobbing into the sheets that still smell like them. But here's the thing. While you sit up there in the gables, gazing forlornly and longingly out of the window, you are choosing to feel alone.

Below the floorboards of the tower room, love scurries around, lighting candles, laughing at bad jokes, making macaroons, teeming away like a hidden rabbit warren. When the tower room is suddenly vacated, it's understandable to want to spend some time up there mourning the loss.

But then, come the heck downstairs. Spend your time warming yourself by the fire in the family room, or playing ping-pong in the games room with a bunch of mates, or gossiping over a whistling kettle in the colleagues room.

Ultimately, when the tower room is empty, it's no big deal. Because your house has 36 other rooms, which are all abuzz with love, connection and respect. The other lodgers hold just as much potential happiness, even though you don't snog them. Your heart is so much bigger than just one room. So don't give that one room ultimate precedence.

Even if the lodger in the tower room appears to become a permanent resident, even if you get a beagle called Baxter, and a set of posh tea *towels from Liberty, even if you become betrothed and/or have a baby, remember that the heart house belongs to you. The deeds are in your name. If infidelity or indifference chill and cobweb the room, or if the reapers of divorce or death sweep in, it will all be A-OK eventually; you can renew yourself by spending your time in the 36 other rooms.*

Your heart is vast and labyrinthine. Wander through it, redecorate rooms that are looking tired, enjoy every lodger, welcome new ones, all-the-while remembering that you will never, ever be alone, or lonely, unless you purposely barricade yourself into that one room.

You own your heart. It's yours. And incidentally, I'll always be out here in the conservatory, tending to (read: slowly killing) defiantly browning plants. I'll be waiting for you with tea and cuddles and Nineties indie, when you've had a nasty shock in the tower room. Come see me anytime.

Love,

Auntie Catherine
XOXO

Have you written your letter yet? If not, go do it. I'll wait here...

Done it now? OK, great. Now try this. I will too. Mentally erase the kids' name from the top and replace it with your own. It's a curious quirk of humans, that we are great at giving the advice, at dispensing the exact wisdom that we really need to heed ourselves.

Re-read that letter as if it's to yourself and take on what it says in a soul-deep way. That's exactly what you need to hear.

MY SINGLE JOY MISSION CONCLUDES

'Ever loved someone so much, you would do anything for them?

Yeah, well, make that someone yourself and do whatever the hell you want.'

– *HARVEY SPECTER*, SUITS

When I pitched this book to my publisher, my original pitch contained the line: 'Obviously, healthy relationships have the ability to make you *happier*, but that doesn't mean you have to be *unhappy* without one'.

I had to go back and delete it, both from the manuscript and from my brain. As I got deep into the actual research, I started to de-programme and re-wire all of my received wisdom about the happiness levels of singles and marrieds. And *then*, my therapy sessions revealed that I, personally, am no happier in a relationship, even a good one, than I am single. Mind – blown. Wide open.

When I commenced writing this, I knew I was happy single, and I knew I'd be happy single 'til say, 45 or 50. But the thought of being single forever? FOR THE LOVE OF GOD, NO. Now, I really don't fear that fate. I know I could be satisfied and happy as a forever-single. I've walked around in it, sat down in it, and felt how peaceful it would be.

Psychologists talk about our 'possible selves', or the future selves we imagine we may one day become. Before now, my 'single forever' self tiptoed around my imagined future malevolently, like Glenn Close's character in *Fatal Attraction*, trying to sabotage my 'nuclear family' self, attempting to boil the rabbit, and sneaking into the bathroom to write sinister messages in steam.

But now, I've invited her in, befriended her, given her a cup of tea and seen that, actually, she's rather lovely. Now, I like that possible self. Which means she can no longer skulk around outside scaring the shit out of me.

My love-addicted voice tried to stop me from writing this book. It whispered things like, 'But what if a future potential boyfriend reads this and then gives you the flick because he thinks you're ring-a-ding-ding crazy?' And then it would leave me alone for a while, before popping back up, like a meerkat of doom, saying, 'And have you even considered the fact his mum might read it and fire you from the chance of being in her family?'

I simply told the voice to shut up. The rational me knows that any man/woman (I may switch sides, who knows) worth their salt will not be put off by this, 'I was a love addict and now I'm trying not to be' confessional.

Here are my final thoughts, both for myself and for you.

I'M STILL A ROMANTIC 'TIL I DIE

Alain de Botton makes a compelling point that whereas singles are perceived as anti-romantic, they are often the most romantic of us all. He cautions that, 'Fervent romantics should be especially careful of ending up in mediocre relationships.'

You can be a starry-eyed romantic, like I am, and still be happy as a clam being single. You can choose to see ridiculously romantic scenes as a sign of the wealth of romance in the world, rather than a rude reminder of your perceived lack of it.

Today I watched a 70-year-old couple walk to the end of the beach and turn at the end, in perfect unison, and peck each other, before starting the walk back, like runners passing a baton in a relay. #couplegoals.

Rather than an ache of longing, I felt a stir of sentiment. Because I now believe in abundance, rather than scarcity.

EVERYONE HAS 'I'M BROKEN' MELTDOWNS

Seriously, EVERYONE. I'm not unique, and nor are you, if you've had them too. Eckhart Tolle wrote, 'That feeling that something is wrong with you, is not a personal problem of yours. It is a universal, human condition.' He goes on to say that there are millions – nay, billions – of people who have the exact same thought pattern. It's merely a thread woven into every human, that we pick at and stare at every now and then, throughout our lives. You're not broken, there's nothing wrong with you, or me, but thinking that *there* is something wrong is merely an inescapable part of the human experience.

THE OPEN-HAND PHILOSOPHY

We can't ever own people. If someone wants to go, try simply bidding them farewell. There's a saying in recovery land that things an addict lets go of have 'claw marks all over them'. That used to be true of my boyfriends. If they wanted out, I would clench my fist around them and fight with all my might not to let them go.

Now, I don't even close my hand. I keep my hand wide open, palm up, so that they can fly off at any time. They were never mine to begin with, they will never *be mine*, because people are not property. And if they do indeed bugger off, I may stare forlornly at the sky for a while, but I don't chase after them with a butterfly net, shouting reasons they shouldn't go. Or hop into a helicopter to slash through the sky after them.

OUR SISTER LIFE IS A SHIP THAT HAS SAILED

Wanting to change the past is a futile waste of your precious energy. 'I'll never know and neither will you about the life you didn't choose,' writes Cheryl Strayed. 'It was the ghost ship that didn't carry us. There's nothing to do but salute it from the shore.'

WE HAVE THE ABILITY TO SAVE OURSELVES

'No one saves us but ourselves, no one can and no one may,' goes the Buddhist philosophy. I fiercely believe this, with every fibre of my being. Other people can *help*, for sure, but you are responsible for your own rescue.

If you're waiting for someone else to ride up and throw you on the back of their horse and gallop away towards safety, you'll be waiting forever. Find a horse yourself. Name it (I vote Sparky) and hop on.

ATTRACTIVE PEOPLE ARE NOT THE ENEMY

You might be like, 'Well of course they're chuffing not', but I didn't know this until my thirties. I now know that envy is not a fait accompli. That stone-cold fox/tall drink o' water sashaying/swaggering past does not carry jealousy with them like an aura, that taints me like second-hand smoke. I choose how I react. Jealousy is an activity, a hot coal we choose to grasp.

I've always seemingly gone out of my way to pick up beautiful friends, but I simultaneously saw any stranger beauties as threats to whatever-relationship-I-was-in. Stranger danger! Now I go out of my way to admire and smile at them. Because it's not their fault they're beautiful. And their beauty does not rob me of anything.

Now that I feel secure with my entire package, I wouldn't dream of doing an early morning make-up dash. What, and miss out on sleep? I spend most of my life make-up free with frizzy hair. I am simultaneously aware and cool with where I sit in the universal pecking order. I'm not the most attractive woman on my street, let alone in any boyfriend's world. And that's A-OK. Because interiors are more important than exteriors. I had it all upside down, in my teens and twenties.

MARRIAGE IS NOT A ONE-SIZE-FITS-ALL GARMENT

I'm not entirely sure marriage is a wise goal for all. Some blossom within it, while others wilt. It's certainly not for everyone, which is probably why so many of us are now choosing not to go there. It's like Jim Carrey tweeted once. 'Whoever invented marriage was creepy as hell. Like I love you so much I'm gonna get the government involved so you can't leave.'

Tim Burton and Helena Bonham Carter knocked two houses together and maintained separate sleeping spaces while married. 'We see as much of each other as any couple, but our relationship is enhanced by knowing we have our personal space to retreat to,' she said at the time. 'It's not enforced intimacy. It's chosen.'

Goldie Hawn and Kurt Russell chose never to marry, even after three decades together. Instead, every morning they wake up and choose to be together. 'Marriage is an interesting psychological thing,' said Goldie. 'If you need to feel bound to someone, then it's important to be married...If you have enough money, and enough sense of independence and you *like* your independence, there's something psychological about *not* being married. It gives you the freedom to make decisions one way or the other.'

I know now that I need freedom inside a relationship. I'm like a savannah creature in that I need big open spaces to run around in. I'm open to the idea of a four-days-off, three-days-on set-up, or separate bedrooms. Who knows if marriage is for me, eventually. Is it for you? Dig deep; get beneath that societal conditioning that says all people must point towards betrothal.

MARRIAGE WILL BE INCREASINGLY REGARDED AS OPTIONAL

It looks like there's hope on the horizon, for future generations, when it comes to the 'failed' feeling around being unmarried. Marriage is being seen as optional, rather than compulsory, among our youngsters.

A poll of Girl Guides aged from 7 to 21 found that only one in five of them thought marriage to be a 'mark of success' to shoot for. How lovely. Moreover, only a third of these Girl Guides said that married people 'make better parents'. I basically want to put these Girl Guides in charge of the future world. Can we? Please?

It's thought that even couples with kids will increasingly stop getting married. A think tank estimates that by 2031, only six in ten families will be headed up by a married couple.

The future is shape-shifting. We are dynamite-blasting new tunnels of choice in this canyon. The question now is not so much *who* to marry, but *whether* to marry.

A sign of progress in itself is the very fact this book has been published. I read an article in the *Observer* that told me that a book called *It's Okay to be Single* was rejected by every horrified publisher back in 1999, with one editor writing back to say, 'Fundamentally, people want to be in a relationship, no matter how confining or awful'. The authors wound up self-publishing.

Fortunately, times have moved on. I didn't need to self-publish this book, nor did you need to read it on the dark web. Happy days.

TAKING A SINGLE STATE OF MIND

If you do end up decamping from singledom and getting hitched, CONGRATS, I am genuinely happy for you. Kate Bolick is in a long-term relationship now, but has taken a 'spinster state of mind' into it. And I'll take a 'single state of mind' with me too, no matter how married I get.

What is being single, really? It's freedom, space, financial independence, emotional autonomy, mastery of all the tasks, sourcing love and romance in your friends and family. Being single for an extended period gives you a set of skills that make you feel slightly invincible, so to ever put those down just because you have a ring is madness.

USING YOUR SINGLE FREEDOM

Whenever I feel like playing it safe, rather than stretching my legs, I think of Mohini the tiger, as my cautionary animal tale.

Tara Brach, a lauded psychologist and meditation teacher, tells the story of Mohini, who lived in a 12-metre-squared cage in the National Zoo in Washington, DC. Thanks to progress, the staff built a new habitat for her, one that covered several acres and featured hills, trees and a pond. 'With excitement and anticipation they released Mohini into her new and expansive environment,' writes Tara on her website. 'But it was too late. The tiger immediately sought refuge in a corner of the compound, where she lived for the remainder of her life. Mohini paced and paced in that corner until an area twelve by twelve feet was worn bare of grass.'

Use the space you have. Leap over the hills. Roll around in the pond. Scratch your ass on the trees. Run tiger, run.

EMBRACING YOUR *WALDEINSAMKEIT*

The Germans did it with *schadenfreude*, nailing something we don't have a word for: that trill of pleasure at another's misfortune. They also did it with *fremdschämen*, which means embarrassment on behalf of someone else. And they've done it again with *waldeinsamkeit* which roughly translated means – the exquisite feeling of being happily alone in the forest.

I can't pronounce it, but I do feel it.

EXHILARATED IN BARCELONA

AUGUST 2018

I'm lying beside a lido writing this final entry when I realize something with a jolt. It's like I've stepped inside the jacket of this book. Swap my nautical bikini for an orange swimsuit, plus chuck in a few palm trees and the shark-fin-shaped W** hotel....and the scenes are identical.

And yet, I had no idea I was going to elope to Barcelona and finish the book here, when we brainstormed the 'diving at a lido' concept. If I wasn't a Godless heathen, if I wasn't about as spiritual as a McDonald's Happy Meal® toy, I'd suspect divine intervention. But I am a non-believer, so I'll just call it an almighty cosmic coincidence instead. (Unless I mysteriously develop the art of the backflip dive.)

The horizon is so ruler-straight it's trippy. No wonder everyone once thought the world was flat. A cruise ship sits on it, as titchy as a plastic Battleship piece. If it falls off and clatters to the ground, the spell will be broken and we'll realize we're all just on a gigantic gameboard.

The cable-car tower's steel body stands above the lido, hoisting tinned people into its mouth, and then transferring them into an elevator. A seagull as big as a Jack Russell swoops inelegantly over my head, doggedly flapping its way beachward as the wind tries to hijack it and take it inland.

That's sometimes how it feels to be single, I realize. Sheer bloody-minded determination. Not giving in, fighting to stay on the path you know to be right, rather than settling for the path of least resistance. I am the seagull.

It's possible I'm starting to develop sunstroke. I seek shade.

I moved to Barcelona for three months this summer since I was breaking my London lease anyhow, and I'm more in the habit of asking 'Why not?' now rather than 'Why?' It costs the same to rent a one-bedroom apartment here, as it would do a studio in a questionable bit of London.

I have come to finish this book, to gawp at Gaudi, to starfish in the sunshine (the moment I leave England, the best British summer ever commences, of course), and to speak terrible Spanish while the locals cock their heads at me and look bewildered. I diligently learn the Spanish for, 'May we speak English please?' and wonder why locals frown slightly and reply, 'Errr, we'll try'. Turns out I have been bouncing into shops and banks and announcing, 'Hello! We should all speak English please!'

My cute rented flat is on the fourth floor. Hanging out the washing feels like an extreme sport, since I have to lean over a 40-foot drop. There are three-inch cockroaches in the building's hallway, which I have taken to calling 'Brian', in order to try to convince my brain I'm not scared. 'It's only Brian! Hey Bri!'

Spookily enough, my flat is exclusively decorated with solo women. Prints of Art Nouveau doyennes by Mucha, flamenco dancers clicking their heels defiantly, a lady with actual dragons (Khaleesi!). This is a couple-free zone.

It's important to me that you know I'm not fixed. On the flight here, I felt a rush of delicious independence as the plane defied logic and tipped itself into the sky. 'I couldn't do this if I was in a relationship,' ticker-taped through my mind. I practically punched the air with euphoria.

Closely followed by the crush of arriving at a strange flat at midnight with two enormous suitcases, asking myself, 'What the hell am I doing here?' and feeling mocked by my singleness. I can't manage both suitcases myself, it's a four-flight climb and I don't want to leave one unattended. I'm tired and a little frightened. Then, a nice lady helps me with my suitcases, and everything is fine.

So, I do still feel the occasional squeeze of single sorrow. It would be disingenuous of me to pretend otherwise. I am not a vessel of constant single joy. I am not a font of endless unattached delight.

Lying and saying otherwise, would be like me saying that I haven't had 'Fuck this shite, my kingdom for a glass of wine' moments in my five sober years. Of course I have. Everyone does, no matter how long they've been sober; no matter how much they know they don't actually want a glass of wine.

The difference is, you don't listen. You listen to the part of you that's wise, rather than the part of you that's a toddler. The part of you that knows better. The rational part of me knows that I don't need a boyfriend as some kind of suitcase Sherpa. That I was just knackered and feeling the aloneness that is inevitable to the human experience. That everyone feels, no matter how married they are.

My point is, single joy and single sorrow can co-exist, and they do inside me, but the ratio overwhelmingly tips towards joy nowadays. I am nine parts joy, to one part sorrow. I don't let fear define how I live my life now; I let adventure lead the way. I'm not going to sit motionless in London looking as pretty as possible, like a daisy waiting to be picked. I'm going to move, and if a moving target is harder to catch, then so be it.

DATING SABBATICALS

I've now been single, aside from brief flings that never even got into 'boyfriend/girlfriend' territory, for the past two-and-a-half years. And they've been the best years of my life.

Four months ago, I decided to take a dating sabbatical, even though I was moving to Barcelona, and Spanish men are totally my bag, because I knew this. I was starting to feel the panic again, the fixation, the frantic scroll of the app.

And when that happens now, I just drop my phone and opt out. Drop and roll. I let go. I take a break and only re-enter the dating atmosphere when I feel strong and serene enough to do so.

Ten years ago, at 28, being date-free for four months would have been unthinkable. I had to find a husband, yo! I can see her in my mind's eye, bowling out of the door in a Warehouse mini-dress, Marlboro Light in hand, saying, 'Why the fuck would I not date?!', blowing smoke in my face and slamming the door.

But now, aged 38, I know that my mind feels so much calmer when I'm not dating. It drops a deep hush over my soul, and strokes my anxiety bird into a flat-feathered snooze. Dating is fun, but also hard. So now I do it if-and-when I feel up to it. Only when I know I can do it in moderation.

I'm not pledging to be single forever, but I am reserving the right to choose single, and to be puffed-out-chest proud of it, if I don't find something that feels better than this does.

SINGLE AND MARRIED ARE EQUALLY VALID

As I lie by the pool, feeling less like a seagull and more like a person now that I've cooled down, I look around for a single role model. I alight upon a ring-free woman, perhaps aged 47, with a solid yoga body, silver and honey hair, and Sanskrit tattoos on her almond thighs. I'd be more than happy to turn into her. She's like Vinyasa Flow Cheetara. She smiles to herself as she reads.

Beside her is a married mother, wrangling two toddlers tenderly and deftly, looking both harried and happy. I realize, there is no right or wrong. No better. Both lifestyles are equally valid, and come with their perks and pitfalls. You don't have to choose to be anti-marriage or marriage-hungry. I think the secret is merely to enjoy whichever camp you happen to find yourself in, and think, 'What will be will be' as to where you will end up.

The single life is, however, definitely simpler. I read recently that the Latin root of single is simplex, or 'simple'. And that sums it up, doesn't it? It's going to take someone spectacular for me to want to de-simplify my life.

I do know I have a challenge ahead though. I've dismantled the story I was telling myself, that 'Each break-up has made me weaker', knowing now that I'm stronger for them. But what is true is this. I am more wary, compared to my dunderheaded, naive twentysomething self. Like Elizabeth Gilbert, back in my twenties I entered relationships with all of the forethought of a Labrador lobbing itself into a swimming pool. Geronimo! *Splash*

My heart is not as wide open as it once was, it's merely ajar, and prone to shutting sharply with the slightest gust of wind. One of my friends once carried a fuzzy heart around Africa with her to remind her to keep her heart soft even when she was afraid; I think of that often.

MOVING IN WITH MYSELF

I leave the pool and bike past one of my favourite Barcelona vistas, a hotchpotch of palm trees, ship-masts and Gothic towers at Port Vell. I feel like I'm flying as I glide through the hawkers one-handed, not quite brave enough to go hands-free.

There was once a study into what women want, which found that even more than marrying or having children, women want to feel 'exhilarated by their lives'. Men too, I'm sure. And of this I am certain; I am exhilarated by mine on a daily basis. Exhilaration seems to me to be a fine raison d'être to point towards, whether it's something you find in Barcelona or in Bolton.

But I'm also hankering for a stable home, for in-between my travelling, so when I return to the UK, I'm going to move into my first actual flat by myself, beside the sea in Brighton. Not just for a few months, or a year, into a flat decorated by someone else, but into an empty shell that I will inhabit and fill, and make my own. (I am more excited about this, than I ever was about moving in with a boyfriend. This too, gives me 'exhilaration'.)

I'm going to fill it with plants, and twelve types of tea, and hang a hammock on the balcony, and have a yoga station, and set about slowly, surely saving a deposit to buy, so I can stop chucking rent money away (ba-bye money *waves*) indefinitely.

LEAVING THE TOWER ROOM

So, I'll be in Brighton physically. But, metaphorically, if you need me, you won't find me in the tower room, weeping, staring forlornly at the moon and listening to Stay by Lisa Loeb, waiting for the thud of hoofbeats to signal the approach of a prince. Nah. Sod that. I'll be in the 36 other rooms of the house, having a blast. The Waiting Place is tiresome; I've moved to the living place.

~~I cycle up Montjuïc~~ I huff, puff and finally push my bike up Montjuïc. In my pocket, I have two padlocks. I've often walked past those love-lock padlocks and thought 'If only', 'One day' or 'I wish'. Well, that is no longer my style. 'One day' is no longer how I roll. Let's do this – now.

So I'm going to join the love-lock people, given I have just as much love in my life as them. I have a padlock that simply says 'CG' and represents a pledge to myself.

I find the place I seek, near a graffiti wall that announces 'Fuck being polite' and looks defiantly down on to the city. The sun dips behind the fairytale spires atop Tibidabo. Barcelona's lights start to blip on in unison, resembling a fallen constellation. I click the lock and throw the key far into the bushes beneath.

I've locked something in. It's a pledge that I will never again abandon myself in the pursuit of a romantic ideal. That I will never again place the importance of being couple-shaped above my own happiness. It means I have my own back, I don't need another set of initials, and I now self-preserve rather than self-sabotage.

Today is also the one-year anniversary of my dad's death, so alongside my padlock pledging devotion to myself, I click one in that simply says 'Dad'. This one means something different. It is a letting-go padlock. A forgiving padlock. It means that I forgive him for the outdated notions he filled my head with, those of 'Find a husband before it's too late': those of depreciating women and appreciating men.

One of his mottos was, 'Give other people the right to be wrong', and I decide to extend that to him. As he so often did to me, when I was being a drunken nightmare, pre-2013. He was merely a product of his time. And now, I can move past that, beyond those damaging beliefs that I have held on to for far too long.

I am on a mountain in Barcelona, not on a dusty shelf in a wife supermarket. I miss my dad terribly, but in some ways his death has freed me. I can no longer disappoint him, because he's no longer here, which is at once heartbreaking and emancipating.

But then, I wonder how much our minds Velcro the negatives, and let the positives Teflon-slide away, when it comes to our parents. Perhaps I've done that with Dad. At his memorial, his best friend gave me one of the best gifts I've ever received. It was as if he'd peered inside my mind and spotted the one thing I needed to know, for closure. 'Your dad was very proud of you, y'know. He just didn't know how to tell you, or show it.'

I stand overlooking Barcelona, and listen to 'Romeo and Juliet' by Dire Straits as a tribute to my dad. I think of the very best side of him, the him that would belt out, 'When you gonna realize, it was just that the TIME was wrong', while expertly driving one-handed (and much too fast) around the serpentine Antrim coast.

I remember the fantasist in him, which I have in me too. When I was 13, I asked him if God was real. He said that, personally, he thought not. Then he picked up a speck of sand and said, 'Maybe Earth is a speck of sand on the beach of a giant's planet. Who knows'.

I remember the animal-lover in him. He would crouch next to his gorgeous tortoiseshell cat, Tinker, who would be swirled on the sofa looking smug. Dad would tell Tinker that she was, 'the bestest, most beautifulest cat in the world' and she would kiss him on the nose, and I would actually wish I was the dang cat. But in 1950s Ireland, little boys were not raised to be emotionally literate, or affectionate towards their kids. Just as I was conditioned to place too much importance on romantic relationships, he was conditioned too.

Sudden, urgent tears flow, since this Dire Straits song is like the 'push for instant grief' button. Next up, I listen to 'Gypsy' by Fleetwood Mac, which has now become my single anthem. 'Her face says freedom with a little fear.' The biggest perk of singledom, for me, is that it allows me to answer the fierce call-to-departures of my wanderlusting gypsy blood.

Barcelona deepens to indigo velvet and stars push out of the pin-cushion sky. The Sagrada Familia soars like an enchanted forest, a tracing-paper butterfly flaps past on a mysterious insect-land mission, while the roar and backfire bang of a motorbike announces its importance beneath.

I feel grief swirled in with relief; ink dancing in water. The grief is for my dad, but the relief is for myself. I know now that if I ever find myself in a toxic relationship, as I have done too many times, I won't hesitate to hightail out of it. Since I'm no longer remotely scared of being single, now that I know I can be happy single, I don't need to stay; nor do I need him to stay. I can leave.

With that, I hop on my bike and free-wheel downhill. There's no meet-cute with a Spanish man after my padlock moment. That's how the film would end, right? And frankly, amigos, I just don't give a damn. Because I am in the midst of a scorching love affair with Barcelona.

• Want more? Follow @unexpectedjoyof on Instagram.

SOURCES

PREFACE

Alain de Botton singlehood-prestige quote: 'Reasons to Remain Single', The School of Life's YouTube channel.

INTRODUCTION

Ten times the rate, people live alone for fifteen years: cited in John Bingham, 'Bridget Jones takeover: number of singletons growing 10 times as fast as population', Telegraph, 8 May 2014.

2016 single data, 42 per cent divorce: Office for National Statistics, Statistical bulletin, 'Population estimates by marital status and living arrangements, England and Wales: 2002 to 2016', July 2017.

Average marriage ages data: Office for National Statistics, Statistical bulletin, 'Marriages in England and Wales: 2015', 28 February 2018.

Four in ten brides under 30: cited in Steve Doughty, 'Rise of the older bride: Average age for women to walk down the aisle is now over 35', Daily Mail, 28 February 2018.

LOVE ADDICTION DEFINED

Priory Definition: Dr Vik Watts and Mel Davis, 'What is sex and love addiction?', Priory website, priorygroup.com

FILMS AND FAIRYTALES

58 per cent: bechdeltest.com stats as of August 2018.

Men outnumber women two to one, women sexual, men violent: Amy Bleakley, Patrick E Jamieson, Daniel Romer, 'Trends of Sexual and Violent Content by Gender in Top-Grossing U.S. Films, 1950–2006', Journal of Adolescent Health, 51 (1), July 2012, 73–9.

BODY/BRAIN

Dragons: Rob Dunn, 'The Top Ten Deadliest Animals of Our Evolutionary Past', smithsonianmag.com, June 2011.

Anticipated loneliness lowers IQ: Roy Baumeister, Jean M Twenge and Christopher K Nuss, 'Effects of social exclusion on cognitive processes: Anticipated aloneness reduces intelligent thought', Journal of Personality and Social Psychology, 83 (4), October 2002, 817–27.

Heartbreak causes physical pain: Jacquelyn H Flaskerud, 'Heartbreak and Physical Pain Linked in Brain', Issues in Mental Health Nursing, 32, November 2011, 789–91.

Symptoms of early-stage romantic love: Arthur Aron, Helen Fisher, Debra J Mashek, Greg Strong, Haifang Li and Lucy L Brown, 'Reward, Motivation, and Emotion Systems Associated With Early-Stage Intense Romantic Love', Journal of Neurophysiology, Vol.94, Issue 1, July 2005, 327–37.

Mammalian Antecedents quote: Helen E Fisher, Xiaomeng Xu, Arthur Aron and Lucy L Brown, 'Intense, Passionate, Romantic Love: A Natural Addiction? How the Fields That Investigate Romance and Substance Abuse Can Inform Each Other', Frontiers in Psychology, May 2016.

Romantic rejection similar to cocaine withdrawal: Helen E Fisher, Lucy L Brown, Arthur Aron, Greg Strong, Debra Mashek, 'Reward, Addiction, and Emotion Regulation Systems Associated with Rejection in Love', Journal of Neurophysiology, 104 (1), July 2010, 51–60.

Amir Levine quote: Amir Levine and Rachel S F Heller, Attached: The new science of adult attachment and how it can help you find – and keep – love, TarcherPerigee, 2011, 209.

INDIFFERENT PEOPLE

Women prefer men who are 'uncertain': Erin R Whitchurch, Timothy D Wilson, Daniel T Gilbert: '"He loves me, he loves me not...": Uncertainty can increase romantic attraction', Psychological Science, Association for Psychological Science, 17 December 2010.

YEAR OFF

Topshop 900 per cent rise: Nicola K Smith, 'Could Singles Day be the new Black Friday for British retailers?', Guardian, 8 November 2016.

Sweden 60 per cent and single commune: 'Single Swedes find ways of being alone together', Sverige Radio website, sverigesradio.se, August 2013.

80 per cent global rise in single households: Eric Klinenberg, 'I want to be alone: the rise and rise of solo living', *Guardian*, 30 March 2012.

One in five: Olivia Rudgard, 'Proportion of women who never have children has doubled in a generation, ONS figures show', *Telegraph*, 25 November 2017.

South Korea: Nicola Smith, 'Dating mandatory for South Korean students of love', *Sunday Telegraph*, 19 November 2017.

America 45 per cent: United States Census, Profile America Facts for Features 'Unmarried and Single Americans Week: Sept. 17–23, 2017', press release 14 August 2017.

Irish women not allowed to buy homes: Suzanne McGee and Heidi Moore, 'Women's rights and their money: a timeline from Cleopatra to Lilly Ledbetter', *Guardian*, 11 August 2014.

Women bank account, loan, credit card: Mark Molloy, Jamie Johnson and Izzy Lyons, '1918 vs 2018: 13 things women couldn't do 100 years ago', *Telegraph*, 6 February 2018.

All marriage rates 1950s–2015: Office for National Statistics, Statistical bulletin, 'Marriages in England and Wales: 2015', 28 February 2018.

Plato's other-half theory, *c*.378BC: 'Plato's Other Half', *Lapham's Quarterly*, laphamsquarterly.org.

Over 2,000 babies: 2,119 babies born to over-45 mothers in 2015; 'Babies born to women aged 45 and over rises by a third', BBC News, 24 September 2016.

Corsages and lemons: Rebecca Traister, *All the Single Ladies: Unmarried Women and the Rise of an Independent* Nation, Simon & Schuster, 2016, 65.

76 per cent, 35 per cent, 9 per cent, 14 per cent: cited in Aziz Ansari with Eric Klinenberg, *Modern Romance: An Investigation*, Penguin, 2015, 22–4.

Jam study: cited in Aziz Ansari with Eric Klinenberg, *Modern Romance: An Investigation*, Penguin, 2015, 132.

Japan details: cited in Aziz Ansari with Eric Klinenberg, *Modern Romance: An Investigation*, Penguin, 2015, 154–7.

Fertility statistics: cited in Hannah Barnes, 'The 300-year-old fertility statistics still in use today', BBC News, 18 September 2013.

Old French data: Jean M Twenge, 'How long can you wait to have a baby?', *Atlantic*, July/August 2013.

Over-forties rate overtaken under-twenties: David Batty, 'Fertility rate higher among over-40s than under-20s for first time since 1947', *Guardian*, 13 July 2016.

GROWING SINGLE JOY

Life-expectancy estimates: Office for National Statistics, Statistical bulletin, 'National life tables, UK: 2014 to 2016', 27 September 2017.

Caitlin Moran quote: 'What young women really need to know', *The Times*, 18 November 2017.

Skin hunger: Kory Floyd study of 509 adults, cited in Floyd, 'What lack of affection can do to you', *Psychology Today*, 31 August 2013.

Sympathetic joy: Johann Hari, *Lost Connections: Uncovering the Real Causes of Depression – and the Unexpected Solutions*, Bloomsbury, 2018.

Hunger and depression: Peter Bongiorno, 'Is there a blood sugar monster lurking within you?', *Psychology Today*, 14 November 2013.

Unwanted thought suppression and dreams: Fiona Taylor, Richard A Bryant, 'The tendency to suppress, inhibiting thoughts, and dream rebound', *Behaviour Research and Therapy*, 45 (1), 2007,163–8.

Social costs of suppression: Sanjay Srivastava, Maya Tamir, Kelly M McGonigal, Oliver P John, and James J Gross, 'The Social Costs of Emotional Suppression: A Prospective Study of the Transition to College', Journal of Personality and Social Psychology, Vol.96 (4), April 2009, 883–97.

Gratitude re. sleep, heart, cortisol and depression: 'Gratitude is good medicine', UC Davis Health, UC Davis School of Medicine website, 25 November 2015.

Gratitude hope and happiness boost: Charlotte vanOyen Witvliet, Fallon J. Richie, Lindsey M. Root Luna and Daryl R. Van Tongeren, 'Gratitude predicts hope and happiness: A two-study assessment of traits and states', *Journal of Positive Psychology*, 15 January 2018.

Cheryl Strayed quotes: Cheryl Strayed, *Brave Enough: A Mini Instruction Manual for the Soul*, Atlantic, 2015.

SINGLE SCARCITY

Harry Benson quote: Jessica Elgot, 'Marriage problems: more than a third of people are single or have never married', *Guardian*, 8 July 2015.

51 per cent, 98 per cent and rise of 92 per cent: Mintel, 'Single Lifestyles – UK – September 2017'.

Boom in single-person households, Euromonitor Research, 'Households in 2030: Rise of the Singletons', Euromonitor International, 20 March 2017.

Two thirds: cited by Kate Bolick, 'It's time to reclaim the word "spinster"', *Grazia*, 19 June 2018.

28 per cent of households: Office for National Statistics, Statistical bulletin, 'Families and Households: 2017', 8 November 2017.

POOR JEN

Dodai Stewart quotes on Jennifer Aniston: Dodai Stewart, 'When Motherhood Never Happens', jezebel.com, 8 May 2012.

Dodai Stewart quotes on George Clooney: Dodai Stewart, 'George Clooney vs Jennifer Aniston: A Tale of Two Singles', jezebel.com, 28 April 2014.

THERAPY OPENS DOORS

Hungry shoppers quote: Anna Maxted, 'How our fathers influence the partners we choose', *Telegraph*, 16 June 2014.

60 per cent of over 85s widows: Office for National Statistics, Statistical bulletin, 'Population estimates by marital status and living arrangements, England and Wales: 2002 to 2014', 8 July 2015.

A 4 per cent drop: David B Dunson, Bernardo Colombo, Donna D Baird, 'Changes with age in the level and duration of fertility in the menstrual cycle', *Human Reproduction*, Vol.17, Issue 5, 1 May 2002, 1399–403.

Over-forties higher than under-twenties: Office for National Statistics data cited in David Batty, 'Fertility rate higher among over-40s than under-20s for first time since 1947', *Guardian*, 13 July 2016.

Newsweek retraction terrorist blooper: Liz Cox Barrett, '*Newsweek* Discovers Doomed Spinsters Marrying', *Columbia Journalism Review*, 30 May 2006.

Esther Perel quote: 'Let Go of Being the "Perfect Partner"', estherperel.com, undated.

Rachel Greenwald quotes: *Find a Husband After 35: (Using What I Learned at Harvard Business School)*, Ballantine, 2004.

WHO ARE SINGLE PEOPLE?

1,000-people survey: Thair Shaikh, 'Single living is the new way to find happiness', *The Times*, 3 August 2005.

Two-friends loss in relationship: cited in Ian

Sample, 'The price of love? Losing two of your closest friends', *Guardian*, 15 September 2010.

Germans who live alone are less lonely: M Luhmann and L C Hawkley, 'Age differences in loneliness from late adolescence to oldest old age', *Developmental Psychology*, 52(6), June 2016, 943–59.

Bella DePaulo quote: TedX talk by DePaulo, *What no one ever told you about people who are single*.

One hour 36: Kei M. Nomaguchi and Suzanne M. Bianchi, 'Exercise Time: Gender Differences in the Effects of Marriage, Parenthood, and Employment', *Journal of Marriage and* Family, Vol.66, Issue 2, May 2004, 413–30.

70 per cent not looking: Mintel, 'Single Lifestyles – UK – September 2017'

Matthijs Kamijn, 'The Ambiguous Link between Marriage and Health: A Dynamic Reanalysis of Loss and Gain Effects', *Social Forces*, Vol.95, 1 June 2017.

Tracy McMillan quote: cited in Rebecca Traister, *All the Single Ladies*, Simon & Schuster, 2016,129.

Neith Boyce quote: cited in Kate Bolick, *Spinster: Making a Life of One's Own*, Corsair, 2015.

Single men less happy: Mintel, 'Single Lifestyles – UK – September 2017'

63 per cent would prefer a relationship: Justin R Garcia, Chris Reiber, Sean G Massey and Ann M Merriwether, 'Sexual Hookup Culture: A Review', *Review of General Psychology*, 16, no.2 (2012).

MARRIAGE MYTH

Happiness levels return to same after wedding: TedX talk by Bella DePaulo, *What no one ever told you about people who are single*.

24,000 people using data from the German Socio-Economic Panel study: cited in

Jennifer L Taitz, *How to be Single and Happy*, TarcherPerigee, 2018, 18.

10,000 Australian seventysomething women: cited in Gabrielle Frank, 'Single ladies: You might be healthier and happier than married friends', Today.com, 5 August 2016.

20,000 adults, 45 per cent, two-thirds and a quarter stats: Ipsos Global Public Affairs, 2012; cited in Jonathan Allen, 'Partners main source of happiness around the globe – poll', reuters.com, 14 February 2012.

LATER MARRIAGES

Marrying after 25: Casey E Copen, Kimberly Daniels, Jonathan Vespa, and William D. Mosher, 'First marriages in the United States: Data from the 2006–2010 national survey of family growth' *National Health Statistics Reports* 49 (2012).

Charlotte Brontë quote: cited in Rebecca Traister, *All the Single Ladies*, Simon & Schuster, 2016, 111.

Thirties and forties women marriage doubled: cited in Mandy Francis, 'Wife begins at 40!', *Daily Mail*, 12 June 2012.

REASONS NOT TO GET MARRIED

Divorce £70,000 (including loss of assets and legal fees): Jonathan Ames, 'Divorce costs £70,000 (and nearly half goes to lawyers)', *The Times*, 5 December 2018.

COLOUR YOURSELF IN

£266,000 more: Thair Shaikh, 'Single living is the new way to find happiness', *The Times*, 3 August 2005.

Double the wealth: Jay L. Zagorsky, 'Marriage and divorce's impact on wealth', *Journal of Sociology*, Vol.41, Issue 4, 1 December 2005, 406–24 .

£1,800, £2,000, savings would run out in a fortnight: cited in John Bingham, 'Bridget Jones takeover: number of singletons growing 10 times as fast as population', *Telegraph*, 8 May 2014.

36 per cent, 52 per cent and 29 per cent

source: Mintel, 'Single Lifestyles – UK – September 2017'.

A third of renting single Brits say they won't be able to buy without partner: Research by Skipton Building Society, cited in: Rachel Hosie, 'One third of single Brits think they need to couple up to buy a property, survey finds', *Independent*, 12 July 2018.

Knot yet report: cited in Rebecca Traister, *All the Single Ladies*, Simon & Schuster, 2016, 175.

DATE RESPONSIBLY

Oprah and Maya Angelou: video on *Huffington Post*, 'Oprah's Life Lesson from Maya Angelou: "When people show you who they are, believe them"', posted 14 March 2013.

Kindness 500 people study: S Katherine Nelson, Kristin Layous, Steven W Cole, Sonja Lyubomirsky, 'Do unto others or treat yourself? The effects of prosocial and self-focused behavior on psychological flourishing', *Emotion*, Vol.16, No.6, September 2016, 850–61.

Dr Ian Robertson quote: cited in Sarah Knapton, 'Forget relaxing – use your stress to become a high achiever', *Telegraph*, 10 July 2016.

Cheryl Strayed quote: *Brave Enough: A Mini Instruction Manual for the Soul*, Atlantic, 2015.

G T Wilson and D M Lawson, 'Effects of alcohol on sexual arousal in women', *Journal of Abnormal Psychology*, Vol.85, No.5, 1976, 489–97.

G T Wilson and D M Lawson, 'Expectancies, alcohol, and sexual arousal in women', *Journal of Abnormal Psychology*, Vol.87, No.3, 1978, 358–67.

V J Malatesta, R H Pollack, T D Crotty and L J Peacock, 'Acute alcohol intoxication and female orgasmic response', *Journal of Sex Research*, Vol.18,1982, 1–17.

Harvard study break-ups: cited in Jennifer L Taitz, *How to be Single and Happy*, TarcherPerigee, 2018.

Epstein quote: cited in Carrie Sloan, 'Learn to Love: How to Live Happily Ever After', elle.com, 26 March 2010.

IDEALIZING PEOPLE

Hyperpersonal Interaction, Joseph Walther: cited in Simon Lindgren, *Digital Media & Society*, SAGE, 2017.

HEARTBREAK TORMENT

'Mobile snoop' stats: cited in Sophie Curtis, 'Men twice as likely to "mobile snoop" than women', *Telegraph*, 10 September 2013.

Banksy 'Love Poem': Banksy, *Wall and Piece*, Random House, 2007.

Nine out of ten exes Facebook: Veronika A Lukacs, 'It's Complicated: Romantic Breakups and Their Aftermath on Facebook', unpublished thesis, The University of Western Ontario, London, Ontario, 2012.

SINGLE JOY CONCLUDES

Observer article: Liz Hoggard, 'Let's say it loud: We're single...and proud', *Observer*, 1 February 2004.

Cheryl Strayed quote: under her 'Sugar' alias, 'Dear Sugar, The Rumpus Advice Column #71: The Ghost Ship that Didn't Carry Us', therumpus.net, 21 April 2011.

Girl Guides and think-tank future of marriage: cited in Judith Woods, 'What do women want? To be married, of course', *Telegraph*, 9 October 2012.

Alain de Botton romantics quote: 'Reasons to Remain Single', The School of Life's YouTube channel.

EXHILARATED IN BARCELONA

Latin root of single: Jennifer L Taitz, *How to be Single and Happy*, TarcherPerigee, 2018, 215.

What women want exhilaration study: Sylvia Ann Hewlett and Melinda Marshall, 'Women Want Five Things', Center for Talent Innovation, December 2014.

INDEX

ACKNOWLEDGEMENTS

I've never been happier in my writing career than I am right now, which is mainly down to two indomitable, effervescent, sharp and big-hearted women: my agent Rachel Mills and my publisher Stephanie Jackson.

The team at Aster continue to be patient, lovely and professional despite my limitations of being excessively detail-oriented (euphemism for a control freak), akin to a startled horse when it comes to public speaking, and thinking I can bend time (read: over-promising on deadlines). In particular, I'm directing much gratitude at Karen Baker, Pauline Bache, Yasia Williams and Harriet Walker.

I salute the ever-illuminating and wise Hilda Burke and Dr Alex Korb, who have continued to give their expert insight to me freely. I also send appreciation to Kate Bolick and Dr Jenny Taitz, who were both an absolute pleasure to interview. And a high five to my married friends and the single men who devoted time and energy to giving me such funny, clever, thought-provoking testimonies.

A colossal thanks to my first readers, who supplied invaluable feedback and much-needed cheerleading: my mum, Kate Faithfull-Williams, Laurie McAllister, Karl Williams, Suzy Cox, Louise Gray and my travel wife Holly Whitaker.

And last but definitely not least, I'm sending platonic (and equally as powerful) love to all of my friends and family, many of whom have already been mentioned, who have magnanimously nodded and brightly said, 'Well, we'll see!', when I've told them some guy I barely know is The One. Who have had the forbearance to tolerate my forensic analysis of my latest romantic dilemma, showdown or Greek tragedy. And who have then hugged and consoled me through many wine-exacerbated breakdowns of the fun 'I'm going to be alone forever' variety.

I feel insanely lucky to have found so many soulmates already. I look forward to spending the rest of my life with you all.